ALSO BY RICHARD KOSTELANETZ

Books Authored
The Theatre of Mixed Means (1968)
Master Minds (1969)
Visual Language (1970)
In the Beginning (1971)
The End of Intelligent Writing (1974)
I Articulations/Short Fictions (1974)
Recyclings, Volume One (1974)
Openings & Closings (1975)
Portraits from Memory (1975)
Constructs (1975)
Numbers: Poems & Stories (1975)
Illuminations (1977)
One Night Stood (1977)
Tabula Rasa (1978)
Inexistences (1978)
Wordsand (1978)
Constructs Two (1978)
"The End" Appendix/"The End" Essentials (1979)
Twenties in the Sixties (1979)
And So Forth (1979)
More Short Fictions (1980)
Metamorphosis in the Arts (1980)
The Old Poetries and the New (1981)
Reincarnations (1981)
Autobiographies (1981)
Arenas/Fields/Pitches/Turfs (1982)
Epiphanies (1983)
American Imaginations (1983)
Recyclings (1984)
Autiobiographien New York Berlin (1986)
The Old Fictions and the New (1987)
Prose Pieces/Aftertexts (1987)
The Grants-Fix (1987)
Conversing with Cage (1988)
On Innovative Music(ian)s (1989)
Politics in the African-American Novel (1991)
The New Poetries and Some Olds (1991)
Solos, Duets, Trios & Choruses (1991)
On Innovative Art(ist)s (1992)
Partitions (1992)
Wordworks: Poems Selected and New (1993)
On Innovative Performance(s) (1993)
A Dictionary of the Avant-Gardes (1993)

Books Edited
On Contemporary Literature (1964, 1969)
Twelve from the Sixties (1967)
The Young American Writers (1967)
Beyond Left & Right (1968)
Possibilities of Poetry (1970)
Imaged Words & Worded Images (1970)
Moholy-Nagy (1970)
John Cage (1970)
Social Speculations (1971)
Human Alternatives (1971)
Future's Fictions (1971)
Seeing Through Shuck (1972)
In Youth (1972)
Breakthrough Fictioneers (1973)
The Edge of Adaptation (1973)
Essaying Essays (1975)
Language & Structure (1975)
Younger Critics in North America (1976)
Esthetics Contemporary (1978, 1989)
Assembling Assembling (1978)
Visual Literature Criticism (1979)
Text-Sound Texts (1980)
Scenarios (1980)
Aural Literature Criticism (1981)
The Literature of SoHo (1981)
American Writing Today (1981, 1989)
The Avant-Garde Tradition in Literature (1982)
Gertrude Stein Advanced (1991)
Merce Cunningham (1992)
Writings about John Cage (1993)

Books Co-authored & Edited
The New American Arts (1965)

Books Co-compiled & Introduced
Assembling (Twelve vols, 1970-1981)

Performance Scripts
Epiphanies (1980)
Seductions (1986)
Lovings (1991)

Portfolios
Numbers One (1974)
Word Prints (1975)

Audiotapes
Experimental Prose (1976)
Openings & Closings (1976)
Foreshortenings & Other Stories (1977)
Praying to the Lord (1977, 1981)
Asdescent/Anacatabasis (1978)
Invocations (1981)
Seductions (1981)
The Gospels/Die Evangelien (1982)
Relationships (1983)
The Eight Nights of Hanukah (1983)
Two German Horspiel (1983)
New York City (1984)
A Special Time (1985)
Le Bateau Ivre/The Drunken Boat (1986)
Resumé (1988)
Onomatopoeia (1988)
Carnival of the Animals (1988)
Americas' Game (1988)
Epiphanies (1982-)
More or Less (1988-)
Kaddish (1990)

Extended Radio Features
Audio Art (1978)
Text-Sound in North America (1981)
Hörspiel USA: Radio Comedy (1983)
Glenn Gould as a Radio Artist (1983)
Audio Writing (1984)
Radio Comedy Made in America Today (1986)
New York City Radio (1987)
Orson Welles as an Audio Artist (1988)
Schallplatten Hörspiel (1989)
Norman Corwin (1991)

Videotapes
Three Prose Pieces (1975)
Openings & Closings (1975)
Declaration of Independence (1979)
Epiphanies (1980)
Partitions (1986)
Video Writing (1987)
Home Movies Reconsidered (1987)
Two Erotic Videotapes (1988)
Americas' Game (1988)
Invocations (1988)
The Gospels Abridged (1988)
Kinetic Writing (1989)
Video Strings (1989)
Stringtwo (1990)
Onomatopoeia (1990)
Kaddish (1991)

Films Produced & Directed
Epiphanies (in German, 1983; in English, 1981-)

Films Co-produced & Directed
Constructivist Fictions (1978)
Ein Verlorenes Berlin (1983)
Ett Forlorat Berlin (1984)
A Berlin Lost (1985)
Berlin Perdu (1986)
El Berlin Perdido (1987)
Berlin Sche-Einena Jother (1988)

Holograms
On Holography (1978)
Antitheses (1985)
Hidden Meanings (1989)

Retrospective Exhibitions
Wordsand (1978)

JOHN CAGE: WRITER

WRITER

PREVIOUSLY UNCOLLECTED PIECES

Selected and Introduced by
Richard Kostelanetz

Limelight Editions
New York 1993

First Edition February 1993

Library of Congress Cataloging-in-Publication Data:

Cage, John.
    [Literary works. Selections]
    John Cage, writer / selected and introduced by Richard Kostelanetz. — 1st ed.
        pp.   cm.
    ISBN 0-87910-163-6 (cloth) — ISBN 0-87910-164-4
    1. Music—History and criticism. I. Kostelanetz, Richard.
II. Title.
ML60.C125 1993   92-41359
780—dc20   CIP MN

Designed and typeset by Mitchell Corber.

From both JC and RK
To Lou Harrison

CONTENTS

ACKNOWLEDGMENTS

The chapters of *John Cage: Writer* first appeared in the following publications, sometimes in different form:

"Listening to Music" (c. 1937), "Remarks Before a David Tudor Recital" (c. 1959), "Program Notes (c. 1959)," "Three Asides on the Dance" (late 1950s), all previously unpublished, reprinted by permission of the author

Most notes and instructions for Cage's musical compositions, "Prefatory Note for Cowell's *Quartet Romantic* and *Quartet Euphometric*" (1974), from *Contemporary Music Catalogue* (1975), reprinted by permission of C.F. Peters Corporation

Musical examples reproduced courtesy of Henmar Press, Inc. (C.F. Peters Corporation)

"East in the West (1946)," *Modern Music* XXIII/2 (April 1946), by permission of the author

"A Composer's Confessions (1948)," *Musicworks*, 52 (Spring 1992), by permission of the publisher, © 1992 by John Cage

"Contemporary Music Festivals Are Held in Italy (1949)," *Musical America* (June 1949), by permission of the publisher

"A Few Ideas about Music and Film (1951)," reprinted from *Film Music News* (Jan.-Feb. 1951), by permission of the author

"Preface to *Indeterminacy* (1959)," from notes to a Folkways record, by permission of the author and Folkways/Smithsonian

"Remarks on *Theater Song* and *Ikon* (1961)," reprinted from a Wesleyan University publication, by permission of the author. Copyright © 1961 by John Cage

"A Movement, A Sound, A Change of Light (1964)" and other texts contributed to the publications of the Merce Cunningham Dance Company, by permission of David Vaughan, administrator

"On Nam June Paik's *Zen for Film (1962-64)*" (1968), reprinted from *Cinema Now* (University of Cincinnati, 1968), by permission of the author

"Art and Technology," origins unknown, reprinted by permission of the author. Copyright © 1969 by John Cage

Dust-jacket notes to the hardback edition of *Notations* (Something Else, 1969), by permission of Richard C. Higgins

"Political/Social Ends?" (1969), reprinted from *Source No. 6*, III/2 (1969), by permission of Larry Austin, editor/publisher

Foreword to Richard Bunger's *The Well-Prepared Piano* (1973) by permission of the Colorado College Music Press

"7 Out of 23" (1977), reprinted from *Tri-Quarterly*, 38 (1977), by permission of the author

"If There Isn't Any, Why Do You Wear Them?" reprinted from *Unmuzzled Ox*, IV/3 (1977); "Mushrooms," *Poets Encyclopedia* (1979), by permission of Michael Andre

"Music and Particularly Silence in the Work of Jackson MacLow," reprinted from *Paper Air*, II/3 (1980), by permission of the publisher

"More on Paik" (1982), English original reprinted by permission of Toni Stoss, Kunsthaus Zürich

"Music and Art," from Karin von Maur, *Von Klang der Bilder-Die Musik in der Kunst des 20 Jahrhunderts* (Staatsgalerie Stuttgart, 1985), by permission of Dr. van Maur

"Writing through 'Howl,'" reprinted from *Best Minds* (Lospacchio Press, 1986), courtesy of Bob Rosenthal for the publisher and Allen Ginsberg

"Tokyo Lecture and Prefaces to Three Mesostics (1988)," reprinted from *Perspectives of New Music*, XXVI/1 (Winter 1988), by permission of the publisher

"Storia dell'Opera" and "Synopses" (1988), reprinted from the catalogue *Europera* by permission of the Frankfurt Opera

"Time (Three Autokus)" (1988), from *Musik-Konzepte* (1990), by permission of the author

"Marshall McLuhan," from *Marshall McLuhan: The Man and His Message* (1989), by permission of George Sanderson and Frank Macdonald, Fulcrum Press, Colorado

"Sports," *New Observations*, 66 (April 1989) by permission of the publisher

"Macrobiotic Cooking," *Aerial 6/7*, edited by Rod Smith, by permission of the publisher, © 1991 by Aerial/Edge

"Music Without Horizon Soundscape That Never Stops (1991)," reprinted from *Festival Wiener Klassic* (1991), by permission of the publisher

"Mirakus 2," *Mirage Verbal*, by permission of the publisher, © 1990 by John Cage & Ulysse Fin de Siecle (74 rue de Velars, F-21370 Plombiers-les-Dijon, France)

"An Autobiographical Statement," *Southwest Review* (Winter 1991) by permission of the author and publisher

Everything by John Cage, by permission of John Cage. Copyright © 1993 by The Estate of John Cage

"Introduction," by Richard Kostelanetz, reprinted from *Talisman* (1993), by permission of the author and publisher

"Second Preface," by Richard Kostelanetz, reprinted from *Exquisite Corpse*, 39 (1992), by permission of the author

PREFACE

One day as I was sitting for a long time outdoors in our wooded dance-deck, I became aware of light on a tree, a red berry that fell at my side, a fog horn in the distance, and children shouting; and I wondered if they were really in trouble or just playing. These chance relationships, each independent of the other, seemed beautiful to me.

Anna Halprin
The Theatre of Mixed Means (1968)

To me, John Cage has always been a writer as well as a composer, as major a writer as he is a composer; and so for the past quarter century I have been writing about his writings, as well as anthologizing selections from them as poetry, as social thought, as esthetic philosophy. That accounts for why it is a pleasure to edit a selection of his previously uncollected writings—pieces that haven't appeared in any books published under his name or with his name in the title. Customarily, such writings might be classified as poetry or esthetics or reportage, but since those categories don't work for Cage, here they appear in chronological order, in sum illustrating my thesis about Cage as a major American author.

The richest appreciation of Cage's poetry is Jackson MacLow's, which is reprinted in another anthology of mine, *Writings about John Cage* (University of Michigan Press, 1993), that also contains my review of Cage's longest and best poem, *I–VI*.

I am grateful to Cage's original publishers for permissions to reprint work here; to Melvyn Zerman of Limelight Editions for commissioning this book as an appropriate sequel to earlier books of mine published by him; to Mitchell Corber for his typesetting, design, and conscientious considerations, in sum reflecting his prior involvement in the production of his videotape *John Cage: Man and Myth* (1990); to Don Gillespie of C.F. Peters Corporation, Cage's music publishers for sharing archives and intelligence; to Tennessee Jerry Hunt for preparing Cage's notes on his compositions; to Andrew Culver for manning Cage's computer; to Nicole Hinrichs for proofreading; and, of course, to John Cage himself, for letting me compose his words once again.

Richard Kostelanetz
New York City
14 May 1992

EPIGRAPHS

Cage has often called the use of chance operations and the composition of works indeterminate as to performance "skillful means" (Skt. *upaya*, a Buddhist term for means employed by Boddhivistas to help all sentient beings attain enlightenment). I think he views the experiences of composing, performance, and hearing such works as being equally conducive to the arousal of *prajn'a* — intuitive wisdom/ energy, the essence/seed of the enlightened state — by allowing the experience of sounds perceived in themselves, "in their suchness," rather than as means of communication, expression, or emotional arousal or as subordinate elements in a structure.

These considerations are as relevant to his writing as to his music — especially to the poems he has written since about 1970, most of which are alogical and asyntactical collages (i.e., ones "departing from conventional syntax") or language elements: letters, syllables, words, phrases, and/or sentences, freed from "the arrangement of an army" (the original meaning, as Norman O. Brown informed him, of "syntax"), and therefore — like the sounds in the music he wrote after 1950 — perceivable in themselves as are objects of perception when one regards them with "bare attention" during *vipasyana* (skt., contemplation), the basic form of Buddhist tradition.

Jackson MacLow
"Something About the Writings of John Cage" (1992)

There has been a kind of prejudice against [John] Cage as a visual artist, although he has made visual art for much of his life. The art world does not like cross-cultural figures, particularly when, like Cage, they are best known for their work in another discipline, when their visual art might be no more than a sideline. Cage's drawings, prints, and installations are so wonderful as to belie that observation, and there is little doubt that he is one of the key artists of the century. As soon as he performs the art-historically correct art of dying he will be recognized as such, and I would argue that within a generation he, like Duchamp, will be totally lionized after being totally neglected, and that, as time passes, the works of his more visually active disciples and acolytes such as Jasper Johns and Robert Rauschenberg might begin to appear to recede in significance.

James Yood
"Taking Stock"
New Art Examiner (Jan. 1992)

Allen [Ginsberg] must be taken seriously as a serious composer in the music-historical music, as Cage must be taken so as a writer.

Nam June Paik
Best Minds (1986)

SECOND PREFACE

As this book was passing through proofs, John Cage died suddenly of a stroke. It was August 12, a Wednesday; the stroke had occurred the evening before, as he was preparing the customary evening tea for his principal companion in both life and art, the choreographer Merce Cunningham.

I had first met Cage twenty-six years ago, likewise in the late summer, at his house in Stony Point, New York. Actually, it was less a house in a compound of houses (most of them occupied by artists and musicians) than an attachment having only two rooms, each about twenty feet by ten, one behind the other, with a utility core in the middle. He lived at the time with few possessions; and when artists tried to give him their works, as they often did, he merely handed them back, with the excuse that he evidently had no space.

I had come to interview him for the *New York Times Magazine*, for a double profile of him and Milton Babbitt that appeared the following winter and has since been reprinted in my book *On Innovative Music(ian)s* (Limelight, 1989). When I returned to this house a few years later to collect material for the documentary monograph that appeared in 1970 (and was reprinted by Da Capo), he found his "archive" by lifting up his bed. That's why I was surprised to discover, once he moved back to Manhattan, a loft filled with plants.

Notwithstanding his advocacy of freedom in art, the man lived a disciplined life. He answered the telephone politely; and if he promised to do something, you did not need to remind him. He answered his mail promptly, even when he was traveling. Though he did not always write music, my sense is that he wrote words every day, for language was as important to him as sounds.

His competence at proofreading never ceased to awe me. (Should you compliment him about it, as I did, he would attribute its meticulousness to having been born in early September.) Two days after receiving the final proofs of *Conversing with Cage* (Limelight, 1988), he telephoned to say that he had to read them three times, because he found in the text a passage that duplicated something that appeared earlier; but not until his third time through the proofs did he discover that a passage near the end of the book also appeared as an epigraph!

Cage possessed a strong memory, perhaps reflective of the quality of his attention. Since he was so swamped with commitments relating to celebrations of his upcoming eightieth birthday, I gave him not the manuscript of this book but only its table of contents. What is "If There Isn't Any, Why Do You Wear Them?" (1977), he asked me. It's a mesostic, I told him, referring to a poetic form he pioneered and has used recently in countless texts. "Oh yes," he replied. "The one about shoes." On his *Indeterminacy* record (1957) is a story declaimed in a Japanese accent I thought so peculiar perhaps it should be removed from the forthcoming reissue. Oh, no, he replied, the weekend before he died, it describes an incident told to him by "Malcolm Roberts, in Seattle" — which must have been over fifty years before.

One professional rule important to Cage was that one should always be as generous as possible with colleagues. When I first mentioned the possibility of a selection from his uncollected writings, he thought he should do it, since all these writings were his. I acceded to that wish until he told me that, since he was not going to do it, I should; that is how this book happened. By leaving so much in the performance of his scores to the choices of the performers, he was, some say, permitting "chance." I think the theme was *trust*, which I, as the performer/interpreter of his texts, respect no less than his instrumentalists.

Although my creative work (poems, stories, and audiotapes) are not customarily classified as Cagean, I find it hard to note all the ways in which they are indebted to him; they would not have happened as they have without his influence.

Richard Kostelanetz
New York City
14 August 1992

INTRODUCTION

My theme holds that, regardless of what you think of his music, John Cage (1912–1992) should be considered a major American author.

Progress in the acceptance of avant-garde art is a tricky business, and when someone does distinguished experimental work in two or more arts, with work in one art no less radical than the work in another, we get to measure from the process (no, progress) of acceptance how the art worlds might differ, at least in regard to experimental work.

From the time that his name first entered my critical imagination, a quarter century ago, Cage has been as much a distinguished writer as a distinguished composer; and so it was appropriate that his work was included in my 1970 comprehensive anthology of post–WWII American work, *Possibilities of Poetry.*

His work as a composer has found more acceptance in our cultural world, as music departments sponsor festivals of his work, but to this day I know of no other general, as distinct from sectarian, anthology of poetry in which his writings appear. You won't find his name in many (if any) broad-based histories of American poetry; and although Marjorie Perloff honors him in her preface to the third edition of *Contemporary Poets* (St. James Press, 1980), which contains individual critical appreciations of several hundred English-language poets, not even in the fifth and most recent edition (1991) is there an entry on Cage's work! It is no small achievement for a major eighty-year-old American artist/writer to do work that is so widely unacceptable. (Try to think of another example.)

If his poetry is about audacious technical inventions, his prose, especially about his own work and its esthetic implications, realizes an interesting, persuasive manner of talking about art, emphasizing technical details in a modest way, even when they could be radically original and provocative, never claiming anything that might not be true. To get a sense of the difference between Cage and his colleagues, consider the following from Aaron Copland:

Dance Panels is in seven contrasting sections: the introduction, with long sustained notes, is in slow waltz tempo; a second section continues the waltz rhythm; the third is a light transparent scherzando; the fourth is a melancholy and nostalgic *pas de trois* featuring solo flute; the fifth is characterized by brisk rhythms and jazzy drum patterns; the sixth is a lyrical episode with a finale in jagged irregular rhythms; and the seventh section ends the piece as quietly as it began.

Within these confines, the separate sections are varied in character and easily identifiable, although they are to be played without pause. The score begins and ends with related material. The music is composed in a simple and direct style. The lyrical parts are very diatonic, "white-notey," one might say, while the lively and bouncy portions have more complexity of texture.

Note especially the use of words descriptive of emotional effect, as though the composer knew how his music would be (or should be) taken. There is none of that sort of pretense in Cage. Instead, he writes about his most ambitious compositon of the early 1950s:

The *Music of Changes* is a piece in four parts in the rhythmic structure 3, 5, 6¾, 6¾, 5, 3⅛ expressed in changing tempi. The composing means involved chance operations from the *I Ching*, the Chinese Book of Changes, a detailed description of which is given in *Silence* (Wesleyan University Press). The notation expresses a relation between time and space such as exists in the case of sound recorded on magnetic tape. Here a quarter-note equals 2½ centimeters.

In my considered opinion, no American composer has written about his work as modestly and yet elegantly, as concisely and yet at times wittily; and one, essential purpose of *John Cage: Writer* is reprinting all his program notes, a history of his inventive designs, apart from descriptions that are really musical scores (and thus should not be reprinted).

A second feature of Cage's critical prose is esthetic resonance; so that while he is talking about music, say, or an individual painter, his remarks can be often understood with reference to art in general.

The principal themes of Cage's poetry have been technical invention and then his own wavering between personal expression and the use of favored texts in lieu of his own words. The first technical invention appeared in the Diaries of the late 1960s, in which remarks of various lengths are printed in various typefaces, as made available on an IBM Selectric. To Jackson MacLow, the result is "a mosaic of ideas, statements, words, and stories." The only poet who could have written such poetry before would have had to have been a printer as well, like William Blake. It goes without saying, almost, that such poetry provided not only a different look but a different read from what every other American writer was doing.

Later inventions include the mesostic made with rub-off letters, the poem composed of fragments drawn from another author's texts (Henry David Thoreau's remarks about music, later James Joyce's *Finnegans Wake*), prose whose typography represents the rhythm of his speech, and the typographical mesostic, which he has used not only for recomposing other writers' texts (Allen Ginsberg's *Howl*, Pound's *Cantos*, the Bible), but for occasional verse about favorite subjects and for favored people. A later commentator will no doubt identify other inventions in the writings of this profoundly innovative mind. Our purpose behind many (though not all) of these inventions is to increase the degree of unintentionality.

Among academic critics, this work has had only one admirer really, Professor Marjorie Perloff, who differs from me in tending to emphasize the less radical and thus more acceptable qualities of Cage's writing, perhaps because she is addressing fellow academics, acknowledging their limited range of esthetic understanding, rather than pursuing radical implications to unfamiliar ends. Not even Perloff acknowledges Cage as a writer of distinguished creative prose (as distinct from criticism/esthetics). I would begin with the ninety stories that comprise his 90-minute *Indeterminacy*, each meant to be one minute long, which are read differently (in *Silence*) after you've heard the record or a live performance (at times as an accompaniment to Merce Cunningham dances). Cage is also capable of writing humor in the tradition of Twain, with ironies entwined in ironies.

The cataloguing of Cage's music I gladly leave to others. But since his writings and speakings have meant so much to me, it has been a pleasure to collect them into several volumes now.

RK

NOTES ON COMPOSITIONS I (1933-48)

Nearly all of Cage's notes on his compositions to 1961 come from a catalogue, John Cage, *published by C.F. Peters (Henmar Press) in 1962, with the preface also reprinted below.*

Not all of my work is in this catalogue. Many scores have seemed to me inferior in quality. I have not destroyed them. But the works which are listed represent all the various paths my musical thought has taken: chromatic composition dealing with the problem of keeping repetitions of individual tones as far apart as possible (1933-34); composition with fixed rhythmic patterns or tone-row fragments (1935-38); composition for the dance, film and theatre (1935-); composition within rhythmic structures (the whole having as many parts as each unit has small parts, and these, large and small, in the same proportion) (1939-56); intentionally expressive composition (1938-51); composition using charts and moves thereon (1951); composition using chance operations (1951-); composition using templates made or found (1952-); composition using observation of imperfections in the paper upon which it is written (1952-); composition without a fixed relation of parts to score (1954-); composition indeterminate of its performance (1958-). I have written a brief note for each of the entries in this catalogue, hoping to enable the reader to get an idea of the character of a particular piece.

John Cage
Stony Point, New York
July 1962

Sonata for Two Voices (1933), for any 2 or more instruments encompassing the following ranges: I, c' to c"; II, c to c", is a chromatic composition in three movements (sonata, fugato and rondo) dealing with the same problem as that of *Composition for 3 Voices.*

Solo with Obbligato Accompaniment of Two Voices in Canon, and Six Short Inventions on the Subjects of the Solo

(1933), for any three or more instruments encompassing the range g to g", is a chromatic composition dealing with the problem of keeping repetitions of individual tones of a twenty-five tone range, the same for each voice, as far apart as possible, though each voice is obliged to express all twenty-five tones before introducing a repetition.

Solo for Clarinet (1933) is an unaccompanied chromatic work in three movements, the last of which though not rhythmically is a retrograde canon of the first. Octave transpositions are employed.

Six Short Inventions (1934) deals with the same problem as that of *Composition for 3 Voices*. The limitations here, however, are greater since all three voices employ the same twenty-five tone range. The instrumentation [for 7 players] is recent (1958).

Composition for 3 Voices (1934) is a chromatic composition dealing with the problem of keeping repetitions of individual tones of the three superimposed twenty-five tone ranges as far apart as possible, even though each voice is obliged to express all twenty-five tones before introducing a repetition of any one of them.

Quartet (any percussion instruments, 1935) is a work in three movements wholly composed of fixed rhythmic patterns.

Three Pieces for Flute Duet (1935) are studies in two-part chromatic writing.

Trio (1936) is a suite of three movements (*Allegro, March* and *Waltz*) wholly composed of fixed rhythmic patterns. The waltz was later incorporated in *Amores* (1943) as the second trio. The instruments are skin and wood.

Five Songs for Contralto (1938) are chromatic songs employing unorthodox uses of twelve-tone composing means. The e.e. cummings poems are *little four paws, little Christmas tree, in Just-, hist whist,* and *another comes.*

Metamorphosis (1938), a twelve-tone piece [for piano] in five movements, is wholly composed of row fragments never subjected to variation. The transpositions of these fragments were chosen according to the intervals of the series.

Music for Wind Instruments (1938) is a twelve-tone piece wholly composed of row fragments never subjected to variation. The transpositions of these fragments were chosen according to the intervals of the series. Silences were also composed of durations equal to those of the row fragments.

First Construction (in Metal) (1939) is written in the rhythmic structure 4, 3, 2, 3, 4, sixteen times sixteen measures of 4/4. The first four 16's are an exposition of individual bodies of material characterized by differences of rhythmic pattern and instrumentation. The remainder is development (without re-exposition), to which is added a 12–measure coda.

Imaginary Landscape No. 1 (1939) is for two variable-speed phono-turntables, frequency recordings, muted piano, and cymbal; to be performed as a recording or broadcast.

Four 15–measure sections divided into three equal parts alternate with three interludes and a coda. Each interlude is one measure longer than the preceding one. The first, one measure long, introduces three rhythmic elements which one by one are subtracted from the interludes to be added one by one to the middle parts of the second and third and to the final part of the fourth 15–measure section. The completion of this process reestablishes the original form of the interlude, which, by means of repetition (first of the whole and then of the second half only), is extended, concluding the piece.

Bacchanale (1940) is the first piece composed for the prepared piano. The need to change the sound of the instrument arose through the desire to make an accompaniment, without employing percussion instruments, suitable for the dance by Syvilla Fort for which it was to be composed.

Living Room Music: A Story (1940), for percussion and speech quartet, is a suite of three pieces: *To Begin With*, *A Story*, and *To End With*. The percussion instruments are those to be found in a living room—furniture, books, paper, windows, walls, doors.

Second Construction (1940) (percussion quartet) concludes with a "fugue" which is placed in opposition to the rhythmic structure, 4, 3, 4, 5. The instruments are predominantly metal and skin with string piano (manually muted and productive of a siren-like sound by means of a cylinder sliding on the strings while a trill is produced on the keyboard).

Double Music (in collaboration with Lou Harrison) (1941) is a percussion quartet. Specific instruments are called for, but performers are permitted to make substitutions, if necessary, keeping the soprano-alto-tenor-bass relation of parts clear. Dynamics are scarcely indicated. The piece does not progress from soft to loud but is continuously festive in intention, the changes in amount and nature of activity producing changes in amplitude. The alto and bass parts were composed by Lou Harrison.

Third Construction (percussion quartet, 1941) has a rhythmic structure of 24 times 24. This is differently expressed in each part. An attempt was made to compose rhythmic "cadences." The instruments are rattles, drums, tin cans, claves, cowbells, lion's roar, cymbal, ratchet, teponaxtle, quijadas, cricket caller and conch shell.

Credo in Us (1942) is a suite of satirical character composed within the phraseology of the dance by Merce Cunningham and Jean Erdman for which it was written. The instruments used are muted gongs, tin cans, tom-toms, an electric buzzer, piano and radio or phonograph.

Forever and Sunsmell (1942), with words by e.e. cummings, is a piece in two parts (the first dramatic, the second lyrical) connected by an unaccompanied hummed interlude. The work follows the phraseology of the dance by Jean Erdman for which it was composed.

March (Imaginary Landscape No. 2) (percussion quartet, 1942) has a rhythmic structure of 3, 4, 2, 3, 5. The percussion instruments (tin cans, conch shell, ratchet, bass drum, buzzers, water gong, metal wastebasket, lion's roar) are combined with an amplified coil of wire.

Imaginary Landcape No. 3 (percussion sextet, 1942): The rhythmic structure is 12 times 12 (3, 2, 4, 3). The percussion instruments, tin cans and a muted gong, are combined with electronic and mechanical devices including audio frequency oscillators, variable speed turntables for the playing of frequency recordings and generator whines, and a buzzer. An amplified coil of wire and a marimbula amplified by means of a contact microphone are also used.

The Wonderful Widow of Eighteen Springs (1942), voice and closed piano: The voice production is without vibrato, as in folksinging. The singer may make any transposition of the written notes in order to employ a low and comfortable range. The accompaniment is percussive, fingers and knuckles on the wooden structure of a closed piano. The music resulted from impressions received from the text from *Finnegans Wake*.

Totem Ancestor (for prepared piano, 1942) was written for the dance by Merce Cunningham and its phraseology corresponds to that of the dance.

Amores (1943), two solos for prepared piano, with the addition of two trios for percussion: Nine screws, eight bolts, two nuts and three strips of rubber, acting as mutes, were placed between the strings pertaining to eighteen keys. Upon this instrument an attempt was made to express in combination the erotic and the tranquil, two of the permanent emotions of Indian tradition. The second solo is written in the rhythmic structure 3, 3, 2, 2.

The first trio is written in the rhythmic structure ten times ten. The second employs fixed rhythmic patterns which are never subjected to variation; it was written several years earlier being also a part of the *Trio* (1936). The piano preparation is not elaborate. The work is an attempt to express in combination the erotic and the tranquil, two of the permanent emotions of Indian tradition. The second solo is written in the rhythmic structure 3, 3, 2, 2.

Tossed As It Is Untroubled (1943) is a lively dance in periodic rhythm written in the rhythmic structure 7 times 7. The piano preparation is not elaborate.

A Room (1943) is the third piece in a projected concert employing various instruments and musicians which was never completed. The first pieces are those of *She Is Asleep*. Their rhythmic structure, 4, 7, 2, 5; 4, 7, 2, 3, 5 is continued in this piece. The notation is conventional and the piano preparation is not elaborate.

She Is Asleep (1943): The *Duet* is a vocalise, the sounds of which (mainly vowels) are to be determined by the singer. The piano preparation is very simple: four pieces of rubber between the strings of four high piano keys.

She Is Asleep (1943), quartet for tom-toms, with the addition of a Duet for voice and prepared piano. Center and edges of tom-toms are distinguished in the notation. The performers play with fingers; right and left hands are not distinguished. The rhythmic structure is 4, 7, 2, 5; 4, 7, 2, 3, 5. A method controlling the number of attacks within the small structural divisions was used to differentiate the structural parts.

A Book of Music (for 2 prepared pianos, 1944) is a piece in two large parts written in the rhythmic structure 2, 7, 2, 3; 2, 7, 2, 3, 3 when the tempo is 66 (Part I), expressed as 5, 21, 5, 7; 5, 21, 5, 7, 7 when the tempo is 176 (Part II). The notation is conventional, the piano preparations relatively elaborate. The expression concerns feelings, both personal and musical. The work was written especially for virtuoso performance.

The Perilous Night (1944) is a suite of six pieces of varied character and differing rhythmic structures using a moderately elaborate piano preparation.

Root of an Unfocus (1944) is in a rhythmic structure corresponding to that of the dance by Merce Cunningham for which it was written. The piece is dramatic in character and the piano preparation is not extensive.

Prelude for Meditation (for prepared piano, 1944) uses four tones in a rhythmic structure five times five.

A Valentine Out of Season (1944) is a suite of three pieces of varying character, the more dance-like being centrally placed. Difficulties of piano preparation and performance were intentionally avoided.

Three Dances (for 2 prepared pianos, 1945) is written to the rhythmic structure 2, 5, 2; 2, 6, 2; 2, 7, 2 when the tempo is 88. These numbers change when the tempo changes, an attempt having been made to maintain actual time proportions. The notation is conventional and the piano preparations are more elaborate than in *A Book of Music*. The expression is physical and moves from simplicity to complexity. This piece was written especially for virtuosos.

Daughters of the Lonesome Isle (for prepared piano, 1945) is a piece of atmospheric character, conventionally notated. Its phraseology is that of the dance by Jean Erdman for which it was written.

Experiences I (1945-48) [for 2 pianos] was written in the rhythmic structure of the dance by Merce Cunningham, the same employed for *Experiences II* (for voice). The melodic line, modal in character, is nearly the same in both pieces.

Experiences II (1945-48) [for solo voice; text: e.e. cummings] was written in the rhythmic structure of the dance by Merce Cunningham, the same employed for *Experiences I* (for two pianos). The melodic line, modal in character, is nearly the same in both pieces.

Mysterious Adventure (for prepared piano, 1945), written for the dance, followed the rhythmic structure given by Merce Cunningham. The notation is conventional.

Ophelia (for piano, 1946) is a piece of dramatic character having a phraseology corresponding to that of the dance by Jean Erdman for which it was composed.

Sonatas and Interludes (1946-48) are an attempt to express in music the "permanent emotions" of Indian tradition: the heroic, the erotic, the wondrous, the mirthful, sorrow, fear, anger, the odious and their common tendency toward tranquility. The first eight, the twelfth, and the last four sonatas are written in AABB rhythmic structures of varying proportions, whereas the first two interludes have no structural repetitions. This difference is exchanged in the last two interludes and the sonatas nine through eleven which have respectively a prelude, interlude, and postlude. The preparation of the piano is relatively elaborate, requiring two or three hours to effect. The compositional opinions involved are the subject of an article, "Forerunners of Modern Music," which is included in *Silence* (Wesleyan University Press).

Music for Marcel Duchamp (1947) has a simple piano preparation: seven pieces of weather-stripping, one of rubber and a small bolt. Notated in the alto clef, the rhythmic structure is 11 times 11 (extended); 2, 1, 1, 3, 1, 2, 1. The performance depends on the sustaining of resonances with the pedal.

Nocturne for Violin and Piano (1947): An attempt is made to dissolve the difference between string and piano sounds though the convention of melody and accompaniment is maintained. The character of the piece is atmospheric and depends for its performance on a constant rubato and the sustaining of resonances.

The Seasons, a Ballet in One Act (1947), commissioned by the Ballet Society, is an attempt to express the traditional Indian view of the seasons as quiescence (winter), creation (spring), preservation (summer), and destruction (fall). It concludes with the *Prelude to Winter* with which it begins. The rhythmic structure is 2, 2, 1, 3, 2, 4, 1, 3, 1. It was written for the ballet by Merce Cunningham. The sounds are a gamut (variously orchestrated) of single tones, intervals and aggregates.

The scenario given me by Mr. Cunningham was the basis for a study of numbers with which I find it congenial to begin a musical composition. His remark, "the fullness and stillness of a summer day," suggested that Summer would be the longest section; that, together with his desire that each season would be developed by continuous invention and preceded by a short formal prelude (formal by means of exact repetitions), and that the entire work would be cyclical and concise, brought about the following numerical situation: 2,2; 1,3; 2,4; 1,3; 1. The number, 4, represents Summer, since it is the largest number (it is also the smallest number which could be the largest number in this situation); the first 3 is Spring, the second, Fall (3's are, like these seasons, asymmetrical, un-static): they suggest both the approach to and away from 4. The second 2 is Winter, for 2 suggests the place between two 3's, opposite a 4. The other numbers are the Preludes. Summer (4) has a Prelude of 2 (fittingly, the longest). Spring and Fall have Preludes of 1. Winter has a Prelude of 2 which is actually 1 repeated.

This was done to provide an instrumental description of atmosphere before the actual dancing begins (the ballet begins with Winter), and to provide an end-piece which was the same, but suitably proportioned to the other preludes as dance accompaniment. This made 2 to begin with and 1 to end with. The entire series of numbers occurs throughout the ballet, not only with respect to the length of sections, but, as is my custom in works for percussion and "prepared" piano, also with respect to phraseology. Thus within each 1, the series given above occurs as the determinant of breathing. Within the 4 of Summer, it occurs 4 times, etc. The tempo changes the actual number of measures as it changes: actual time length being the basis of this plan. Naturally, a plan like this is made not only to be followed, but also that it may be broken. Yet the pleasure of breaking a law can only exist if the law is existent. The question arises whether one can know this rhythmic structure from a first hearing. The answer clearly is: No.

Dream (for piano, 1948) was written in the rhythmic structure of the dance by Merce Cunningham. It employs a fixed gamut of tones and depends in its performance on the sustaining of resonances either manually or with the pedal.

In a Landscape (for harp or piano, 1948) was written in the rhythmic structure of the dance by Louise Lippold. It is similar to *Dream* but the fixed gamut of tones is more extensive. Its performance depends on the sustaining of resonances with the pedal.

Suite for Toy Piano (1948) employs a restricted gamut of tones, that of the nine "white" keys from E below middle C to F above. These nine tones appear only in the third and fourth of the five pieces of this suite, the first and last of which employ only five tones, G to D. The rhythmic structure is 7, 7, 6, 6, 4.

SUITE FOR TOY PIANO

JOHN CAGE
(1948)

Edition Peters 6758

LISTENING TO MUSIC (1937)

Written in Seattle about 1937, this has not been previously published. Like all Cage's early essays, it contains lines that prophesize his later artistic endeavor.

When I was asked to speak concerning the instruments of the orchestra, I was, at first, not interested, for two things occurred to me: (1) that I might catalogue those instruments and their characteristics much as is done by a theorist writing on orchestration (perhaps interspersing anecdotes to relieve the recital), or (2) I might give hints as to how to improve at that game of identifying the sounds of instruments, a game through the aid of which so many people pass an otherwise tiresome hour of symphonic music. We have all been annoyed by our neighbor's asking us if that was a clarinet or an oboe, and what made that sound. When we're guilty ourselves, we have often realized that the curiosity as to labels, the desire to identify and pigeon-hole a pleasure, had separated us from the real job of listening to the whole thing, the rich continuous music, which, itself, never stops for annotation.

I have talked with several musicians who have seriously claimed that music is not made of sound, but rather of the relationships of the sounds, and that in order to appreciate it we must understand its structure. From such a musical point of view, a talk on the instruments of the orchestra would be quite unnecessary. A solo for clarinet might be played on the piano: the music would not change, for the relationships of the sounds would remain the same. Many transcriptions of music have been the result of this point of view, and we have the sad result that very few organists play organ music, satisfying themselves by playing anything else: songs, orchestral overtures, etc.

After remembering this point of view, it seems to me that a talk on the instruments of the orchestra, or rather their relation to music, is of more importance than I had at first thought. Certainly the idea that music is not made of sound requires examination. It might prove false.

In a world in which music is not made of sound, it would seem logical to expect that painting is not made of color and shapes. It would also seem that the two arts might be exchanged, one for the other: The relationships of sound for the relationships of shapes. Our first question can be: Why any shapes or why any sounds? Why not relationships of numbers or relationships of apples?

For fear that you already agree with my inferred contention: that music *is* made of sound, let me remind you of all the recent lectures on music and painting which pretend to help the listener or the observer by pointing out, with emphasis, the structure, form, composition, etc. of music and painting. One is asked, in other words, not to listen to the sound of the music, but to listen to relationships of the sounds. We have here the beginning of another game: HERE COMES THE THEME or What On Earth is Happening Now? Most people will get completely mixed up unless they have learned the rules by heart.

Let us now take, in particular, the Sonata form, which as a matter of fact everyone takes when he is giving a talk on listening to the relationships of music. For one thing, it is a form which has been widely used by the composers of the last century; almost every quartet, symphony, in fact every major musical work has as its first movement the sonata form. We are told that the piece opens with the principal theme in such and such a key. (Those of us who don't know G major from F minor without seeing it written out are already bewildered; what of those unfortunate music lovers who can't read music?) Furthermore there comes next a transition to the group of secondary themes in another related key. How is it related, we may rightfully ask. And the cold but musical answer: it is the key of C major, related to G major as its subdominant, a rather startling innovation, for we should have expected D major, the dominant. Well, we shall let that pass. What happens next? The Development of these themes. But whereas we might have expected a development to be something simple we would understand, such as the development or growth of a seed into a tree, or a child into a man, we find in the sonata form, that it is nothing more or less than more keys—the carrying of the subjects through many different keys. The last part of the sonata form is the one, listening to music in this way, we all love, for it is the recapitulation or repetition of the beginning themes. Knowing beforehand that the recapitulation is going to come, many people listen for it and for it alone, feeling pleased when they recognize it and slightly annoyed when it escapes their notice.

This is an outline of an elementary appreciation of the Sonata form. More advanced formal appreciation will include all the details of the construction of the piece of music, details by which scarcely ever are acquired by the layman. However, if we agree with the premise that music is made of relationships and that, in order to appreciate it these relationships must be discerned, we can give the layman a book on Formal Analysis and dismiss his plight from our minds.

But, after a knowledge of the workings of the sonata form would come analyses of other forms, but with the advent of the new forms of modern music (on which no books are yet written), or the strange forms of oriental music, any layman would surely be lost, no matter how successfully he may have been with the conventional forms. If he thought the appreciation of music lay in the direction of an understanding of its form or the relationships of sounds, he would necessarily devote his life to music alone, as musicians do.

Music then becomes a lonely art, made for those who learn the rules, a rather bleak game, no matter how great some may choose to think it.

How often we hear people say: I don't know anything about it but I know what I like. And in the presence of a musician, the high priest who alone reads the books, most people are afraid to admit any reaction to music, for fear it be the wrong one, or that they mistook the Development for the Recapitulation. This state existing between audience and musicians amounts to an ever-widening gulf and is largely due to the musicians making music obscure, that is: difficult to understand.

I propose a solution.

Let us take a premise which seems apparent and elementary: music is made of sound. Every one with ears may hear it. The music is made to be heard. A piece of music is constructed, much as a chair or building is constructed. But there is no greater need to appreciate it through analysis of the details of its construction than there is that need with regard to our own home, or chair. The chair is useful for sitting, the home for dwelling, the music for hearing.

From this point of view, the one which I am proposing, music need not be understood, but rather it must be heard.

Just as the chair is made of materials, wood and cloth, or metal and leather, just as the house is made of stone or glass, so the music is made of sound. The dimensions of this musical material, sound, are four: Duration or rhythm; Frequency or pitch; Amplitude or dynamics, that is, loudness and softness; and last Timbre, or quality of sound. This last constitutes the only difference between an oboe and a clarinet, when the two instruments are playing the same tone with equal dynamics for the same length of time. From these materials a composer makes music. To be sure, he uses a method in writing, just as the carpenter uses a method in building; and furthermore, he uses his method to make a chair or house. What has been accomplished is an organization of the materials. In the case of music, we often find that this organizing has made otherwise startling sounds seem natural. From the beginning to the end of a fine piece of music the sounds follow one another in a natural sequence. The whole problem (it is really a natural thing, no problem at all) of listening to music is this: Hear the sounds as belonging together. Let the composer spend his days making them belong together. That is scarcely anybody's job but his.

By no means do I think that one should ignore the construction of music, provided he has acquired a knowledge of it. What I do think is that listening to music is one thing and making, composing music is another: two different pleasures. Just as sitting in a chair is quite different from constructing a chair.

Although one might be tempted to think that a knowledge of musical construction would lead to a deeper appreciation of music than the one I am suggesting, this is not the case. Particularly with advanced or modern music, we find it to be definitely not true. Stravinsky was acclaimed not by musicians, but by laymen who knew nothing about music, but who had open ears. George Antheil was recognized by Ezra Pound, a poet. Knowledge often becomes a prejudice. The prejudiced ear is listening not to the sounds, but to the relationships of the sounds, and, not hearing the expected relationships, closes itself.

There are certain popular pitfalls when music is being played that make it well-nigh impossible to hear the music.

First and foremost is the making of sounds which don't belong in the atmosphere at the same time: humming the theme as it returns, or beating audible time to the secondary themes, or as has already been mentioned, asking your neighbor what instrument is playing or who played that instrument, which leads to the second pitfall:

Thinking about something else while the music is being played. This is very easy to do and requires no effort at all. One reason that modern music is not liked by some people is that it is more difficult to wonder what sort of weather there will be tomorrow when Bartok is being played than it is when we are listening to a symphony which we have heard at least twenty-five times. Just as I would recommend not keeping on one's walls pictures which one no longer sees, so I would recommend not listening at all to music which one no longer hears.

And to return to the idea which I am stressing: Thinking about the construction of the music is very apt to be a pitfall to real hearing. I remember turning pages for a performance of Bach's *Art of the Fugue*. One bit of counterpoint engaged my attention; I forgot to turn the page and I forgot to listen. Fortunately it was not a concert performance.

What can we expect to be the result of attentive listening to music? I believe that listening to music makes for our lives another world, living in which, somehow, our hearts beat faster and a mysterious excitement fills us. And the natural flow of sounds which music is reassures us of order just as the sequence of the seasons and the regular alternation of night and day do.

THE EAST IN THE WEST (1946)

On several occasions early in his career, Cage wrote extended essays both critical, as in this example from the most prestigious professional journal of its time, Modern Music, XXIII/2 (April 1946).

In Western music at the present time, certain practices are similar to or characteristic of Oriental classical music, specifically, that of Hindustan. I should like to report on them and advance a possible explanation for the tendency they represent towards a fusion of cultures.

Not relevant to my point are the frank transcriptions of Eastern music, like those, for instance, of the Balinese by Colin McPhee. Faithful to the original, they signify a love of the Orient as it is, rather than a desire to bring elements of it together with those of the Occident to create a new music. Nor am I concerned with music unfaithful to the Oriental original (e.g., Mozart's *Rondo alla Turca* or anyone's *Orientale*), the motivation of which is a taste for the exotic.

The theory of Schoenbergian music, as distinguished from its sound, does represent an action of the type which concerns us. The use of a different twelve-tone row for each composition is similar to the Hindu use of a special raga, or scale, for particular improvisations. The enormous number of ragas which exist is perhaps equalled by the number of possible variations of the order of the twelve tones in a row. This great variety of available "scales" obviously differs from the conventional Western adherence to only two. Each twelve-tone row differs from a major or minor scale in not proceeding in a straight pitch line (from low to high) but, instead, in what may be called a curve; whether a tone in the row is lower or higher than those which precede and follow is not a matter of theory but of individual choice. By not too great a stretch of the mind, this "curve" characteristic of twelve-tone rows may be likened to the characteristic of the Hindu raga, which often uses two series of tones, one in ascending, and a different one in descending. This duality of the Hindu raga is, of course, more like the same characteristic of the Western minor scale. But another characteristic, that a higher octave may present different intervals than does the lower, suggests an arabesque in pitch-space, which is also implicit in the twelve-tone row.

Certainly the Schoenbergian theory is not a conscious imitation of the Hindu raga, and the parallel between the two cannot be accurately drawn. That there is a closer relationship between them than between the minor scale and the raga might be argued. Interestingly enough, Schoenberg places unusual emphasis on the minor scale in his teaching of counterpoint. He requires that all ascending tones be resolved scale-wise upwards in each voice before the introduction of descending tones, and likewise all descending tones downwards by step in each voice before the introduction of ascending tones. This discipline is made the basis of his teaching of "modulation" (all cross-related tones being so handled). Moreover, Schoenberg's insistence that modulation is not a change of scale but merely an emphasis on a particular degree of the original scale brings to mind the Hindu adherence to a single raga for a single improvisation. His erstwhile avoidance of harmony is neither Eastern nor Western. It suggests the Orient, since the East does not practice harmony; but, at the same time, since avoidance is an admission of presence, it suggests the Occident. Schoenberg's use of the twelve-tone row, being motival and thematic, is definitely Western (an Oriental use would be more freely improvisatory). By the term "motival," I mean that method of composition which employs conscious and consistent repetition and variation of a short motive, method which Schoenberg, in his analyses, finds practiced by Beethoven, Bach, Brahms and other composers. Likewise, by "thematic," I mean the use of themes, through repetition and development, for structural purposes. The parallel between twelve-tone and Oriental music attempted above, both begins and ends with the similarities of theory pointed out, for there is no likeness in their sound.

Unlike the Schoenbergian, the music of Alan Hovhaness, young composer of Scottish-Armenian descent, is a conscious fusion of Orient and Occident. Hovhaness diverges both from the Orient and the Occident, and he does this at his own discretion. To the degree that he follows his own ideas in matters of theory, he is Occidental. His music sounds Armenian, but this impression is due largely to our general unfamiliarity with Oriental music. For Hovhaness's music is by no means the faithful transcription, for instance, that McPhee's is; it is the evidence purely of its composer's imagination. Freely invented ragas are used which may change in the upper octaves and which may ascend in one way and descend in another. For purposes of expressivity, he allows a change of one or more tones (generally only one) after the raga has been established. Furthermore, he allows a change of raga altogether, with or without a return to the original one, if the expression so demands. He also combines different ragas by letting them appear simultaneously between voices. The use of raga is Oriental; the idea of changing its tones, of letting others appear either at the same time or later is characteristic of Occidental musical thought. The absence of harmony in Hovhaness's music is Eastern. The fact that his compositions are notated and may be played more than once is Western.

Hovhaness's practices with regard to rhythm suggest the Hindu tala, or metrical plan. But he treats his freely invented talas in Occidental fashion, changing them, introducing or combining others, according to his feeling. The Oriental sound of Hovhaness's music is realized with Occidental instruments (basically string orchestra with or without solo instruments), not by preparing the instruments, nor by employing microtones, but solely through the character of the melodies which they play. This character, which is Oriental, is a gliding along the raga without unresolved leaps. Hovhaness's music (and this characteristic likewise is Eastern) is not motival or thematic, but is continuous invention.

The integral use of percussive sound which appears in the music of Edgard Varèse is also a characteristic of Oriental music. The battery in the West is generally only auxiliary to the other instrumental bodies. Even in his combinations of pitched sound (e.g., *Octandre*), we are reminded more of percussion events than of harmonies. Varèse's frequent use of repeated tones, which bring to his music the image of telegraphic messages, is less melodic than it is percussive. Although he employs generating motives, his use of them is not strict, and his procedure is Orientally non-thematic. His music does not sound Oriental probably because of the absence of anything corresponding to raga or tala.

The microtonality of Alois Haba and others presents an Oriental characteristic not found in any of the music discussed above. Although the Hindu ragas employ generally only seven tones, these seven are chosen from some forty-odd tones in the octave. Haba, as is well known, employs quarter and even one-sixth tones. He uses them, not to make seven-tone scales, but to enrich the possibilities of melodic and harmonic nuance, and to facilitate his non-thematic, non-motival procedure, which he practices in purist fashion. But what I have heard of his music has not sounded Oriental, and, as with Varèse, I think this due to the absence of structural rhythm and integral use of scale. Carrillo's *Cristobal Colon* is the only example of Western microtonal music I know of that uses its scale in step-wise manner with all leaps resolved.

In general, then, there may be pointed out certain large musical conditions which are characteristically Oriental. They are: that the music be non-thematic, non-harmonic, non-motival; that it have (a) an integral step-wise use of scale, (b) structural rhythm, (c) an integral use of percussive sound and (d) pitch distances less than a semi-tone.

One other characteristic, not technical, must be added to the above. It is the quality of being static in sentiment rather than progressive. In Hindu esthetic, the emotion of serenity or tranquility is considered a necessary adjunct to the proper expression of any of the "permanent" emotions, e.g., the erotic, the heroic. In Western music, this point of view is ably expressed in the work of Erik Satie. His *Socrate* presents a vocal line which is continuous invention, which is like an arabesque, and never seems to move towards or away from a climax. Its accompaniment is in the form of musical situations (rather than themes) which recur unaltered. They apparently take place in relation to a predetermined planning of time-lengths. This is a special instance of structural rhythm, and indicates not so much an imitation of Hindu tala systems as it does a fusion of the principle underlying them with that underlying sophisticated Occidental phraseology.

Orientalisms occur in music where we least expect to find them. The non-thematic procedure of Virgil Thomson produces such impressions, reinforced in much of his music (notably the Stein opera) by his integral use of scale. There is, I believe, a similarity also between Western medieval music and Oriental. In other fields than music, Dr. Ananda K. Coomaraswamy has discussed such a relation. The idea is pertinent because a community of purpose has shown itself between those composers whose work is "Oriental" and those whose work is "neo-Gothic" (dissonant total polyphony, e.g., Carl Ruggles, Lou Harrison, Merton Brown). This purpose is to express lofty sentiments in the most direct manner possible, rather than to evoke in any way the "classical" tradition of music.

This is also the purpose of Messiaen, whose music, like a changeable silk, shows now aspects of the Orient, now of the medieval world, and now of twentieth-century French impressionism. It is, incidentally, the emphasis on harmony in Messiaen's music which accounts for its occasional bad taste. This element, harmony, is not medieval nor Oriental but baroque. Because of its ability to enlarge sound and thus to impress an audience, it has become in our time the tool of Western commercialism. Messiaen's use of invented scales and rhythmic structures and his non-thematic procedure (the medieval subject or ground, expressed either melodically or rhythmically, being used instead) account for the congruity between his music and its avowedly spiritual program. These devices, to paraphrase Virgil Thomson, are suitable to "opening up the heavens"; his harmony to "bringing down the house."

Hovhaness's subject matter is also openly religious (the Armenian Church and its precedent mythology). Although Harrison has no direct connection with an organized Church (as do both Hovhaness and Messiaen), his *Motet for the Day of Ascension* is of sacred, rather than secular, intent. Other composers feel more individually along these lines, their music being dedicated, but not destined for liturgical use. Varèse, through the force of his imagination, creates an explosive present between an ancient past and an unknown future. Ruggles, with his *Evocations*, suggests, less literally but more vividly than Ives, the transcendentalism of New England. Thomson, in his *Symphony on a Hymn Tune*, by placing the sublime in constant juxtaposition with the ridiculous, allows each to give measurement to the other in an act of faith, a procedure not unlike that of medieval Christianity which covered its churches with gargoyles. Schoenberg analyzes and fragmentizes his music, so that he seems with Freud to be a founding father of today's cult of the neurosis.

The composers who today wish to imbue their music with the ineffable, seem to find it necessary to make use of musical characteristics not purely Western; they go for inspiration to those places, or return to those times, where or when harmony is not of the essence.

I

_____ = PEDAL   ----- = UNA CORDA.

A COMPOSER'S CONFESSIONS (1948)

This is the original text of the 1948 Vassar College lecture to which Cage frequently refers, because in passing he forecasts two of his more notorious compositions of the early fifties. The text was first published in Musicworks, 52 *(Spring 1992).*

I am going to tell you the story of how I came to write music, and how my musical ideas and my ideas about music developed.

I remember that when I was eight years old, in Santa Monica, California, I saw a sign— PIANO LESSONS —two doors away from where my mother and father and I lived. It was love at first sight; I remember that running and eating became faster and day-dreaming became longer and slower. It made no difference to me what I was taught: the exercises, a piece by Victor Herbert called *Orientale*, and *Für Elise*. I was introduced to "neighborhood music," that branch of the art that all the world loves to play, and I did too.

Neither my mother nor my father took this turn of events with the passion and the intensity that I did. Having before them the examples of two of my aunts and one uncle, they were aware of the economic difficulties which musicians can run into. And deeper than this, my father, who is an inventor and electrical engineer, would have preferred to see me follow in his footsteps, I am sure.

However, they were indulgent and practical: they bought a piano; nothing could have pleased me more. We moved to another neighborhood in Los Angeles and I remember that when the movers were bringing the piano into the new house, before they had its legs on, I was walking along with them playing already by heart Victor Herbert's evocation of the Orient.

My new teacher was my Aunt Phoebe, and she taught me how to sight-read. This was her particular interest, and I am grateful to her for it. She also extended my awareness of the music of the nineteenth century, avoiding, however, that century's masters. Together we played Moskowski's *Spanish Dances* and alone I played Paderewski's *Minuet in G*. Music appeared to be divided according to the technical difficulties it presented to performers: it was first year, second year, third year, and fourth year.

Later on I studied with a teacher who was also a composer, Fannie

27

Charles Dillon. She taught me to play Brahms' *Hungarian Dance No.5*, but my Aunt Phoebe did not agree with Miss Dillon's interpretation.

I remember having a kind of sinking feeling inside myself every time Aunt Phoebe or Miss Dillon played the piano for me or at a recital. The music they knew how to play was fantastically difficult, and my sinking feeling was the realization that I would never be able to perform as well as they.

I stopped taking lessons and fell back on the "open sesame" that Aunt Phoebe had given me: sight-reading. And that, together with a library card, changed music's aspect for me. It no longer was first to fourth year: It was rather A to Z. Of course, my aunt had warned me about Bach and Beethoven (Mozart was not mentioned at all) and her remarks about the *Hungarian Dance* also contained references to a side of Brahms that she felt I would not like. So I confined my curiosity to the minor figures of the last century. I became so devoted to Grieg that for awhile I played nothing else. I even imagined devoting my life to the performance of his works alone, for they did not seem to me to be too difficult, and I loved them.

This was my first ambition. Nothing in school had suggested to me a life-work. Going to church had, indeed, made me feel that I should become a minister. But this feeling was not very strong because two years at college removed it. I was caught in the too great freedom American education offered, and I did not really know what on earth to do with myself. This I did know: that continuing in college would be useless. Therefore, I persuaded my family to send me to Europe for a year, since, as I told them, I had determined to become a writer, and "experience" was certainly more valuable for a writer than education.

After a month in France, the whole place seemed to me to be nothing but Gothic architecture. So I spent another month in the Bibliotheque Mazarin studying stone balustrades of the fifteenth century. A professor from college, passing through Paris, found out what I was doing, literally gave me a kick in the pants, and managed things in such a way that I found myself working in the atelier of a modern architect. He set me to drawing Greek columns when I wasn't running errands. One day he happened to say that to be an architect, one must devote oneself entirely to architecture, that is, give all one's time to it. The next day I told him that I could not do that because there were many things I loved that were not architecture, and there were many things I did not even know, and I was still curious.

One evening in the home of La Baronne d'Estournelles de Constant, I was asked to play the piano. La Baronne found my playing very bad but somehow musical. And she offered to arrange lessons for me with Lazare-Lévy who taught at the Conservatoire. He began to teach me to play a Beethoven Sonata, and he insisted that I should attend concerts of music, particularly that of Bach. I had never gone to concerts before, and now I went every evening. One evening I heard some modern music: Scriabin, Stravinsky. I also had seen modern painting in Paris.

My reaction to modern painting and modern music was immediate and enthusiastic, but not humble: I decided that if other people could make such things, I could too.

In the course of the next three years I left Paris, travelled a good deal, returned to California to find the Depression well under way, but all that time I spent painting pictures and writing music, without the benefit of a teacher in either art.

I remember very little about my first efforts at composition, except that they had no sensuous appeal and no expressive power. They were derived from calculations of a mathematical nature, and these calculations were so difficult to make that the musical results were extremely short. My next pieces used texts and no mathematics; my inspiration was carried along on the wings of Aeschylus and Gertrude Stein. I improvised at the piano and attempted to write down what I played before I forgot it. The glaring weakness of this method led me to study Ebenezer Prout's books on harmony and counterpoint and musical form. However, wishing to be a modern composer, I so distorted my solutions of the exercises he suggested that they took on a tortured contemporary aspect.

I have mentioned the Depression and how it was going on when I returned from Europe. Although nothing in my experience had prepared me to make a living, I now had to do it. I did it by giving lectures on contemporary music and painting. I advertised these lectures as being by someone who was young and enthusiastic about all modern art and that was all. I confessed that I knew nothing about my subject, but promised that each week I would find out as much as I could. In this way I became familiar with quite a lot of modern music. When the music was easy to play I illustrated the lectures at the piano; otherwise I used recordings. When the time approached to give a lecture on the music of Arnold Schoenberg, I asked Richard Buhlig, who was living in

Los Angeles, to play the *Opus 11* because I had read that he played its first performance years before in Berlin. He said he would "most certainly not." However, I had met him and he is a great musician, and he became my friend and teacher. He said that he could not really teach me composition, because he was not a composer, but he could criticize what I wrote. The first pieces I showed him were, he said, not composed at all. And then he conveyed to me the idea that composition is putting sounds together in such a way that they fit, that is, that they serve an over-all plan. One day when I arrived at his house half an hour before I was expected, he closed the door in my face after telling me to come back at the proper time. I had some library books with me which I decided to return, and thus I arrived at his house a half hour late. He then talked to me for two hours about time: how it was essential to music and must be observed carefully and always by anyone devoted to art.

Finally the day came when Buhlig looked at one of my compositions and said he could not help me further. He suggested that I send my work to Henry Cowell who might publish it in his New Music Edition. This encouragement that Buhlig gave me acted to put a stop to my painting, for now I began to feel that I needed all the time I had for music. I had developed a rigid way of writing counterpoint. Two voices, each one having a chromatic range of twenty-five tones, that is, two octaves, and having a common range of one octave or thirteen tones, would progress in such a way that no one tone would be repeated between two voices until at least eleven had intervened, and no tone in a single voice would be repeated until all twenty-five had been employed.

I sent my work to Henry Cowell and he offered to have it performed in San Francisco at a meeting of the New Music Society. This was very exciting, but when I arrived in San Francisco, tired from hitch-hiking but expectant, I discovered that the instrumentalists had not looked at my music and found it too difficult to sight-read. But I met Henry Cowell and I played my pieces for him on the piano. He said that I should study with Schoenberg since, although I used twenty-five tones, my music most resembled that using twelve. He gave me the name of a pupil of Schoenberg, Adolph Weiss, and suggested that I study first with him. I was now anxious to study composition, for working by myself and developing my own ideas had left me with a sense of separation from the mainstream of music, and thus of loneliness. Besides, what I wrote, though it sounded organized, was not pleasant to listen to.

The next year was spent in New York, studying harmony with Adolph Weiss and rhythm with Henry Cowell; and the following two years, back in California, studying counterpoint with Arnold Schoenberg.

There were so many exercises to write that I found little time to compose. What little that I did write was atonal, and based on twelve-tone rows. At that time I admired the theory of twelve-tone music, but I did not like its sound. I devised a new way to write it which consisted of not only establishing an order to the twelve tones but of dividing the row into a series of static, non-variable motives and giving each motive its own ictus pattern. This brought the element of rhythm into an integral relation with that of pitch. The compositions which resulted from this procedure interested some of my friends, particularly the late Galka Scheyer. She brought a friend of hers, Oskar Fischinger, who made abstract films, to listen to my work. He spoke to me about what he called the spirit inherent in materials and he claimed that a sound made from wood had a different spirit than one made from glass. The next day I began writing music which was to be played on percussion instruments.

I was convinced overnight that although twelve-tone music was excellent theoretically, in making use of the instruments which had been developed for tonal music, it had continually to be written negatively rather than straightforwardly. It had always to avoid the harmonic relationships which were natural to the tonal instruments, which instruments it did not so much use as usurp. I was convinced that for atonal music new instruments proper to it were required.

I finished a *Quartet* for four percussion players. I had no idea what it would sound like, nor even what instruments would be used to play it. However, I persuaded three other people to practice the music with me, and we used whatever was at hand: we tapped tables, books, chairs, and so forth. When we tired of these sounds, we invaded the kitchen and used pots and pans. Several visits to junk-yards and lumber-yards yielded more instruments: brake-drums from auto-mobiles, different lengths of pipes, steel rings, hardwood blocks. After experimenting for several weeks, the final scoring of the *Quartet* was finished. It included the instruments that had been found, supple-mented by a pedal timpani and a Chinese gong which lent to the whole a certain traditional aspect and sound.

To write for percussion alone was by no means an original idea with me. I had heard Varèse's *Ionisation* and William Russell's *Three Dance Movements*. I had also heard, through Henry Cowell, many recordings of music from the various oriental cultures. But I did not think of percussion music as being an imitation of or derivation from any exotic music; rather, it had its roots in our own culture: in the work of Luigi Russolo and the Italian Futurists who around 1912 published a manifesto called *The Art of Noise* and gave many concerts in Italy, France, and England using machines especially designed to produce desired noises. Certain works of Henry Cowell, Ernst Toch, Darius Milhaud, and others belong to this same tradition. The term "percussion" in this connection does not mean that all the sounds used are obtained by the act of striking or hitting. It is used in a loose sense to refer to sound inclusive of noise as opposed to musical or accepted tones. Therefore, just as modern music in general may be said to have been the history of the liberation of the dissonance, so this new music is part of the attempt to liberate all audible sound from the limitations of musical prejudice. A single sound by itself is neither musical nor not musical. It is simply a sound. And no matter what kind of a sound it is, it can become musical by taking its place in a piece of music. This point of view requires some adjustment of the definition of music which was given by my Aunt Phoebe. She had said that music was made up of melody, harmony, and rhythm. Music now seemed to me to be the organization of sound, organization by any means of any sounds. This definition has the advantage of being all-inclusive, even to the extent of including all that music which does not employ harmony, which, doubtless, is the larger part of the music which has been made on this planet, since it includes all oriental music, all of the early and middle music of our culture, and a large and not inconsiderable part of our current production.

Like many others before me, from Russolo to Varèse, I looked forward to an exploration of sound by *new technological means*: machinery, electricity, film and photoelectric devices, the invention of new means and new instruments. However, I determined to exercise patience in this regard, because I knew that the equipment required was either not existent or not available, being, if existent, expensive and under the control of large commercial companies. I decided, therefore, to work with whatever producing means came my way, and always to have one ear to the ground in search of a new sound.

Luckily, I joined the faculty of the Cornish School in Seattle, Washington, and found there a large collection of percussion instruments and a well-equipped recording studio. Within a few months, I organized a group of players and presented the first concert of music for percussion instruments alone. Compositions by William Russell, Gerald Strang, Ray Green and myself were performed. Before giving the next concert, six months later, I wrote to many composers listing the instruments available and inviting them to send scores. In this way the literature for percussion instruments alone grew from about three or four pieces in 1934 to about fifty in 1940.

Access to the recording studio of the Cornish School led me to write a series of compositions which I called *Imaginary Landscapes*. These employed records of constant and variable frequencies on turn-tables, the speed of which could be varied. Durations were controlled by lowering or raising the pick-up. This was a use of recording equipment for creative rather than the customary reproducing purposes. I was also able to work with small sounds which to be heard required amplification.

One of the heart-breaking problems that American composers have to meet is how to get their music played once they have written it. I have met very many who have grown bitter and lonely in their studios. I solved this problem for myself by writing music which could be played by a group of literate amateur musicians, people who had not developed instrumental skills on a professional level and therefore still had time to enjoy playing music together with their friends. The number of them who rapidly had become virtuosi was probably due to the natural and uncommercial character of this situation. The problem of performance was also solved for me and for many other composers by the modern dancers, who have always been insatiable consumers of modern music.

In writing for the modern dance, I generally did so after the dance was completed. This means that I wrote music to the counts given me by the dancer. These counts were nearly always, from a musical point of view, totally lacking in organization: three measures of 4/4 followed by one measure of 5, 22 beats in a new tempo, a pause, and two measures of 7/8. I believe this disorder led me to the inception of structural rhythm.

The structural element in tonal music between Scarlatti and

Wagner is its harmony. This is the means by which the parts of a composition are related to each other. Up to this point I had borrowed from twelve-tone music its row procedures, that is, a special place-in-the-row of each individual sound observed for the purposes of composition. This procedure, like the intervallic controls of counterpoint, is extremely useful, but is primarily concerned with the point-to-point progress of a piece rather than the parts, large and small, and their relation to the whole.

If one recognizes that the four physical characteristics of sound are its pitch, its loudness, its timbre, and its duration, one may say that harmony and the intervallic character of counterpoint derive from no one of the physical characteristrics of sound, but rather from the human mind and its thought processes. This, by the way, may account for the cerebral, even psychoanalytical, and non-sensuous aspect of much twelve-tone music. In dealing with the sounds of percussion music, one hears immediately that in the very nature of their material they are for the most part indefinite as to pitch, but autonomous as to duration. For example: no human power can make the sound of a wood-block last longer than it, by its nature, is going to.

Two facts then led me to structural rhythm: the physical nature of the materials with which I was dealing, and the experience I had in writing within the lengths of time prescribed for me by modern dancers.

I also was able to approach this problem objectively because of the aesthetic attitude to which I found myself at that time dedicated. It had nothing to do with the desire for self-expression, but simply had to do with the organization of materials. I recognized that expression of two kinds, that arising from the personality of the composer and that arising from the nature and context of the materials, was inevitable, but I felt its emanation was stronger and more sensible when not consciously striven for, but simply allowed to arise naturally. I felt that an artist had an ethical responsibility to society to keep alive to the contemporary spiritual needs; I felt that if he did this, admittedly vague as it is a thing to do, his work would automatically carry with it a usefulness to others. Any latent longing that I might naturally have had to master expressivity in music was dissolved for me by my connection with the modern dance. For them I had continually to make suitable and expressive accompaniments.

My *First Construction (in Metal)*, which embodies the principles of rhythmic structure to which ten years later I still adhere, I propose now to describe.

It contains 16 parts, each one of which contains 16 measures. Each 16 measures is divided into five phrases: 4 measures, 3 measures, 2 measures, 3 measures, and 4 measures. Likewise, the 16 parts as a whole are divided into 5 large sections in the same proportion: 4, 3, 2, 3, 4. The distinction between this system and that of Indian *Tala* systems is that the latter deal with pulsation, and that not within a closed structure, whereas the idea now being described, independently conceived, concerns phraseology of a composition having a definite beginning and end. I call this principle micro-macrocosmic because the small parts are related to each other in the same way as are the large parts. The fact of the identity of the number of measures and the number of parts, or, in other words, the existence of the square-root of the whole, is an essential *sine-qua-non*, providing one wants to reflect the large in the small, and the small in the large. I can understand that other rhythmic structures are possible. When I first conceived of this one, I thought of it as elementary because of its perfect symmetry. However, its possibilities appear to be inexhaustible, and therefore I have never departed from it since finding it. The particular proportion of the parts is, naturally, a special aspect of each work. In the one I am describing now the special situation is that of 4, 3, 2, 3, 4. It may be noticed that the first number is equal to the number of numbers which follow it: 3, 2, 2, 4. This made a special situation in which an exposition of 4 ideas could be followed by their development in the four subsequent sections (in other words a sonata form without the re-capitulation). For the details of this composition I adhered to the sound-row procedure I had employed previously. I adjusted my materials, however, to number 16, both with regard to their sound and with regard to their ictus patterns.

The next step in my work occurred fortuitously as indeed all else had. I was asked by Syvilla Fort, a dancer later associated with Katherine Dunham, to write music for a dance she had choreographed. She was performing in a theatre that had no room in the wings for percussion instruments; yet her dance, a *Bacchanale*, most evocative of her African heritage, suggested the use of percussion. But for practical purposes, I had to confine myself to the piano. For several days I improvised, searching for an idea that would be suitable. Nothing satisfied me until finally, realizing that it was the sound of the piano itself that was objectionable, I decided to change that sound by placing objects on and between the strings themselves.

This was the beginning of the prepared piano, which is simply an ordinary grand piano muted with a variety of materials: metal, rubber, wood, plastic, and fibrous materials. The result is a percussion orchestra of an original sound and the decibel range of a harpsichord directly under the control of a pianist's fingertips. The instrument makes possible the invention of a melody which employs sounds having widely different timbres: as far as I know this is a genuinely new possibility. Its correlates exist in singing where a variety of colors is exploited, for example, in the Navajo *Yei-be-chai*, and in the playing of stringed instruments, where all the possibilities of variety in sound quality are used (examples of this cross the world and the ages from ancient China to the music of Anton Webern).

The actual muting of an instrument is, as anybody knows, not a new idea at all. We are familiar with the mutes of the brass instruments, and with that of the violin. The altering of the sound of a piano had been effected by hot jazz musicians in New Orleans by placing paper between the strings. Henry Cowell, who had used his fists and arms to play the keyboard of the piano, had muted the strings themselves with the fingertips and palms of his hands. Bach societies, lacking a harpsichord, had placed thumb-tacks on the hammers of small uprights in order to simulate the sound they needed.

The prepared piano also makes possible the use of microtones, that is, pitch differences less than our conventional half-tones. This provides an auditory pleasure which has long been known in jazz and folk and oriental music, but which had been largely excluded from our standardized serious music, with the exception of the modern uses of 1/4 tones, 1/8 tones, 1/16 tones, and even 43 tones to the octave, in the work of Alois Haba, Julian Carrillo, and Harry Partch. I can't refrain from mentioning here that one of New York's principal opera conductors recently returned from a European visit and, as reported in the Sunday *Times*, said that nothing new in the field of opera was going on in Europe with the exception, in Czechoslovakia, of Alois Haba's recent work in quarter tones, which, our informant said, we in America would of course not find of interest.

I learned many essential things about the prepared piano only in the course of the years. I did not know, at first, for instance, that very exact measurements must be made as to the position of the object between the strings and I did not know that, in order to repeat an obtained result, that particular screw or bolt, for instance, originally used, must be saved. All I knew at the beginning was the pleasure I experienced in continual discovery. This pleasure remains to this day undiminished because the possibilities are unlimited.

I was now involved in the presenting of percussion concerts. A tour was made giving programs at the universities of the Northwest. I went to Bennington when it went to Mills College and gave a concert there [Bennington College as a whole joined Mills College in Oakland for a summer.—Ed.]; the next summer, with Lou Harrison, I was again at Mills. Lou Harrison had written, of the literature for percussion instruments I mentioned earlier, at least half. Our common musical interests began to make us the very best of friends. Just as the weather never tires of repeating the seasons, so Lou and I never tire of discussing again and again problems involved in musical composition.

I spent the next year writing letters and seeing people by appointment, all with the end in view of finding financial support for establishing a Center of Experimental Music. This Center was to be a place where the work with percussion could continue, and where it would be supplemented by the results of close collaboration between musicians and sound engineers, so that the musical possibilities might be continually refreshed with new technological instruments. Composers were to be regularly advised of the new instruments available, and performances were to be periodic. Such an active relationship between music and science might be expected, I felt, to enrich and enliven the whole field of music.

Although I approached many universities, foundations, companies, and individuals, nothing happened. I remember in particular two hours spent at MGM with Douglas Shearer, head of the Sound Department. He showed me a room provided with a library of sound recorded on film and all the auxiliary equipment: light tables, film recorders and film phonographs, equipment with which a composer could compose music exactly as a painter paints pictures, that is, directly. I begged to be allowed to use this room for a few hours a day. But that was impossible, considering the objectives of Hollywood: the doors were closed.

I returned to San Francisco and with Lou Harrison gave a concert of our recent compositions for percussion. To end this concert appropriately we wrote a piece called *Double Music* which meant that we both wrote it. We did so in the following way: we each wrote independently within agreed-upon time lengths and using agreed-upon instruments. The result required no change, and indicates to me that there is a deeply rewarding world of musical experience to be found in this way. The peculiarities of a single personality disappear almost entirely and there comes into perception through the music a natural friendliness, which has the aspect of a festival. I hereby suggest this method of composition as the solution of Russia's current musical problems. What could better describe a democratic view of life?

Trying to establish the Center of Experimental Music had made me ambitious, and giving performances had brought me before increasingly large audiences. The natural outcome of this was to come to New York which is the center and the marketplace. Later, when Lou Harrison was leaving Los Angeles to come to New York, Schoenberg asked him why he was going east. He said he didn't know. Schoenberg replied: "Ah! You are going for fame and fortune. Good luck! Study Mozart every day."

On my way to New York I stopped in Chicago where I gave a concert at the Chicago Arts Club and conducted a class in Sound Experiments at the late Moholy-Nagy's School of Design. This class was confined to theory for, the school being in a single enormous room partitioned off into separate areas, any sound made disturbed the other classes.

While I was in Chicago I was commissioned by CBS to do a workshop production with Kenneth Patchen. Patchen wrote a script called *The City Wears a Slouch Hat*. My idea was to use the actual sound effects developed in radio studios, but to use them not as effects, but as sounds, that is, as musical instruments. This, I felt, would provide an accompaniment proper to the play since it would be the organization of those sounds typical of the environment of the dramatic action. The sound effects engineer was agreeable, so I asked him to show what the possibilities were. He was too busy to do this, but said that anything was possible. So I wrote 250 pages of score for instruments, the timbre, loudness, and relative pitch of which I described, but the existence of which I only guessed. A week before the performance over a nationwide hookup, I took the score to the radio station. They said it was utterly impractical and could not be done, which indeed was true. I spent the next week scarcely sleeping, writing and rehearsing with six players a new score which used the instruments with which I was already familiar: percussion, recordings, and amplification of small sounds.

Many letters were received in Chicago from listeners in the West and Middle West and they were all enthusiastic. So I came to New York expecting to be received with open arms by the highest officers of the Columbia Broadcasting System. The letters they had received from listeners in the East, however, were the reverse of enthusiastic. The Company decided that I had gone too far, and that they themselves would not go further.

The first thing one notices about New York is that an incredible number of things are going on. In Seattle, I remember, there would be a show of modern painting that would last a month, and it was the only one, and we would go to it often and think and talk and feel about it. We would play music and we even had time for simple games. No such thing in New York. There are so many shows of painting, concerts of music, cocktail parties, theatrical events, telephone calls, such a continuum of business, that it is a wonder any one there maintains his wits. When I arrived the war was under way: I took a job doing library research work in connection with a secret government project which I hasten to say was not the atom bomb. I wrote lots of music for modern dancers. I organized a group of twelve players and gave a concert of percussion music for the League of Composers and the Museum of Modern Art. The difficulties involved in twelve people getting together in New York City for something as uncommercial as a non-union rehearsal are enormous, and in this case we had something like thirty or forty rehearsals. Thirteen of us did it but at present I can't imagine how.

Being involved in the complexities of a nation at war and a city in business-as-usual led me to know that there is a difference between large things and small things, between big organizations and two people alone in a room together. Two of my compositions presented at the Museum concert suggest this difference. One of them, the *Third Imaginary Landscape*, used complex rhythmic oppositions played on harsh sounding instruments combined with recordings of generator noises, sliding electrical sounds, insistent buzzers, thunderous crashes and roars, and a rhythmic structure whose numerical relationships suggested disintegration. The other, four pieces called *Amores*, was very quiet, and, my friends thought, pleasing to listen to. Its first and last movements were for the prepared piano and were the first pieces using this instrument independent of the dance.

My feeling was that beauty yet remains in intimate situations; that it is quite hopeless to think and act impressively in public terms. This attitude is escapist, but I believe that it is wise rather than foolish to escape from a bad situation. I now saw harmony, for which I had never had any natural feeling, as a device to make music impressive, loud and big, in order to enlarge audiences and increase box-office returns. It had been avoided by the Orient, and our earlier Christian society, since they were interested in music not as an aid in the acquisition of money and fame, but rather as a handmaiden to pleasure and religion.

The *Amores* concerned the quietness between lovers. *The Perilous Night* concerned the loneliness and terror that comes to one when love becomes unhappy. *The Book of Music for 2 Pianos* was less concerned consciously with my personal feelings and more concerned with my idea about Mozart, that his music strictly adheres to three different kinds of scales: the chromatic, the diatonic, and that consisting of the larger steps of thirds and fourths. It is thirty minutes long, and employs the rhythmic structure I have described earlier. In this case, however, the number of sections is 31 and each section has 31 measures except when the tempo changes. The number of measures then changes accordingly, thus showing that actual time-length is the basis of this plan rather than arbitrary numerical relationships. The two pianos are prepared at the same points on the same strings but with different materials.

The absence of harmony in my music frequently suggests to listeners oriental music. Because of this, the *Book of Music* was used by the OWI [Office of War Information] during the war as *Indonesian Supplement n. 1*, which meant that when there was nothing urgent to do on the radio-beamed-to-the-South-Pacific this music was used, with the hope of convincing the natives that America loves the Orient.

Next I wrote the *Three Dances*, also for two pianos, which Merce Cunningham recently choreographed under the title *Dromenon*. Considering the theme of this conference, the inter-communication between society and the arts, I may be forgiven for advertising that a recording of the *Three Dances* is available, published by the Disc Company of America. Notes to the album by Lou Harrison describe the structure of the piece so adequately so I will not decrease possible sales by describing it here. The *Three Dances* are written as a gesture of friendliness towards the dance as an art with which I have long been associated. Since doing this was suggested to me by a passing remark of Virgil Thomson, I open the third *Dance* with a quotation from his *Hymn Tune Symphony*, which, due to the preparations, I am afraid he has never recognized.

Another passing remark, this time by Edwin Denby, to the effect that short pieces can have in them just as much as long pieces can, led me two years ago to start writing twenty short *Sonatas and Interludes* which I have not yet finished.

They have all been written in my new apartment on the East River in Lower Manhattan which turns its back to the city and looks to the water and the sky. The quietness of this retreat brought me finally to face the question: To what end does one write music? Fortunately I did not need to face this question alone. Lou Harrison, and now Merton Brown, another composer and close friend, were always ready to talk and ask and discuss any question relative to music with me. We began to read the works of Ananda K. Coomaraswamy and we met Gita Sarabhai, who came like an angel from India. She was a traditional musician and told us that her teacher had said that the purpose of music was to concentrate the mind. Lou Harrison found a passage by Thomas Mace written in England in 1676 to the effect that the purpose of music was to season and sober the mind, thus making it susceptible of divine influences, and elevating one's affections to goodness.

After eighteen months of studying oriental and medieval Christian philosopohy and mysticism, I began to read Jung on the integration of the personality. There are two principal parts of each personality: the conscious mind and the unconscious, and these are split and dispersed, in most of us, in countless ways and directions. The function of music, like that of any other healthy occupation, is to help to bring those separate parts back together again. Music does this by providing a moment when, awareness of time and space being lost, the multiplicity of elements which make up an individual become integrated and he is one. This only happens if, in the presence of music, one does not allow himself to fall into laziness or distraction. The occupations of many people today are not healthy but make those who practice them sick, for they develop one part of the individual to the detriment of the other part. The malaise which results is at first psychological, and one takes vacations from his job to remove it. Ultimately the sickness attacks the whole organism. In this connection let me remark that a composer may be neurotic, as indeed being a member of contemporary society he probably is, but it is not on account of his neurosis that he composes, but rather in spite of it. Neuroses act to stop and block. To be able to compose signifies the overcoming of these obstacles.

If one makes music, as the Orient would say, *disinterestedly*, that is, without concern for money or fame but simply for the love of making it, it is an integrating activity and one will find moments in his life that are complete and fulfilled. Sometimes composing does it, sometimes playing an instrument, and sometimes just listening. It very rarely happens to any one I know in a concert hall. (Although Lou Harrison and Mimi Wollner told me a few days ago that hearing the Boston Symphony Orchestra play Charles Ives' *Three Places in New England* made them feel very good; the same thing happened for me and many of my friends when I heard Webern's *Five Pieces for String Quartet* about a year ago.)

I don't think it is a matter here of communication (we communicate quite adequately with words) or even of expressivity. Neither Lou nor Mimi in the case of Ives, nor I in the case of Webern, had the slightest concern with what the music was about. We were simply transported. I think the answer to this riddle is simply that when the music was composed the composers were at one with themselves. The performers became disinterested to the point that they became unselfconscious, and a few listeners in those brief moments of listening forgot themselves, enraptured, and so gained themselves.

It is these moments of completeness that music can give, providing one can concentrate one's mind on it, that is, give one's self in return to the music, that are such deep pleasure, and that is why we love the art.

So I don't believe it is any particular finished work that is important. I don't sympathize with the idealization of masterpieces. I don't admire the use of harmony to enlarge and make music impressive. I think the history of the so-called perfecting of our musical instruments is a history of decline rather than of progress. Nor am I interested in large audiences or the preservation of my work for posterity. I think the inception of that fairly recent department of philosophy called aesthetics and its invention of the ideas of genius and self-expression and art appreciation are lamentable. I do not agree with one of our most performed composers who was quoted in a recent Sunday *Times* article called *Composing for Cash* as saying that what inspired him and should inspire others to write music today is the rising crescendo of modern industrialism. I think this and the other ideas I have just been ranting about may be labeled along with others, that at present I haven't the calmness to remember, as being sheer materialistic nonsense, and tossed aside. Since Petrillo's [leader of musicians' union] recent ban on recordings took effect on the New Year, I allowed myself to indulge in the fantasy of how normalizing the effect might have been had he had the power, and exerted it, to ban not only recordings, but radio, television, the newspapers, and Hollywood. We might then realize that phonographs and radios are not musical instruments, that what the critics write is not a musical matter but rather a literary matter, that it makes little difference if one of us likes one piece and another another; it is rather the age-old process of making and using music and our becoming more integrated as personalities through this making and using that is of real value.

In view of these convictions, I am frankly embarrassed that most of my musical life has been spent in the search for new materials. The significance of new materials is that they represent, I believe, the in-cessant desire in our culture to explore the unknown. Before we know it, the flame dies down, only to burst forth again at the thought of a new unknown. This desire has found expression in our culture in new materials, because our culture has its faith not in the peaceful center of the spirit but in an ever-hopeful projection on to things of our own desire for completion.

However, as long as this desire exists in us, for new materials, new forms, new this and new that, we must search to satisfy it. I have, for instance, several new desires (two may seem absurd but I am serious about them): first, to compose a piece of uninterrupted silence and sell it to Muzak Co. It will be 3 or 4½ minutes long—those being the standard lengths of "canned" music—and its title will be *Silent Prayer*. It will open with a single idea which I will attempt to make as seductive as the color and shape and fragrance of a flower. The ending will approach imperceptibility. And, second, to compose and have performed a composition using as instruments nothing but twelve radios. It will be my *Imaginary Landscape No. 4*. Twice when I have been offered commissions, once by the New Music Society and the other time by a young recitalist, for whom I would have willingly turned the idea into a piece for solo violin and two radios, the commission has been retracted when I explained my intentions. These experiences have proved to me the essentially conservative character of musical attitudes today. Due to this conservatism, my third desire will seem innocuous. It is simply to write again for symphony orchestra as I did last year when I wrote *The Seasons* for Merce Cunningham's ballet which was produced by the Ballet Society. Writing for orchestra is, from my point of view, highly experimental and the sound of a flute, of the violins, of a harp, of a trombone, suggest to me most attractive adventures. I also want to finish my *Sonatas and Interludes* for prepared piano and I am looking forward to working with Joseph Campbell on several operas, and with Lou Harrison and Merton Brown on finding a means whereby *Triple Music* can be written combining the techniques of their secundal chromatic counterpoint and my structural rhythm, and thereby providing a means with which three or four people can collaborate on a single piece of music. The pleasure here would be in friendliness and anonymity, and thus in music.

These desires of mine and the equally intensely felt desires of each other composer, not only as to new materials and such things, but also as to fame, money, self-expression and success, bring about the state of music as it is today: extraordinarily disparate, almost to the point of a separation between each composer and every other one, and a large gap between each one of these and society.

Insults and bouquets are flung across these gaps. Teachers teach what they can, lighting up and sometimes obscuring an atmosphere which is for the most part empty of response and understandably so.

Each one of us must now look to himself. That which formerly held us together and gave meaning to our occupations was our belief in God. When we transferred this belief first to heroes, then to things, we began to walk our separate paths. That island that we have grown to think no longer exists to which we might have retreated to escape from the impact of the world, lies, as it ever did, within each one of our hearts. Towards that final tranquility, which today we so desperately need, any integrating occupation—music is one of them, rightly used —can serve as a guide.

CONTEMPORARY MUSIC FESTIVALS ARE HELD IN ITALY (1949)

This piece of criticism-reportage originally appeared in Musical America
*(June, 1949). It indicates Cage's growing disappointment with the European
"avant-gardes."*

MILAN, ITALY. Nothing world-shaking took place at either the 23rd
Festival of the International Society for Contemporary Music (Palermo-
Taormina, April 22–30) or the First Congress for Dodecaphonic Music
(Milan, May 4–7). The quantity of music was not great on either occasion, since in Sicily elaborate arrangements had been made to
acquaint the visitors with Greek ruins and Norman-Saracenic architecture, while in Milan the twenty-odd composers who gathered there
found talk about the twelve tones more engaging than the twelve tones
themselves. High quality remained the unchallenged property of works
known for some time to possess it (Schoenberg's *Pierrot Lunaire* and
Anton Webern's *Variations*). On each occasion, mediocrity reigned to
such an extent that the simple entering of a concert hall became in itself
a stupefying act. Many veterans were of the opinion that the fairly
venerable ISCM should give up the ghost, while the First Dodecaphonic
Congress very wisely voted itself out of existence on its fourth day.
Comic relief was provided in Palermo by a book of program notes in
four languages, translated so literally from the Italian, and with a result
so hilariously funny, that all the foreigners were kept in good humor.
And everyone was kept jumping, both in Milan and in Sicily, never
knowing what music to expect or when; since programs were not only
continually changed, but were in some cases cancelled, and in
still others sprung up unannounced and at strange hours (midnight,
for example).

Of the forty-four works heard by this reporter, two used
advanced sounds; ten were by established masters (Willem Pijper,
Alfredo Casella, Charles Koechlin, Arnold Schoenberg, Alban Berg,
Anton von Webern, Ernst Krenek, Wallingford Riegger, and Luigi
Dallapiccola); fourteen were *nuovo-dodecaphonique*; and seventeen
were miscellaneous varieties of contemporary music, some more
impressionistic than neo-classical, others vice versa, and one was not
modern at all (Giuseppe Mule's *Music for The Cyclops*).

Neither of the two experimental works (both given at the ISCM

Festival)—Bruno Maderna's *Concerto for Two Pianos*, and percussion ensemble and harps; and Yvette Grimaud's *Three Pieces*, for voice, Martenot waves and percussion—was performed correctly. Mr. Maderna, who conducted his concerto, stood with his back to the duo-pianists, and was of no assistance to a group of unrehearsed players who, not understanding their music, and lacking some of their instruments, wandered about trying to obtain information from each other as to where and when to play. The piece was long, noisy and un-integrated, and may help to account for Maderna's recent conversion to dodecaphony. Miss Grimaud's work also suffered from insufficient rehearsal, absence of a singer, and missing instruments. Her quarter-tone counterpoints of melodies characterized by large skips were played very quietly in a single color, although the Martenot waves employed are capable, as was demonstrated before the performance, of great variety in both timbre and amplitude. According to the program note, "The essential idea of the one-fourth-non-tempered-tune-songs rests on one cell, be it rhythmic as well as melodic, which engenders all together, and sometimes two songs, cells in constant transformation and development." This music was excessively timid in expression, and it seemed put together over-minutely. But then, as the program note explained, "Each last particle has its reasons of being."

Both in Sicily and in Milan the listener was introduced to the work of twelve-tone composers who in most cases had enjoyed no direct contact with the Viennese trinity—Schoenberg, Berg, and Webern. The will to set out on this unpopular path implies in some cases courage and originality of thought, but in others it is an expression of a European weakness for tradition. Jelinek, Jemnitz, Togni, Hartmann, Searle, and Apostel bolstered up their dodecaphony with well-known forms from the past—respectively, Bach *Inventions*, Music the Whole World Loves to Play, Italian Impressionism, German Neoclassicism, student counterpoint exercises, and Beethoven—implying on their part a possible lack of faith in the new dispensation.

On the other hand, one can report with delight that Elizabeth Lutyens' *The Pit*—a dark, dreary, depressing stage work characterized by slow, aimless, melodic leaps — was not only original but unique. Miss Lutyens is a twelve-tone composer who heard Schoenberg's *Pierrot Lunaire* for the first time in Palermo; she is also the wife of the President of the ISCM, and her work is presented at each Festival of the Society. This information is retailed because it helps to explain the present schism between the United States Section and the rest of the organization. The constitution of the ISCM expressly forbids the performance of music composed by its officers, and, Miss Lutyens, although not exactly an officer, is in daily contact with the most influential one. Actually, she is not the only offender; over one-fourth of the music in the 1949 ISCM Festival programs was written by officials in the organization.

Wladimir Vogel's *Thyll Claes Suite II* was a labored, programmatic work in which the program was never clear. Percussive effects were applied as though they were bandages, but no resolution of the problem of percussion in twelve-tone composition was presented.

Riccardo Nielsen's *Three Movements for Strings* and H.J. Koellreutter's *Nocturnes*, for contralto and string quartet, were more acceptable—the first because a consistent sonority, one of the valid contemporary twelve-tone objectives, was achieved, in this case by means of intervallic control; and the Koellreutter, because of its strict but poetic use of the basic row.

Serge Nigg's *Variations*, for piano and ten instruments, heard at Taormina, was the most unpopular work of the Festival. An uncomfortable silence following its performance was broken by general hissing. Nigg is apparently in a state of transition, for, although he was one of the organizers of the Milan Congress, he resigned from it by means of an involved letter, which, without being clear about his present musical position, stated his convictions of a social-political nature. The *Variations* were willfully ugly and uncompromisingly intellectual. They proceeded from relative simplicity to thorough complexity with a ruthless absence of humane feeling. Nigg does not seem to have yet taken the walk around himself that Satie remarked was necessary before sitting down to compose.

The outstanding new twelve-tone works were Matyas Seiber's *Fantasia Concertante*, for violin and string orchestra, convincingly played by Max Rostal and conducted by Constant Lambert; and Wladimir Woronoff's *Sonnet to Dallapiccola*, a piano piece sensitively played by Genevieve Joy. Both were heard at the Palermo Festival. The Seiber work avoids the usual twelve-tone sound by freeing the accompaniment from the tone-row when the soloist is confined to it, and vice versa. This composer is English, but his Hungarian birth is evident in the fiery and rhapsodic nature of his continuity. The Woronoff piece, utilizing a wide variety of piano sonorities, is distinguished by a rhythmic structure derived from an intelligent and perceptive study of versification. This work, as adventurous in the field of structure as the Grimaud and Maderna pieces were in that of instrumentation, was defined in the program notes as a "Piece of Poli-variations." "But," as the note continued, "it is important to underline that it constitutes the first essay and the first step in the perspected direction, without any pretense towards immediate efficacy."

Stage works by Françaix and Riisager; chamber music by Schibler, Dutilleux, Contilli and Brokovec; symphonic works by Berkeley, Kabelac, Tommasini, Petrassi, Ghedini, Mihalovici, Legley, and Martinet; and music for "little complexes" by Orrego-Salas and Binet were played without influencing one's faculties one way or another.

The Françaix work, *Le Diable Boiteux*, inferior to similar works by Poulenc, stood out because Hugues Cuenod, with Gallic wit and brilliance, sang both its tenor and bass parts, thus at the last minute turning an unexpected gap in the cast into a *tour de force* to be remembered.

Of the other pieces, Victor Legley's *Miniature* Symphony, and G.F. Ghedini's *Concerto dell'Albatro*, for violin, cello, piano, recitation, and orchestra deserve special praise — the first for its balance of thought and feeling, its clarity and conciseness; the other, on a subject from Herman Melville, for its having beautifully conveyed an impression of mystery and the sea. Both these works survived performances by the orchestra of the Festival (the same cannot be said for J.L. Martinet's *Orphee*), the Orchestra Sinfonica di Roma della Radio Italiano, which, regardless of its conductor, requires the filtering process of radio broadcasting in order to make its characteristic weaknesses of rhythm, sonority, and intonation in the least endurable. The Legley work, although not adventurous, is not pretentious—"Each part is treated in its shortest expression; each element is reduced to the very necessary. On the whole, it radiates an atmosphere of which subsists in the slow movement too. The orchestra is relatively narrow; none too numerous the strings, the timbres and the brasses, always perdue and the battery formed only of the timpani."

In Milan, the performance of Webern's *Symphony*, which this reporter would have given his eye-teeth to hear, was cancelled, along with other works by Paz, Hauer, and Vogel. Cancellations here and in Sicily were generally blamed on difficulties with the Italian Customs. A rumor, in the case of a Hartmann Symphony, was that it had been accidentally omitted from the rehearsal schedule. In view of the fact that many unrehearsed works were performed, this unofficial explanation seemed beside the point.

Just as Cuenod was the hero of the Palermo Festival, so Marcelle Mercenier, playing Anton von Webern's *Variations for Piano*, at a moment's notice, beautifully and sensitively, as the heroine of the Milan Congress. her playing was particularly welcome after that of Massimo Toffoletti, who had made Arnold Schoenberg's *Suite*, Op. 25, unrecognizable. Alban Berg's *Lyric Suite* also suffered at the hands of the Vegh Quartet, who gave it a polished but sugar-sweet rendition. The principle of balance requires that this music, more than most, be read with restraint. Dallapiccola's *Five Fragments from Sappho*, a work that makes audible the beauty of the Italian countryside, its flowers, ruins, and vital nostalgia for the past; and Riegger's *Third Symphony*, a vigorous, thoroughly American work, received happier treatment. They were performed by the Orchestra dei Pomeriggi Musicali di Milano, under the direction of Hermann Scherchen. Krenek's *Kafkalieder*, for voice and piano, were exactly if not beautifully performed by Margherita de Landi and her husband, Edward Staempfli. The couple's concern for details of rhythm and intonation kept this music, which is not without character and vitality, flat and unwinged.

The masterworks in Palermo were less in number than in Milan, and, with one exception, inferior in quality. (This writer did not hear Karol Szymanowski's opera, *King Roger*, nor some Stravinsky songs— the first because he was suffering from a passing fever at the time, and the latter because they were presented at one of the unannounced concerts he failed to attend.) They were Casella's *La Fayola d'Orfeo*, an opera in one act, distinguished by its warm and gentle transparency; Koechlin's *Primavera*, for five instruments (flute, harp, and three strings), "written in 1936 to celebrate the return of spring," noisily performed by an Italian ensemble, but worthy of a sweeter usage; and Pijper's last work, the unfinished *Fifth String Quartet*, a pale but workmanlike example of the motive method applied to polytonality.

Above these, and above everything heard at Milan, too, rose Schoenberg's *Pierrot Lunaire*, reminding one of the way Mt. Etna rises above Taormina. Marya Freund, at the age of 74, spoke-sang this work, accompanied by an extraordinary Italian ensemble directed by Pietro Scarpini, who also played the piano. This performance, on April 23 in the Villa Igliea at Palermo, was such that anyone who heard it will never forget it. A member of the audience who came all the way from Australia said that she understood then why she made the long voyage.

This reporter found himself trembling for some time afterwards and noticed others weeping. The hermetic nature of this work was given on this occasion an almost oracular character, so that one seemed to be hearing a special and profoundly necessary truth. The president of the organizing committee had written in his Welcome to the Festival, "When later in our life, each and everyone of us shall have, as a sweet leitmotif in the symphony of souvenirs, the vision of this Sunny Island on the background of limpid blue skies and celestial harmonies, we shall feel to have been fully paid up for the enthusiastic preparation of nine days of spiritual retreat." His wish, through *Pierrot Lunaire*, came true.

NOTES ON COMPOSITIONS II (1950-63)

A Flower (1950), for voice and closed piano, is in the rhythmic structure of the dance by Louise Lippold for which it was written. The dance being suggestive of flora, an attempt was made to suggest fauna in the music. The vocalise within a single octave may be sung in any transposition low and comfortable for the singer.

Six Melodies for Violin and Keyboard (Piano) (1950): These pieces, melodic lines without accompaniment, employ single tones, intervals and aggregates requiring one or both of the instruments for their production. These constitute a gamut of sounds. The violin strings to be used for the production of tones are specified. The rhythmic structure is 3½, 3½, 4, 4, 3, 4.

String Quartet in Four Parts (1950): The subject is that of the seasons, but the first two movements are also concerned with place. Thus in the first movement the subject is Summer in France while that of the second is Fall in America. The third and fourth are also concerned with musical subjects, Winter being expressed as a canon, Spring as a quodlibet. Throughout the work the tempo is constant, but predominant quantities change from movement to movement. The composition, a melodic line without accompaniment, employs single tones, intervals, triads and aggregates requiring one or more of the instruments for their production. These constitute a gamut of sounds. The strings are played without vibrato and those to be used for the production of tones are specified. The rhythmic structure is 2½, 1½, 2, 3, 6, 5, ½, 1½.

Concerto for Prepared Piano and Chamber Orchestra (1951) is a composition in three parts in the rhythmic structure 3, 2, 4; 4, 2, 3; 5. The solo part is, in the first movement, in opposition to the orchestra, since it is composed freely, whereas the orchestra part employs a fixed gamut of single tones, intervals and aggregates arranged in a chart, systematic moves upon which determine the succession of events. Later the solo part gives up its independence, its tones (those of an elaborate piano preparation) being incorporated in the master chart. The notation is conventional.

Music of Changes (1951) is a piece [for piano] in four parts in the rhythmic structure 3, 5, 6¾, 6¾, 5, 3⅛ expressed in changing tempi.

The composing means involved chance operations derived from the *I Ching*, the Chinese Book of Changes, a detailed description of which is given in *Silence* (Wesleyan University Press). The notation expresses a relation between time and space such as exists in the case of sound recorded on magnetic tape. Here a quarter-note equals 2½ centimeters.

Imaginary Landscape No. 4 (March No. 2) (1951), for 12 Radios, 24 Players and Conductor: The rhythmic structure—2, 1, 3—is expressed in changing tempi. The notation is in space where ½ inch equals a quarter note. Kilocycle, amplitude, and timbre changes are notated. Two players are required for each radio. The composing means are the same as for *Music of Changes* and are the subject of an article which appears in *Silence* (Wesleyan University Press).

Sixteen Dances (1951) was composed in the series of rhythmic structures of the dances by Merce Cunningham. The sounds are a fixed gamut of noises, tones, intervals, aggregates requiring one or more of the players for their production. The composing means involved the establishing of this gamut in a chart. Systematic moving upon this chart determined the succession of events. The notation is conventional.

Two Pastorales (1951): Both pieces are written in the rhythmic structure 2, 3½, 5½ expressed in changing tempi. The notation of durations is in space where 2½ centimeters equal a quarter tone. The composing means involved chance operations derived from the *I Ching* (Chinese Book of Changes). The second pastorale, though using the same fairly simple piano preparation, also makes use of two whistles.

For M.C. and D.T. (for piano, 1952) employs the same composing means used in *Seven Haiku*. Here, however, the page itself was taken to be a "canvas" of time.

4'33" (1952), tacet, any instrument or combination of instruments: This is a piece in three movements during all three of which no sounds are intentionally produced. The lengths of time were determined by chance operations but could be any others.

Imaginary Landscape No. 5 (1952) is a score for making a recording on tape, using as material any 42 phonograph records. Each graph unit equals three inches of tape (15 ips). Differences of amplitude (1-8) are given. The rhythmic structure is 5 times 5. The composing means involved chance operations derived from the *I Ching*.

The recording on magnetic tape used in the first performances was made by the composer and David Tudor with the technical assistance of Louis and Bebe Barron.

Music for Carillon No. 1 (1952): On the graph, one inch horizontally equals one second, and three vertical inches equal any pitch range. A performer may use this graph to make any version he requires. The 2- and 3-octave versions have been notated. The composition means involved the use of template stencils with respect to a rhythmic structure at points in it determined by chance operations.

[In the 2- and 3-octave versions] whole notes are notated on conventional staves where one system equals seven seconds. When two notes are to be played simultaneously, they are connected by a stem. The player uses a stop-watch in performance.

Music for Piano 1 (1952) is written entirely in whole notes, their duration being indeterminate. Each system is seven seconds. Dynamics are given but piano tone production on the keyboard or strings is free. The notes correspond to imperfections in the paper upon which the piece was written. Their number was the result of applying a time limitation to the act of composition itself, changed for each system.

Seven Haiku (for piano, 1952): The composing means are those of the *Music of Changes*. The seventeen-syllable Japanese poem-structure is rendered as a space of time where a quarter-note equals ½ inch, having seventeen units (5, 7, 5), within which chance operations determined the musical events.

Waiting (for piano, 1952) employs ostinati on a page where a whole note equals 2 inches.

Water Music (1952) for a pianist, using also radio, whistles, water containers, deck of cards; score to be mounted as a larger poster: The composing means were chance operations derived from the *I Ching*. The notations are in space equal to time, the musician using a stop-watch in performance.

Williams Mix (1952) is a score (192 pages) for making music on magnetic tape. Each page has two systems comprising eight lines each. These eight lines are eight tracks of tape and they are pictured full-size (15 ips) so that the score constitutes a pattern for the cutting of tape and its splicing. All recorded sounds are placed in six categories, modified by whether or not their frequency, overtone structure and amplitude are predictable or not. Double categories (mixed sounds) are also designated, as are loops. Approximately 600 recordings are necessary to make a version of this piece. The composing means were chance operations derived from the *I Ching*.

59½″ For a String Player (1953) is a graph in space where 2 cm. horizontally equal metronome indication given. These indications change. Tone productions on the four strings are separately graphed, individual spaces being provided for each string, the range of each of which is determined by the player. Noises on the box, vibrati and bowing pressure are also graphed. Only indications for direction and place of bowing and changes from hair to wood employ conventional symbols. The piece may be played on any four-stringed instrument.

Music for Piano 2, 3, and 20 (1953): Tempo and dynamics are free. Tone production was determined by chance operations, the tones themselves by paper imperfections.

Music for Piano 4-19 (1953): Tempo and dynamics are free. Tone production was determined by chance operations, the tones themselves by paper imperfections. The sixteen pages "may be played as separate pieces or continuously as one piece or . . . ."

Music for Carillon No. 2 (1954) is graphed in a space where time is horizontal, pitch vertical. A performance may use this graph to make any version he requires. A two-octave version has been notated lasting forty-five to sixty-six seconds. The composing means was observation of imperfections in the cardboard upon which the notations, punched through by means of a pin, were made.

Two-octave version: The player uses a stop-watch in performance.

Music for Carillon No. 3 (1954) is the retrograde inversion of *Music for Carillon No. 2*. Inexactitudes result from the process of reading the graph upside down. The player uses a stop-watch in performance.

31′57.9864″ For a Pianist (1954), for prepared piano, is a piece notated and composed like *34′46.776″ For a Pianist* (see below) and its uses are the same. However, the latter composition demands a virtuoso performance, whereas this one is relatively easy to play.

34'46.776" For a Pianist (1954), for prepared piano: To be used (with two previous pieces) in whole or part to provide a solo or ensemble for any combination up to 2 pianists, 5 string players, 1 percussionist; pre-recorded tape may be used to assist in the performance of *27'10.554"*.

The notation is in space equal to time. Notes are played on the keyboard or harp according to indications given. Where these are unclear, the pianist is free to decide what to do. Various ways of using the strings are suggested but not specified. The production of harmonics and the use of pedals is at the pianist's discretion. Noises are distinguished according to three categories, piano preparations according to five, the pianist again making specific choices. Force, distance and speed of attack are graphed. The notation may be read in any "focus," as many or as few of its aspects as desired being acted upon. The rhythmic structure is that of *26'1.1499" For a String Player*, and the composition means the same.

26'1.1499" For a String Player (1955) is graphed like *59½" For a String Player* but in actual time, the amount of space equalling a second being given at the top of the pages. The composition means were complex involving both chance operations and observation of imperfections in the paper upon which the piece was written. These are the subject of a somewhat hermetic article, "45' For a Speaker," hermetic since it was written by similar means, which is included in *Silence* (Wesleyan University Press). The rhythmic structure is 3, 7, 2, 5, 11. This piece may be segmented at structural points indicated by dotted lines and the segments superimposed in any way to make duets, trios, quartets, etc. See also below for other uses of this material.

Music For Piano 21-36; 37-52 (1955): "These pieces constitute two groups of sixteen pieces which may be played alone or together and with or without *Music For Piano 4-19*. Their length in time is free and there may or may not be silence between them or they may be overlapped. Given a programmed time-length, the pianists may make a calculation such that their concert will fill it. A system is two staves with line between. Black notes above this line are noises produced on the interior piano structure, below on the exterior, manually or with beaters." A detailed account of the composing means appears in *Silence*.

Speech (1955), five radios with news-reader: These are six parts, indeterminate as to actions—articles to be read, tunings to be made.

Specific time indications are given and graphic suggestions for the playing of radios. There is no master score, the parts being mobile with respect to one another within certain limitations.

27'10.554" For a Percussionist (1956) is a graph of amplitude with respect to four groups of percussion instruments: metal, wood, skin, and all others (electronic devices, machines, whistles, etc.). The space of each page equals one minute. The player chooses his own instruments which in a virtuoso performance are as varied and numerous as possible. The rhythmic structure and composition means are those of *26'1.1499" For a String Player*. This piece may be segmented as structural points indicated by dotted lines and the segments superimposed in any way to provide duets, trios, etc. See below for other uses of this material. It may also be performed as a recording or with the aid of a recording.

Music For Piano 53-68 (1956): This is a group of sixteen pieces which may be played alone or together and with or without *Music For Piano 4-19, 21-36, 37-52*. Except for the fact that systems are often incomplete, these pieces are notated like those of *Music For Piano 21-52* and were composed in the same way.

Music For Piano 69-84 (1956): This is the final group of sixteen pieces in this series. All of them may be performed, in whole or part, by any number of pianists.

Radio Music (1956), to be performed as a solo or ensemble for one to eight performers, each at one radio: This is a single movement in four sections, the length of each section determined by each performer. Durations of tunings are free, but each is to be expressed by maximum amplitude. Stop-watches are used in performance. The composing means were chance operations.

For Paul Taylor and Anita Dencks (1957) applies to a single system of three minutes, where one inch equals 12 seconds, one of the 84 composing means of the *Solo For Piano* of the *Concert For Piano and Orchestra*, specifically BB where "notes are single sounds, lines are duration, frequency, overtone structure, amplitude and occurrence. Proximity to these, measured by dropping perpendiculars from notes to lines, gives, respectively, longest, lowest, simplest, loudest, and earliest." Here all sounds are noises produced either on the interior of the piano construction or by means of auxiliary instruments.

Winter Music (1957): "The twenty pages may be used in whole or part by a pianist or shared by two to twenty to provide a program of an agreed-upon length. The notation, in space, may be freely interpreted as to time. An aggregate must be played as a single ictus. Where this is impossible, the unplayable notes shall be taken as harmonics prepared in advance. Harmonics may also be produced where they are not so required. Resonances, both of aggregates and individual notes of them, may be free in length. Overlappings, interpenetrations, are also free. The single staff is provided with two clef signs. Where these differ, ambiguity obtains in the proportion indicated by the two numbers notated above the aggregate, the first of these applying to the clef above the staff. Dynamics are free. An inked-in rectangle above a pair of notes indicates a chromatic tone-cluster." The composing means like those of *Music For Piano 4-84* involved both chance operations and observation of imperfections in the paper upon which the music was written.

Concert for Piano and Orchestra (1957-58) is without a master score, but each part is written in detail in a notation where the space is relative to time determined by the performer and later altered by a conductor. Both specific directives and specific freedoms are given to each player including the conductor. Notes are of three sizes referring ambiguously to duration or amplitude. As many various uses of the instruments as could be discovered were subjected to the composing means which involved chance operations and the observation of imperfections in the paper upon which the music was written. The pianist's part is a "book" containing eighty-four different kinds of composition, some, varieties of the same species, others, altogether different. The pianist is free to play any elements of his choice, wholly or in part and in any sequence.

Fontana Mix (1958): Parts to be prepared from the score for the production of any number of tracks of magnetic tape, or for any number of players, any kind and number of instruments. This is a composition indeterminate of its performance. There are ten transparent sheets with points, ten drawings having six differentiated curved lines, a graph having one hundred units horizontally, twelve vertically, and a straight line, the two last on transparent material. A sheet with points is placed over a drawing with curves (in any position). Over these the graph is placed and the straight line is used to connect a point within the graph with one outside. Measurements horizontally on the top and bottom lines of the graph with respect to the straight line give a "time-bracket" (graph units = any time units). Measurements vertically on the graph with respect to the intersections of the curved lines and the straight line specify actions to be made, where the curved lines represent different kinds of actions and the twenty vertical units of the graph represent different degrees of these. Thus, sound sources, their mechanical alteration, changes of amplitude, frequency, overtone structure, the use of loops, special types of splicing, etc. may be determined. The use of this material is not limited to tape music but may be used freely for instrumental, vocal and theatrical purposes.

Aria (1958): To be used alone or with *Fontana Mix*, or any parts of *Concert*.

The notation represents time horizontally, pitch vertically, roughly suggested rather than accurately described. The relation of time and space is free. The vocal lines are drawn in black, with or without parallel dotted lines, or in one or more of eight colors. These differences represent any ten singing styles established by the singer. Black squares are any unmusical uses of the voice or auxiliary devices. The text employs vowels and consonants and words from five languages: Armenian, Russian, Italian, French and English. All aspects of a performance (dynamics, etc.) which are not notated may be freely determined by the singer.

Music Walk (1958), for one or more pianists, at a single piano, using also radios and/or recordings, is a composition indeterminate of its performance. Readings are taken from a transparent rectangle having five parallel lines placed in any position over a sheet having points. There are nine sheets with points and one lacking points (silence). The five parallel lines refer freely to five double categories (having to do with piano or radio playing according to where the performer has walked). The relation of points to lines is interpreted relatively with respect to any characteristic of sound or action. More specific determination of all the characteristics of sound may be made by the use of eight small plastic squares having five lines each. These are used as in *Variations I*. A performance lasts an agreed-upon length of time. When this material has been used by dancers, other categories than those here specified relative to what the dancers choose to do have been used.

Solo for Voice (1958) is two pages, each having eight systems. The time-length of these is free. Any amount of the material may be used.

Notes are of three sizes, referring to differences of amplitude or duration (ambiguously). Semi-circles above notes indicate the position of these latter with respect to vocal phrases to be determined by the singer. Microtonal alterations of conventional pitches are suggested by the position of the notes with respect to the lines of the staves which are far apart. Noises are included. Dynamics within certain limitations are free. The text is a fragmentation and collage of German, French and English. A virtuoso performance includes a variety of singing styles freely chosen by the singer. The composing means were *I Ching* chance operations and the observation of imperfections in the paper upon which the piece was written.

TV Koeln (1958) uses noises produced either on the interior of the piano construction or on the exterior, together with auxiliary instruments and keyboard aggregates specified only as to the number of tones in them. The position of notes with respect to lines is ambiguous, referring either to relative pitch, duration or amplitude.

Variations I (1958), both parts to be prepared from the score, with or without the extra materials; any number of players, any kind and number of instruments, is a composition indeterminate of its performance. Material is provided, by the use of which the performer himself makes his own part. There are six transparent squares, one having points of various sizes, five having five lines each. These latter are five parameters of sound; the points are events, the nature of which is determined by dropping perpendiculars from them to the lines. The material may be read in any position. The "extra materials" have fewer points. They are useful where several performers are preparing their parts at the same time.

Sounds of Venice (1959): Score for solo television performance, involving a large number of properties and four single-track tapes, 7½" per second, 3 minutes each.

The composing means were the materials of *Fontana Mix*. A stopwatch is used in performance.

Water Walk (1959): Score for solo television performance which involves a large number of properties and a special single-track tape, 7½" per second, 3 minutes. The composing means were the materials of *Fontana Mix*. This piece led to my composing the *Theatre Piece*. The large number of properties required is easily available, given the facilities of a television broadcasting company.

Cartridge Music (1960) is for amplified "small sounds"; also piano or cymbal; any number of players and loudspeakers; parts to be prepared from score by performers.

(A cartridge is an ordinary phonograph pick-up in which customarily a playing needle is inserted.) This is a composition indeterminate of its performance, and the performance is of actions which are often indeterminate of themselves. Material is supplied, much of it on transparent plastics, which enables a performer to determine a program of actions. These are insertion, use and removal of objects from the cartridge, manipulation of timbre and amplitude dials of the associated amplifiers, production of auxiliary sounds (also electronic). Since without amplification, the sounds are too small to be heard, one performer's activities interpenetrate radically with those of other performers when they concern the use of amplifiers. Directions are given for the use of this material for making a cymbal or piano duet, a piano trio, etc.

Music for Amplified Toy Pianos (1960), for any number of toy pianos, is a composition indeterminate of its performance. There are eight sheets of transparent material. Two have points which refer to the keys or rods of the pianos. Two have circles which refer to the piano amplification. Two have points within circles which refer to noise. A graph read vertically refers to the pianos (any number), read horizontally refers to time, regular or irregular. All sheets are superimposed in any way for a single reading. Any number of readings may be taken for a given performance. Contact microphones are used on the pianos and associated loudspeakers are distributed around the audience.

Music for "The Marrying Maiden" (1960) is a composition indeterminate of its performance. Transparent material is provided by means of which one can determine the splicing of speech phrases, room silence, speech glissandi, loops and fragments of speech. Readings with respect to time are simply relative: very short, short, medium, long and very long.

The single-track tape (7½" per second) for Jackson Mac Low's play was made by the composer with the technical assistance of Richard Maxfield.

Solo for Voice 2 (1960) is a composition indeterminate of its performance. The singer prepares a program of desired time-length using the material provided. This material is various, some sheets on transparent plastic. Superimposition of these permits the singer to determine many of the details of a vocalise, the vowels and consonants to be used. Several singers doing this independently may present their findings in chorus.

Theatre Piece (1960): Parts are provided for one to eight performers (musicians, dancers, singers, *et al.*) to be used in whole or part, in any combination.

This is a composition indeterminate of its performance. Time-brackets are given within which an action may be made. These actions are from a gamut of twenty nouns and/or verbs chosen by the performer. This gamut changes at given points, so that each part involves a performer in a maximum of 50 to 100 different actions. Means are supplied for the answering of four questions with regard to the activities within any one time bracket. The composing means were the materials of *Fontana Mix*.

WBAI (1960) is a score for the operation of machines. Durations are graphed.

Where Are We Going? And What Are We Doing? (1960): Four single-track tapes (7½″ ips; 45′ each) to be used in whole or part to provide a single-hour lecture, or used in any combination up to four to provide simultaneous lectures. When combinations are made, the loudspeakers are to be separated in space. Variations in amplitude may be made, following the score *WBAI*. The composing means were the materials of *Cartridge Music*. The following four programs for the four tapes give a lecture one hour long. **I:** Start 0″; Stop 25′00″; Start 30′00″; Stop 45′00″; Start 53′30″; Stop 60′00″. **II:** Start 5′00″; Stop 19′00″; Start 26′30″; Stop 58′45″. **III:** Start 2′30″; Stop 12′30″; Start 22′30″; Stop 32′30″; Start 36′00″; Stop 50′00″; Start 51′00″; Stop 59′30″. **IV:** Start 54″; Stop 10′00″; Start 11′00″; Stop 23′00″; Start 26′00″; Stop 30′45″; Start 34′00″; Stop 49′45″; Start 54′00″; Stop 57′15″.

Atlas Eclipticalis (1961-62): Instrumental parts (86) to be played in whole or part, any duration, in any ensemble, chamber or orchestral, of the above performers; with or without *Winter Music* ; an electronic version is made possible by use of contact microphones with associated amplifiers and loudspeakers operated by an assistant to the conductor.

Each part is written in space equal to a time at least twice as slow as clock time. Arrows indicate 0″, 15″, 30″ and 45″. Space vertically equals frequency. Since equal space is given each chromatic tone, notes not having conventional accidentals are microtones. Specific directives and freedoms are given regarding duration of tones. Loudness is relative to the size of notes. Tone production is never extraordinary. Percussion parts are a graph of the distribution in space of the instruments, as various and numerous as possible, chosen by the performer. The composition means involved chance operations together with the placing of transparent templates on the pages of an astronomical atlas and inscribing the positions of stars. The assistant to the conductor prepares his part from *Cartridge Music*. The conductor's part is not a master score but gives information as to the details of the composition.

Music for Carillon No. 4 (1961), for an electronic instrument with electronic accompaniment, is written in whole notes on the treble clef. The range is C below middle C to C two octaves above middle C. Each system is 15 seconds. A line below the staff indicates feedback (taped or produced by means of a microphone). An inked-in square is a low wood thud (samantran) either taped or arranged mechanically with amplification so that the performer can produce the sound by operating a pedal. These sounds are to be varied as much as possible. The composing means was superimposition of a transparent template on pages of an astronomical atlas (*Atlas Coeli*).

Variations II (1961), with parts to be prepared from the score; any number of players, any sound-producing means, is a composition indeterminate of its performance. The material supplied is similar to that of *Variations I*, but in this case no two lines or points are on the same transparent plastic.

Variations IV (1963): For any number of players, any sounds or combinations of sounds produced by any means, with or without other activities.

A FEW IDEAS ABOUT MUSIC
AND FILM (1951)

This essay appeared in Film Music Notes, *a magazine no longer published, in its issue of January-February, 1951.*

It is always a simple matter for someone who does not do it to know something about it, and that is my situation with regard to music for films. Of course I have done a little of it (the Duchamp sequence in *Dreams that Money Can Buy*, a miserable film in my opinion with the exception of this particular sequence—in which by a series of events the relation between music and pictures was botched up—and the Herbert Matter film, *Works of Calder*), but each time when I was working, I knew that I knew nothing about it. The same was true when back in 1942, I did *The City Wears a Slouch Hat* for Columbia Workshop (not a film but a radio play).

Not working, I know that music loses virtue when it accompanies. Nothing in life or art needs accompaniment, because each has its own center (which is no center). To bring about the state of no-accompaniment, there must underlie everything (whether words, pictures, or what have you) a rhythmic structure. In my case, this is micro-macro cosmic. If a film or play or dance is X minutes long, I take a pulse and then know how many measures of 2/2 there are in the work to be done. I let the major structural points in the film give me a particular structural articulation which is small in phraseology and is large in section-delimiting. (The numbers of measures must be capable of having a square root.) E.G., if there are 1600 measures in the film, these will be divided into 40 × 40 measures, and each 40 measures will be phrased in the same proportions that divide the 40 parts into large sections (e.g., 6, 7, 10, 5, 3, 9). This is a structural idea not distant in concept from Hindu tala (except that tala has no beginning or ending, and is based on pulsation rather than phraseology), the work of Anton Webern and Erik Satie and hot jazz.

Given this structure, both film and music may proceed free of one another and everything works out beautifully. It is even possible to have several composers working independently of one another on the same music (the same part of the same music); what they do, when put together, becomes a polyphony anonymous by nature, but alive the way nature is. To understand this, one is obliged to give up harmony, melody, counterpoint, etc. (everything one has learned including genius and the three B's) and accept music for what it is: a way of life devoted to sound and silence, the only common denominator of which two is rhythm (not as pattern but as quantity, free to have or not have accents, for example). This accepted, one may have back, paradoxically, that much of harmony, melody, etc. (including genius and the B's and all else) one wishes to permit oneself.

It may seem artificial and forced (life often does) to clamp a rhythmic structure onto something that doesn't have it. It is of course artificial (so are the houses we live in; they don't, however, keep us from falling in love).

Another idea I have is that if there is a story or pictures, the sounds should be the noises and sounds characteristic of or relevant to what one is following or seeing. This is what I was thinking of in the Calder film and *The Slouch Hat* (Kenneth Patchen) radio play. Not as sound effects but as organized sound (to quote Edgard Varèse). So that in the workshop part of the Calder film, what we hear are noises of mobiles and noises of the making of mobiles and the loudest noise comes when it is least needed, when the little boy smiles (a case of no-accompaniment) and no hammering when Calder is seen hammering, etc. (Opposed to the redundant — otherwise nonpartisan.)

> *Works of Calder*, filmed in color and directed by Herbert Matter, and produced and narrated by Burgess Meredith, has been acquired for exclusive 16mm non-commercial distribution by the Museum of Modern Art Film Library, New York. The music was written by [myself]; narration by John Latouche. Rhythmically composed sequences suggest a parallel between familiar forms and movements in nature and the movements of Calder's mobiles. Between these two sequences, Calder is seen at work in his studio, surrounded by his magical world of moving objects.

I don't know what else there is to say, except that I love the idea of writing for films; but when I am doing it, it is not so good, because either the techniques one is always reading about are not available, or someone connected with it goes blank when it comes to the imagination or something else. In the radio play, for instance, I scored a good deal of escaping compressed air, only to be told that each escape was worth five dollars and what with rehearsals, etc. "Please don't use it."

In the Hans Richter film, the film was changed after the music was written and I was never informed (although, since I am in the phone book, it is the simplest thing in the world to reach me). And then in the Matter film, I had highfaluting ideas about superimposing inaccurate performances of a single prepared piano line with each time micro-tonal shifts of pitch and slight timbre changes (to be achieved by re-positioning of screws and other mutes), all of this arising from the lovely accidents that mobiles by their nature of moving present to the eye. However, the machines necessary to do this were not available.

One more idea and then I am through. Music should not be recorded, and film music should not be a recording of music. It should be a music which could not exist except as a recording, a music which comes into being by virtue of (and only by virture of) the available contemporary (mechanical, electronic, film, etc.) means. (This is not the 18th century.)

More and more in my ears and those of younger composers (Boulez, Feldman, Wolff) are the sounds which radio and film means make available, and our imaginations run swiftly towards the *necessarily* "synthetic." We are in a real-life situation (not an academy, acoustically speaking) and it is impossible to say which is cause and which is effect (our ears or our sounds), which technic and which vision. Technic is Vision and vice-versa, the Sudden School.

What we desperately need in America is a laboratory for useless musical activity, devoted to failure rather than to success (research — *A–1 in other fields — ignored in this one of art), and I record (shout) at this time that first Var*èse tried to interest companies both in Hollywood and in New Jersey in such activity and then I myself spent a year (1940) trying to realize the same dream.

The dream is a simple one: a place for collaboration between com-posers and sound engineers replete with equipment — in Hollywood terms a simple get-together of the Music and the Sound Departments (in Canadian terms, an actuality: Norman McLaren and the National Film Board in Ottawa).

Perhaps this has been accomplished in our United States and I am behind the times. However, if it has and there is such a place, lead us to it. We have work to do!

NOTES ON CUNNINGHAM
CHOREOGRAPHY (1954-62)

This previously unpublished text was among Cage's papers discovered in the late 1960s.

Totem Ancestor was choreographed and presented by Merce Cunningham in 1942, *Root of an Unfocus* in 1944. Both of these first performances were at the former Humphrey-Weidman Theater on 16th Street. *Trio*, originally entitled *Effusions avant l'Heure*, and *Amores* were choreographed in 1949 and first performed with Tanaquil LeClercq and Betty Nichols at the Théatre du Vieux Colombier in Paris. *Two-Step* [composed by Erik Satie], also choreographed in 1949, was first seen at the City Center American Dance Festival that same year.

Variation was choreographed in 1951 and first presented at the University of Washington in Seattle. The music by Morton Feldman was composed especially for the dance as is also the case with three other works in the current repertoire: *Root of an Unfocus*, *Suite by Chance* [Christian Wolff], and *Totem Ancestor*.

Collage [Pierre Schaeffer] was originally entitled *Excerpt from Symphonie pour Un Homme Seul* and was first seen at the Brandeis University Creative Arts Festival (1952). *Suite by Chance* was also choreographed in 1952, but its first performance was not until March of 1953 when, with *16 Dances for Soloist and Company of Three*, it was presented at the University of Illinois Festival of Contemporary Arts.

Solo Suite in Space and Time was choreographed late last spring and first performed at the Louisiana State University Arts Festival (1953) when Mr. Cunningham was for the second time a guest artist. On that occasion the five parts were entitled: *At Random*; *Stillness*; *Repetition*; *Excusion*; and *For the Air*.

Septet [Satie], *Banjo [Louis Moreau Gottschalk]*, *Dime a Dance* [19th century piano music] and the *Untitled Solo* [Wolff] were all choreographed and first performed, August 1953, at Black Mountain College, North Carolina, while Mr. Cunningham was for the third time a member of the Summer School Arts Faculty.

Fragments [Pierre Boulez] is the most recent work in the repertoire, and is another example of Mr. Cunningham's interest in composition by chance which is discussed by Remy Charlip in his article in the current issue of Dance Magazine [reprinted in Richard Kostelanetz's *Merce Cunningham*, 1992]. It may be pointed out, however, that not all the works to be seen in this Holiday Week repertoire are composed by chance. Those choreographed by other means include the early works. Totem Ancestor, Root of an Unfocus, Two-Step [Satie], Amores, Trio and *Rag-Time Parade* [Satie], as well as the more recent works, *Banjo* and *Septet*. The dances in *Dime a Dance* were originally composed as class dances for Mr. Cunningham's advanced pupils in dance technique. They were not composed by chance means, but chance enters into the order in which they are performed.

Marianne Preger and Remy Charlip first appeared with Mr. Cunningham in 1950 at Cooper Union. Jo Anne Melsher joined the company in 1952 and danced both in the Schaeffer work and in Mr. Cunningham's choreography for *Les Noces* (Stravinsky) at Brandeis University. Carolyn Brown, wife of the composer Earle Brown, met Mr. Cunningham while he was on a nationwide tour in 1951. She has danced with him since the autumn of 1952. Anita Dencks, Viola Farber, and Paul Taylor were with the company at Black Mountain College last summer. This is their first appearance with Mr. Cunningham in New York City.

The continuity of *Septet* (1953) is not logical from movement to movement. At times it seems profoundly sad and noble, at others playful and surprising. It provides an experience that one is unable to resolve, leaving one, as a dream often does, uncertain of its meaning.

Satie's music is for piano 4 hands: there are seven pieces in the suite and it is this fact that suggested the title of the ballet. While Satie was working on the composition, he took what he was doing to Debussy who said that the music lacked form. Satie then gave it the title, *Three Pieces in the Form of a Pear*.

The music for *Suite for Five* (1953-58) is *Music for Piano* (4-84) by John Cage, and is played by the composer and David Tudor. The sounds correspond to imperfections in the paper upon which the music was written. The number of sounds on a given page and other aspects of the composition were determined by chance operations. The dynamics, tempo, and the nature of the noises are determined by the pianists.

The music for *Antic Meat* is John Cage's *Concert for Piano and Orchestra*, first performed in 1958 with Merce Cunningham as conductor. The soloist is David Tudor who uses an amplified piano and accessory noise-makers that are also in connection with electrical circuits. Each of the players uses a wide variety of ways of producing sound. The conductor's gestures are like those of the hands of a watch, but a watch that changes speed.

The costumes are basic black tights and leotards, to which are added thirty-five ready-made clothes and objects, such as overalls, slacks, a nightgown, parachutes, and hooped undershirts.

The music for orchestra in *Summerspace* (1958) is *Ixion* by Morton Feldman. Consisting of numbers on graph paper, it is a composition dealing with what Feldman calls "weight." The amount of sound varies and each player is free to play any notes of his choice, providing he plays the number given, and these within the time of a single pulse. All of the sounds are in the high register of each instrument save during one brief moment when they are in the low.

Aeon (1961) is a dramatic, though not a narrative, dance concerned with decisive moments in the relationships between a man and four women. The atmosphere is harsh and erotic. When two people are together, they are bound not only by invisible ties, but by actual elastic bands. In spite of such explicit relationships, Cunningham has made the situation mysterious, so that such questions as "What happened?" and "What does it mean?" are left to be answered differently by each observer.

This dance, *Aeon*, is epic in character, for, as its title indicates, a long time is involved. One event is followed, often overlapped, by another. At one point, as though it were the end of a period in history, the dancers come prostrate on the floor to a complete stop. The events, varied in character, generally elevated but not excluding fantasy and humor, form a history that can be told in many ways. That is, the dance is so made that it can be presented for a longer or shorter time, with more or less events and more or fewer performers, and the order that the events take can change from evening to evening. This work was first performed for the Montreal Festivals Society, in July 1961.

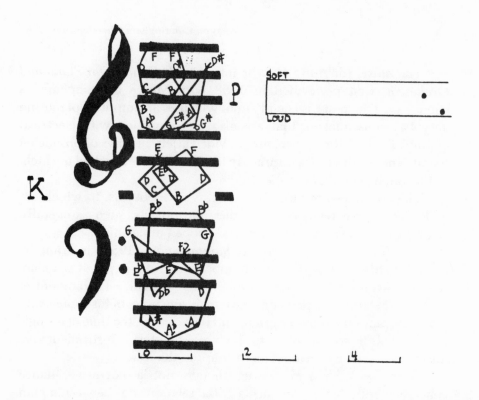

REMARKS BEFORE A DAVID TUDOR
RECITAL (1959)

Cage confesses his inability to remember exactly when these previously unpublished notes were written. Internal evidence dates the first set, subtitled "Remarks Before a David Tudor Recital," to 1958 or 1959; and the third probably introduced a concert at the Village Gate in New York, April 26, 1959.

The piano music you will hear this evening may be called avant-garde. But if one describes it more accurately, it is simply selections from the repertoire of David Tudor. His devotion to the music he plays and his ways of playing piano have aroused the interest of composers on both sides of the Atlantic and have brought changes in their means of composing. The Italian Bruno Maderna and the German Karlheinz Stockhausen, both members of the European avant-garde, have written works especially for David Tudor; a piano concerto by Maderna, a work for magnetic tape, piano, and percussion by Stockhausen.

The influence of Tudor is the result of his several European tours. Going to Europe, he took with him principally the music of Earle Brown, Morton Feldman, Christian Wolff, and myself. Coming back to New York, he brought to America for their performances music by Pierre Boulez, Stockhausen, Henri Pousseur, Bo Nilsson, Bengt Hambraeus, and others. In fact, the music of Franco Evangelisti is heard this evening for the first time on this side of the Atlantic; it was first played by David Tudor at Darmstadt last September (1958).

Naturally, these composers all go in different directions. Frequently one hears the term "post-Webernian" applied to this music. However, I begin to suspect that the term is meaningless if thought to refer to anything other than chronology. The German critic Heinz-Klaus Metzger agrees with me on this point.

The Europeans mostly continue their traditional interests in the organization of sound, bringing this about through new ideas of either order, discourse, or expression. The piece by Olivier Messiaen which opens the program is one that reawakened the interest of the young in his music. It is more purely musical and austere than those other pieces by him which enabled Virgil Thomson to remark that Messaien "opens up the heavens and brings down the house." I have not studied or analyzed the piece by Evangelisti, but I enjoyed hearing it at Darmstadt. It seems to deal with sound and the actions necessary to produce piano sounds more than it deals with ideas of order. And I like that.

The Pousseur piece, in a context such as this evening's, may seem more romantic than the other pieces. This impression may be the result of Pousseur's paying special attention to vertical or harmonious relations of sound in his music. For even in a recent work, *Mobile for Two Pianos*, where the composition is largely indeterminate of its performance, Pousseur nevertheless arranges matters in such a way that harmonious relations planned by him will certainly take place. His involvement with indeterminacy is, of course, the acceptance of an influence brought him from this side of the Atlantic by David Tudor. In tonight's piece that interest in indeterminacy, though present, is slight: the pianist is free to start at any one of several points in the composition, continuing the performance when he arrives at the point just before that at which he began.

The piece by Nilsson interests me because of the prominence in it of inactivity. That is something else that I like. However, there is a difference between a silence and a pause. I suspect that Nilsson gives us pauses. But I like them because I hear them as silences. He was born inside the Arctic Circle and now lives in Stockholm. His knowledge of modern music was gained from radio broadcasts; for in Europe all of the music that you hear this evening and all of the music like it is frequently available on the air. Nilsson's latest piece for piano, *Quantitaten*, written especially for David Tudor, requires for its performance microphone and amplification, reflecting the composer's special interest in the sound of loud-speakers.

The Boulez *Sonata*, his first for piano—there are now three—is an early work. It reveals the composer's delight in vigor, virtuosity, and discourse. I prefer this piece to more recent ones by him, like *Le Marteau sans Maitre* and the *Trosieme Sonate*, both of which are made up of differentiated blocks of composition juxtaposed without transitions.

I do not know precisely how the pieces by Christian Wolff were composed. I consider him the most advanced of American composers, and naturally I consider American composers more advanced than European ones. It was Wolff who made clear to me the necessity to renounce any interest in continuity. It was he who, in order to "let sounds come into their own," wrote music vertically on the page though the music was to be played horizontally, as is conversional. It was Christian Wolff also who, one day as we were walking along 17th Street, said, "No matter what we do, everything turns out to be a melody."

My own piece [from *Music for Piano*] which concludes the program was written simply by noticing imperfections in the paper upon which I was writing, employing that number of imperfections which had been given by a coin oracle in the *I Ching*. In an article describing this process of composition, first published in *Die Reihe* and reprinted in *Silence*, I question whether anything in this instance has been composed.

I now take the liberty of thanking Virgil Thomson for arranging this program, and La Maison Française of New York University for presenting it. One may question the propriety of so much music that is not French being played under a roof devoted to France. It is small help to point out that on my mother's side I have a little French blood, and that Christian Wolff, though of German parentage and American citizenship, was born in Nice. For Pousseur is a Belgian, Evangelisti an Italian, Nilsson a Swede, and Boulez, though a Frenchman, is a resident of Baden-Baden. David Tudor himself is Pennsylvania Dutch. It is more to the point to recall that France, and especially Paris, has always been hospitable to intellectuals no matter what their birthplace. If such persons today do not flock to Paris so commonly as they did in the past, it is perhaps due to the airplane; for nowadays it is possible for anyone to live anywhere in the world just as though he were living in Paris, that is, with a sense of the life of the intellect and the liveliness of the arts, and with a keen response to those of their aspects that we call avant-garde.

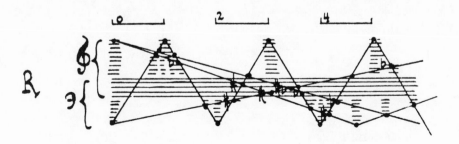

PREFACE TO *INDETERMINACY* (1959)

These brief notes originally appeared in the booklet to Indeterminacy *(1959),
the two-record volume of Cage reading his short (one-minute) stories to the
aleatory pianistic non-accompaniment of David Tudor.*

For over twenty years I have been giving lectures. Many of them have
been unusual as lectures, simply because I employed in them means of
writing analagous to my composing means in the field of music. My
intention was, often, to say what I had to say in a way which would
exemplify it, which would, conceivably, permit a listener to experience
it rather than just hear about it. This means, essentially, that, being, as
I am, engaged in a variety of activities, I attempt to introduce into each
one of them aspects conventionally limited to the others. So it was that
I gave about 1949 my *Lecture on Nothing* at the Artists' Club on 8th
Street in New York City (the artists' club started by Robert Motherwell
that predated the popular one associated with Philip Pavia, Bill
de Kooning, et al). This *Lecture on Nothing* was written in the same
rhythmic structure I employed at the time in my musical compositions
(*Sonatas and Interludes, Three Dances,* etc.). One of the structural
divisions was a repetition of a single page in which the refrain occurred
"if anyone is sleepy let him go to sleep" some 14 times. Jeanne Reynal,
I remember, stood up part way through, screamed, and then said,
while I continued speaking, "John, I dearly love you, but I can't bear
another minute."

She then walked out. Later, during the question period, I gave five
prepared answers regardless of the questions. This was a reflection of
my engagement in Zen. At Black Mountain College, I organized an
event which involved the paintings of Bob Rauschenberg, the dancing
of Merce Cunningham, films, slides, phonograph records, radios, the
poetries of Charles Olsen and M.C. Richards recited from the tops of
ladders, the pianism of David Tudor, together with my lecture which
ends: "A piece of string, a sunset, each acts." The audience was seated
in the center of all this activity, and, later that summer, vacationing in
New England, I visited America's first Synagogue to discover that the
congregation was there seated precisely the way I had arranged the
audience at Black Mountain. As I look back, I realize that this concern
with poetry was early with me. At Pomona College, in response to
questions about the Lake Poets, I wrote in the manner of Gertrude

Stein, irrelevantly and repetitiously. I got an A. The second time I did it
I was failed. And between the *Lecture on Nothing* and the one here
recorded, there are at least a dozen which are unconventionally
written, notably the *London Lecture* which was written by means of
chance operations, and the *Rutgers Lecture* which is largely a series of
questions left unanswered. When M.C. Richards asked me why I didn't
one day give a conventional informative lecture (adding that that
would be the most shocking thing I could do), I said, "I don't give these
lectures to surprise people, but out of the need for poetry." As I see it,
poetry is not prose, simply because poetry is one way or another
formalized. It is not poetry by reason of its content or ambiguity, but
by reason of its allowing musical elements (time, sound) to be
introduced into the world of words. Thus, traditionally, information,
no matter how stuffy (e.g. the sutras and shastras of India), was
conventionally transmitted by poetry. It was easier "to get" that way.
(Karl Shapiro may have been thinking along these lines when he wrote
his *Essay on Rime* in poetry.)

Late in September in 1958 I was in Stockholm in a hotel. I set about
writing the present lecture which I was obliged to give a week later at
the Brussels Fair. I recalled a remark made years before by David
Tudor that I should make a talk that was nothing but stories. The idea
was appealing when he gave it to me but I had never acted on it. A few
weeks before, in Darmstadt, Karlheinz Stockhausen had said, "I'll publish your Brussels talk in *Die Reihe*." I replied, "You'd better wait and
see what it is I write." He said, "No matter what it is, I'll publish it."

When the talk was given in Brussels, it was just the first thirty
stories and without musical accompaniment. A recital by David Tudor
and myself of music for two pianos followed the lecture. The title was
*Indeterminacy: New Aspect of Form in Instrumental and Electronic
Music*. Karlheinz Stockhausen was in the audience. Later when I was
in Milan making the *Fontana Mix* at the Studio di Fonologia, I received
a letter from Karlheinz Stockhausen asking for a text for *Die Reihe*. I
sent the Brussels talk. He published it.

When I got back to America in March 1959, there was a letter
from Jack Arends asking me to lecture at Columbia Teachers College. I
decided to write sixty more stories and to ask David Tudor to make a
ninety-minute accompaniment for the occasion. He did this using
material from the *Concert for Piano and Orchestra*, employing several

radios for noise elements.

A few days after the talk was given at Columbia, I went to see Emile de Antonio. I gave him a copy of the stories. After he read them, he telephoned to say they should be published. I mentioned this to David Tudor. He said, "It should be published as a record." The next day I got a letter from Roger Maren. He wrote to say that he had just seen Moe Asch who was interested in recording something of mine. I telephoned Moe Asch and we made an appointment. The day was set for the recording so that it could be made before David Tudor returned to Europe. David Tudor said, "Instead of radios, I'd like to use tracks from the *Fontana Mix.*" I said, "Fine."

It took about an hour and a half for the recording engineer, Mel Kaiser, to set up the studio. Finally he asked me to speak a little to get the level. Then he did the same for the piano, the whistles, the tape machines and the amplified slinky. Then he said, "We're ready." However, I no sooner started speaking than he stopped me. I said, "What's the trouble?" He said, "You shouldn't pause the way you do between words; you should just speak naturally." I said, "But this is what I have to do. I tell one story a minute, and, when it's a short one, I have to spread it out. Later on, when I come to a long one, I have to speak as rapidly as I can. He said, "O.K. I'll just keep my mouth shut." After the first side was made, he said, "I'm beginning to get the idea. I think we'd better do it over again." What had happened was that he had tried to get some kind of balance, rather than just letting the loud sounds occasionally drown out my voice. I explained that a comparable visual experience is that of seeing someone across the street, and then not being able to see him because a truck passes between.

We then made the first record over again, and continued with the other three. At the end of the session, David Tudor said, "You may want to cut that last sound I made at the piano. It's an ugly one." Editing, which took place the following week, was minimal. I lowered the level on my voice at one point near the end, and took out an echo that had developed on the tape before one sound somewhere in the middle. I didn't cut out the last sound as David Tudor had suggested, for to my ear it sounded perfectly acceptable. All this time, Moe Asch was out of town. When he returned, he listened to the record, and then called to say he was delighted. I said, "I'm glad you are, because I am too." He said, "When you write the album notes, write as much as you wish. Don't stint. And technical information too."

Most of the stories are things that happened that stuck in my mind. Others I read in books and remembered, those, for instance, from Kwang-Tse and Sri Ramakrishna. The 2nd, 15th, 16th, 46th and 75th stories are to be found somewhere in the literature surrounding Zen. The statement, "Split the stick and there is Jesus," (19th story) comes, perhaps, from Huxley's *Perennial Philosophy*, which I read when it first came out. The 29th story I read in one of Martin Buber's books. The 61st story is told in Joseph Campbell's *Hero with 1000 Faces*. Xenia (stories 72 and 73) is Xenia Cage. She was Xenia Andreyevna Kashevaroff whom I married in 1935; we were divorced 10 years later. Malcolm Roberts first delivered the lecture on Japanese Poetry (78th story). We (he, Xenia and I) were sitting, quite drunk, in a Seattle gutter; it was a full moon. He claimed that it had been given at the University of Washington by a Japanese scholar. Virgil Thomson told me the story about Chabrier, "the dirty" composer (story number 58). Henry Cowell told me the story about the Eskimo lady (the 25th). Merce Cunningham picked up, I don't know where, the one about the Japanese Abbott (the 13th). It may be discovered that I have remembered some of these stories inaccurately. However, this is the way they are now as far as I am concerned.

The continuity of the 90 stories was not planned. I simply made a list of all the stories I could think of and checked them off as I wrote them. Some that I remembered I was not able to write to my satisfaction, and so they do not appear. Whenever I have given the talk, someone comes up afterwards and insists that the continuity was a planned one, in spite of the ideas that are expressed regarding purposelessness, emptiness, chaos, etc. One lady, at Columbia, asked, during the discussion following the talk, "What, then, is your final goal?" I remarked that her question was that of the John Simon Guggenheim Memorial Foundation to applicants for fellowships, that it had irritated artists for decades. Then I said that I did not see that we were going to a goal, but that we were living in process, and that that process is eternal. My intention in putting 90 stories together in an unplanned way is to suggest that all things, sounds, stories (and, by extension, beings) *are* related, and that this complexity is more evident when it is not over-simplified by an idea of relationship in one person's mind.

Critics frequently cry, "Dada," after attending one my concerts or hearing a lecture. Others bemoan the interest in Zen. One of the liveliest lectures I ever heard was given by Nancy Wilson Ross about 1937 at the Cornish School in Seattle. It was called *Zen Buddhism and Dada*. There is a connection possible between the two, but neither Dada nor Zen are fixed tangibles. They change; and in quite different ways in different places and times, they invigorate actions. What was Dada in the twenties is now, with the exception of the work of Marcel Duchamp, just art. What I do, I do not wish blamed on Zen, though without my engagement with Zen (attendance at lectures by Alan Watts, D.T. Suzuki, reading of the literature) I doubt whether I would have done what I have. Recently, I am told, Alan Watts has questioned the relation between my work and Zen. I mention this in order to free Zen from any responsibility for my actions. I shall continue making them, however. I often point out that Dada nowadays has a space, an emptiness, in it that Dada formerly lacked. What, nowadays, New York, mid-twentieth century, is Zen?

PROGRAM NOTES (1959)

The present program illustrates two divergent directions character-
izing advanced contemporary music, both stemming from the work of
Anton Webern. Webern's later music, in contrast to that of Berg and
Schoenberg, suggested the application of serial methods to other
aspects of sound than frequency. Thus, concerning himself not only
with the ordering of pitch but with the control, too, of diverse characteristics of amplitude and duration, Karlheinz Stockhausen assumes a
responsibility toward the problem of unification of disparate elements
greater than that previously entertained by European composers.
Continuing the European concern with a musical dialectic, he brings to
it a new complexity. In a recent work he employs group composition,
the group being one of fields, each field defined by specific limitations
of the several aspects of sound. The works by Pousseur and Nilsson represent new directions influenced by Stockhausen.

Webern's music also suggests the autonomy of a sound in time-
space and the possibility of making a music not dependent upon linear
continuity means. The American works, setting out from this
essentially non-dualistic point, proceed variously. Feldman, in his
Intersections, has graphed high, middle, and low frequencies in a given
time unit, entrances within the unit and actual pitches being freely
chosen by the performer. The *Two Pieces for Two Pianos* are conventionally notated: i.e., he has himself interpreted his graph. Christian
Wolff, who found geometrical composing means which freed his work
from simple cause/effect relations, makes his *Suite* a metamorphosis of
timbre, from an unprepared to a prepared piano. Earle Brown's *Galaxy*
(the title is that used by Merce Cunningham and Dance Company; the
music was originally entitled *Four Systems*) is composed as a drawing
of parallel lines of varying length and thickness within a space
equivalent to the 88 piano keys. The drawing is to be read from any of
the four possible directions, and its four systems are to be performed in
any time sequence. The present performance uses two realizations of
this material made by David Tudor. No two performances of this piece
are the same. This is also true of *Winter Music* and *Music for Two
Pianos*; for neither piece has a score, and the parts, sufficient for twenty
and sixteen pianos respectively, though proportionally exact, permit
flexibility of interpretation. These pieces, and *Galaxy*, are played with

chronometers. The inclusion of noises in *Music for Two Pianos* is an admission of the liveliness of sound whether it originates inside or outside the "boundaries of art."

Recent works of Stockhausen and Pousseur indicate a relaxation of the earlier total control. Pousseur's *Variations II* gives the pianist the freedom of beginning at either of the two structural points, proceeding to complete the "circle" in his performance. Stockhausen's *Klavierstucke XI* is an assortment of separate short pieces written on a single large sheet of paper. The pianist is directed to play the piece which hits his eye first, going on to the performance of whichever other one he next notices.

THREE ASIDES ON THE DANCE (1959)

These notes, retrieved from Cage's files, were probably first written in the late fifties, and then collectively entitled by this book's editor a decade later for appearance in his documentary monograph, John Cage (1970, 1991), *from which it was deleted for reasons of space.*

About ten years ago Christian Wolff and I were walking along a street in the Lower East Side of Manhattan. I tried for a way of getting from the River to Union Square without losing sight of growing trees. He asked me what the best way would be to learn to write music for the dance. I told him to start by playing for Merce Cunningham's technique classes, that the best way to learn to do that would be to go and watch a class. Christian Wolff did this. Afterwards, Merce Cunningham asked him when he wanted to begin. Christian Wolff said simply: "I don't intend to begin at all. Your dance doesn't need music."

Why, then, if Cunningham's dance doesn't need music and Wolff perceives this—why has Cunningham choreographed three of his solos (*Untitled Solo*, *Lavish Escapade*, and *Changeling*) to music by Wolff, and why did Wolff compose his *Suite by Chance* and *Rime* especially for the works of those titles by Cunningham?

I propose that these questions are one question: that is, why was something done that didn't need to be done? In order to give an answer to this question, let us briefly and therefore with some over-simplification examine the nature of our actions when they follow from thoughts regarding what is necessary.

At the beginning, curiously enough, doing what one thinks is necessary is simply doing again what has already been done. Thus the dance goes 1, 2, 3, 4. This may be called a one-to-one relationship; it may be dignified by being called first special counterpoint. Second species counterpoint consists in writing two notes in one part against one in the other. After the music and the dance have been doing 1, 2, 3, 4, together for some time, the thought arises that it would be better if they didn't. Thus, against four counts in the dance, we find it necessary to put two in the music or eight. In each case, we have the relation of one to two. We get those of one to three and one to four by making use of the third and fourth species counterpoint. Fifth species of florid counterpoint is any number of notes against any other number. The relationship becomes less one of counts and more one of intervals.

These intervals are said to be consonant or dissonant, but there is nothing exactly like them in the dance. One then finds it necessary to concentrate the mind not on numbers and intervals but on mood and character. And then, curiously enough, having determined that the expressivity of the dance is such and such, one finds it necessary to give the music the same character. Following these lines, one rarely goes farther than what would correspond to second species counterpoint. That is, against a given expressivity in one of the arts, one puts a different expressivity in the other. This is called contrast. It is only considered necessary when it is effective, that is to say, when it is obvious.

Likewise, if there is a climax in one of the arts, the first thing that is thought necessary is to put a climax in the other art and, curiously enough, at exactly the same time. Later, one finds that it is interesting, and therefore necessary, to let a climax in one art take place at a different time than a climax in the other. And coming to the question of structure, that is, the division of the whole work into large parts: the first thought is that the music and the dance should have the same structure. When something new happens in the music, we should have something new in the dance. The next thought is something new happens in one of them, but the other goes on doing the same thing it was doing. What I am saying is this: when we think such and such is necessary we think in extraordinary simple terms, terms corresponding to one against one or at best one against two, three or four. Where does this simplicity come from? Certainly not from the world of sounds or the incalculable world of physical movement. The sounds we are able to hear exceed the limitations of musical notation, and no amount of dance notation will catch the life of a single step. What has happened is that we have used our minds, our thoughts about necessity, to narrow our awareness and limit our actions. This is how we have treated our arts, and even our language. Thus I was told again the other day at Tanglewood, "What you do is perfectly all right, but don't call it music." I had to point out again that we have the opportunity while we are alive to extend our consciousness. Why should we use our language, the word *music*, for instance, to keep us from being able to hear a particularly sonorous situation?

The reason then for doing something that didn't need to be done was to leap beyond mentally imposed limitations. Out of the leap one brings about an art that resembles life when we open our eyes and our ears to experience it. By what useful means was this done?

Wolff wrote a score giving varying amounts of freedom to each instrumentalist within varying amounts of time. That is, for instance, the trombonist within 3¼ seconds plays seven notes out of a group of thirteen, any ones of his choice. Three are to be loud, one is to be muted, and about the other three nothing is said. Or within nine seconds, with two notes given by the composer, one is to be played at any time. More interesting yet is the conclusion of *Rune*: for 4½ minutes, the musicians play from cue sheets. If the viola player hears a high loud tone from the piano, he is to proceed in such and such a way, that way including certain freedoms. Or he gets a cue from the trumpet or another instrument.

The dance is not so indeterminate, for there exists in dance performance the danger of physical catastrophe: someone, that is, getting actually hurt. Therefore, everything is carefully rehearsed. But the choreography is such that it can be different at different performances. And this summer it is not what it was last summer. It is again as new as it was before.

Cunningham and Wolff bring about a dance which is not supported by the music. This is a realistic situation comparable to the fact that a tree is not supported by the breezes that blow through it. The relationship of the music and the dance is unpredictable. It occurs at the moment of performance. Where does this place the experience? Directly where it is perceived, in each person of the audience.

REMARKS ON *THEATER SONG*
AND *IKON* (1961)

It was the composer Richard Winslow who first invited Cage to Wesleyan University.

Richard Winslow's music does not seem offensively modern. Why is that? I think it is because it arises from the European habits of singing, particularly from the Italian. This Italian singing, the *bel canto*, arose from the nature of the Italian language, namely a predominance of vowels. This produces a melodiousness which is to say an attention to continuity rather than discontinuity.

Though they come at it in different ways, most avant-garde composers nowadays are concerned with discontinuity and not with the nature of the Italian language but rather with the nature of language having a high percentage of consonants. An example of this interest is a recent work by the Italian composer, Luciano Berio, which uses an English text. Why this interest in discontinuity and in consonants that break up a line rather than fusing events in it?

Because, I believe, we are either aware or are becoming aware that existence, the existence of a sound for instance, is a field phenomenon — not limited to known discrete points in that field, the conventionally accepted ones — but capable of appearance at any point in the field. Then there is a strong tendency, which has the quality of urgency, to move to extreme points, to employ for instance very high, very low, very loud, very soft sounds and to move to the extremes of timbre which means to move away from so-called musical tones to the world of noises, the world of consonants.

Winslow's music doesn't do this. It is not only melodious. It is content within the range of singing. It all takes place in little more than four octaves, the home of choral music. Also there is one noise in *Ikon* produced by the pianist who plays at that point with his arms on the keyboard. It is so done, however, that the arm cluster goes out from the area of middle C and thus does not reach much beyond the conventional limits of singing.

Where then in this music of Winslow am I going to sense some urgency? Because, I am one among many nowadays who require this experience. Winslow's music uses two conventions, that of the major and minor scales and that of the twelve-tone row. This is technically epitomized by the almost equal presence in *Ikon* of the intervals of the fifth and of the tritone. In or out of either of these intervals he is able to move with the greatest of ease. This produces a flexible situation characterized by disunity and this is refreshing because while I was copying parts I was able to be surprised. I asked myself every now and then, how is this possible? Am I copying the same piece I was copying? This disunity brings us out of the European world of Bach, Beethoven and Boulez, into the American world of Ives.

But Winslow's music contains the repetition of themes. He even repeats themes of *Ikon* in *Theater Song*. This is a technique of unity, not disunity, and has the effect of cluttering up the mind of the listener so that even days later humming a tune he loses his sense of urgency and falls back on his faculty for observing simple relationships. Life is more complex than the simple repetition of themes and music should make us aware of this fact.

Furthermore, the two elements in Winslow's disunity are those of chromaticism and diatonicism, Schoenberg and Stravinsky, so accepted nowadays that the quality of urgency is no longer present there nor in the "consolidation of those composers' acquisitions."

I have to look or listen in some other way to discover in Winslow's music something which in the profoundest sense is revealing, which rouses in me my sense of urgency.

I might be seduced by the silence that takes place at the beginnings and endings of the operas together with the stage inactivity, for I love silence. I noticed that it was here and wherever else there was audio-visual inactivity that the audience was most uncomfortable. It is out of discomfort that liveliness, what I'm calling urgency arises. But I am familiar with silence and I need something from Winslow with which I'm not familiar.

I found it in a quiet short passage given to two trombonists. They are each asked to play the same notes. Musically speaking, this is doubling. It was employed in Europe to increase weight and to make the music more impressive in large concert halls. But in the passage I refer to, the trombones are without competition and they are playing pianissimo and slowly. Doubling is nowadays considered in bad taste. Why in Winslow's music is it so beautiful? The trombonists playing the same line necessarily fail to do so. One of them plays at first not quite as softly as the other. Each alters his amplitude so that he will be with the other. They proceed by means of human frailty. They are unable to hold a tone the same length of time. One gets to the next slightly before the other. The whole passage makes transparently clear the uniqueness of individual action and experience, and its inevitability even at the point where the attempt at togetherness is made. No composer in his right mind would have thought of doubling those two quiet, slow playing trombones. It was by means of his own original awareness that Winslow did it. It is through the door—and I am sure there are others — that I choose to enter into Winslow's music. It shows me discontinuity where I least expected to find it.

An hour or so ago I was out in the woods looking for mushrooms. There didn't seem to be any. Finally up a hill I found a patch of hair-capped moss. I thought here I'll certainly find some cantherellus umbonatos. I wandered around looking carefully through the moss; there didn't seem to be any mushrooms. Finally I noticed one little one. And then, suddenly, wherever I looked there was cantherellus umbonatos flourishing. Now I have enough for dinner.

I have used the world "urgency." That word could mean something other than what I mean. I mean "on the *qui vive*" and "quick: a word of truth or I slit the cat's throat" and "Dear God, I beg you to rid me of God." My intention here is not praise or dispraise of Winslow's music. It is rather to give an instance of how, through the experience of another's work, or indeed, through any experience, one may become aware. I am convinced that this access is constantly available and that it is in cultivated stupidity alone that it is not noticed.

A MOVEMENT, A SOUND, A CHANGE
OF LIGHT (1964)

Throughout his 50-year collaboration with Merce Cunningham, Cage has frequently written general essays, such as the following for the booklet accompanying a 1964 world tour, or program notes for various venues.

The development of theatre-dance in America has followed two paths, that of the ballet and that of the "modern" dance. The modern dance differs from the ballet in that it uses the full body and, rather than holding a traditional approach, favors experiment, research, and discovery. Its first exponents in America were Isadora Duncan, Ruth St. Denis, and Ted Shawn. Their followers were, principally, Martha Graham, Doris Humphrey and Charles Weidman, and Hanya Holm, who, having come from Germany, brought to America influences of Mary Wigman, Harold Kreutzberg, and others.

Where, for subject matter, the ballet had, for the most part, told the story of the prince and princess, the modern dance generally employed contemporary concerns, social or individual. When either the ballet, as in many works of George Balanchine, or the modern dance was "pure" or "abstract," it was so as a relatively exact visualization of the music employed.

Merce Cunnigham, who was for several years on the one hand a soloist in the Company of Martha Graham, and, on the other hand, a member of the faculty of the School of American Ballet, has, since 1944, developed his own school of dancing and choreography, the continuity of which no longer relies on linear elements, be they narrative or psychological, nor does it rely on a movement towards and away from climax. As in abstract painting, it is assumed that an element (a movement, a sound, a change of light) is in and of itself expressive; what it communicates is in large part determined by the observer himself. It is assumed that the dance supports itself and does not need support from the music. The two arts take place in a common place and time, but each art expresses this Space-Time in its own way. The result is an activity of interpenetrations in time and space, not counterpoints, nor controlled relationships, but flexibilities as are known from the mobiles of Alexander Calder. By not relying on psychology, this "modern"

91

dance is freed from the concerns of most such dancing. What comes through, though different for each observer, is clear (since one can only approach it directly—not through an idea of something else than itself), brilliant (the dancers can actually move physically, and they do not cover themselves with disguising costumes), and serene (the absence of an emotionally-driven continuity brings about an overall sense of tranquility, illuminated from time to time by feelings that are, according to the observer's reactions, heroic, mirthful, wondrous, erotic, fearful, disgusting, sorrowful, and angry: these eight emotions, those considered, with tranquility, the permanent ones by Indian tradition, appear thus kaleidoscopically in this choreography). As for the individual movements, they are both derived and discovered; in being derived, they stem as much from the ballet as from the modern dance; in being discovered, they represent the findings of Cunningham himself, who has constantly searched and refined his sense of movement.

Where other music and dance generally attempt to "say" something, this theatre is one that "presents" activity. This can be said to affirm life, to introduce an audience, not to a specialized world of art, but to the open, unpredictably changing, world of everyday living.

NOTES ON COMPOSITIONS III (1967-78)

Most of the following notes on his compositions come from brochures for concerts where Cage's pieces were performed live.

Music for Carillon No. 5 (1967), for a four-octave instrument. The notation (treble and bass staves, giving equal space for each of 47 bells, omitting low C# and E♭) is on plywood, the grain, etc. to suggest what bells are sounded.

Reunion (1968): This event first took place in Toronto. Electronic music was in continuous production by David Tudor, Gordon Mumma, David Behrman, and Lowell Cross. However, Lowell Cross had made a chessboard at my suggestion which acted as a gate, so that the continually produced musics were only heard intermittently according to their connection with the board, and the influence on the board of the moves in a game of chess. Games were played during a five-hour performance by Marcel Duchamp and John Cage and by Madame Alexina (Teeny) Duchamp. The title is in reference to the fact that all the composers involved, good friends who had gone their several ways, were in this manner brought back together for an evening's performance.

Cheap Imitation (1969) for piano solo was written to take the place of the *Socrate* of Erik Satie as an accompaniment for *Second Hand* by Merce Cunningham, the right to arrange the *Socrate* for two pianos having been refused by the French copyright holder. Becoming attached to the imitation as I had for many years been attached to the original, I arranged it for an orchestra of any size between the minimum of twenty-four and the maximum of ninety-five. In 1975 Paul Zukofsky, encouraged by my use in the *Etudes Australes* of not graphic but relatively conventional notation, asked whether I would consider making a similar work for the violin. I am now engaged in that work. But in order to do it, I study under Zukofsky's patient tutelage, not how to play the violin, but how to become even more baffled by its almost unlimited flexibility. *Cheap Imitation* [1977] for violin solo is one of the results of this study. I wrote the notes. The editing is Zukofsky's, though he did it in my presence and often asked me which of several possibilities I preferred. The bowing in the third movement was *I Ching* chance determined. The three movements of the *Socrate* are *Portrait of Socrates*, *On the Bank of the Ilissus*, and *Death of Socrates*.
    The following information regarding the compositional means of *Cheap Imitation* appeared with the version for piano solo: The *I Ching*

(64 related to 7, to 12, etc.) was used to answer the following questions for each phrase (with respect to the melodic line and sometimes the line of accompaniment) of Erik Satie's *Socrate*:

1. Which of the seven "white note" modes is to be used?
2. Beginning on which of the twelve chromatic notes?

Then, in I (for each note excepting repeated notes):

3. Which note of given transposition is to be used?

In II and III original interval relations were kept for one-half measure, sometimes (opening measures and subsequent appearances) for one measure.

This solo (a major third higher than the one for piano, due to the E*b*'s in II: 97, 118, and 163 which are below the violin G string) is essentially the same, though certain passages (e.g. I: 7-10) are not sustained and I: 140-144 do not descend: they go up, keeping, however, the intervallic relations of the piano version. The opposition in III between single tones and octaves is sometimes expressed in the violin version by dynamic changes.

Cheap Imitation (orchestra version, 1972): While the *I Ching* (64 related to appropriate numbers) was used to answer questions for each phrase of the piano solo of my original *Cheap Imitation* (1969), of those orchestra instruments that easily play all the notes of the phrase, how many and which actually do? *For each instrument*: Of those notes of the phrase, how many and which are actually to be played? *For each duration longer than the unit within a phrase*: What quantity of the total duration is to be held? *For single notes and phrase endings*: Is a note left quickly (·), held full length (–), or held slightly more than full length (♪)?

Performance: In order for all of the notes of the melody to be heard, the following 24 parts must be included in a performance: Piccolo, Flute 1, G Flute 1, Oboe 1, English Horn 1, B*b* Clarinet 1, B*b* Bass Clarinet 1, Bassoon 1, E*b* Saxophone 1, F Horn 1, C Trumpet 1, B*b* Trombone 1, B*b* Tuba 1, Guitar, Marimba, Glockenspiel, Harp 1, Celesta, Piano, 1st Violin I, 1st Violin II, 1st Viola, 1st Cello, 1st Double Bass.

In addition, a performance may include any or all of the following parts: Picc. 2 & 3, Fls 2 & 3, G Fls 2 & 3, Obs 2 & 3, E.H. 2 & 3, B*b* Cls 2 & 3, B*b* B.Cls 2 & 3, Bns 2 & 3, E*b* Sax. 2 & 3, F Hns 2 & 3, C Tpts 2 & 3, Tbns 2 & 3, Tubas 2 & 3, Harps 2 & 3, Timpani, Vibraphone, Bells, I Violins 2 to 12, II Violins 2 to 12, Violas 2 & 3, Cellos 2 to 9, Double Bass 2 & 3.

Those who play are to seat themselves together in any unconventional way: not according to instrumental categories. The "Score" (the full melody in small notes) appears in each part (excepting a part having *tacet* to the end of a movement). Below the "score" in larger notes are the notes to be played on that particular instrument. The orchestra's conductor will help the musicians in the preparation of a performance, using *Cheap Imitation, Piano Solo*.

The dynamic levels notated are those of the full orchestra (whatever combination of instruments is performing). Individual musicians, by listening attentively, modify dynamics accordingly.

For the strings, the following unconventional abbreviations have been used: L.B. = *col legno battuto*; L.T. = *col legno tratto*. In some cases, long durations have been written for sounds that cannot be sustained (e.g. Marimba, Strings, L.B.). Make the action, but do not use tremolos, or other means to complete the duration.

Minimum Rehearsal Schedule: Not less than two weeks before a projected performance each musician shall be given his part. During the first week he will learn the melody, at least those phrases of it in which he participates. He is to learn, among other matters, to play double sharps and double flats without writing in simpler "equivalent" notes. During the second week there will be orchestra rehearsals on each day, each rehearsal lasting 1½ hours. If, at anytime, it appears that any member of the orchestra does not know his part, he is to be dismissed. If as a result one of the essential 24 parts (see above) is missing, the projected performance is to be cancelled.

Mureau (1970):

Matsutake ya	mushroom
shiranu ko-no-ha no	ignorance; leaf of tree
hebaritsuku	adhesiveness
Basho	**transliteration.**

R.H. Blythe translates Basho's haiku as follows: The leaf of some unknown tree sticking on the mushroom.

I showed this translation to a Japanese composer friend. He said, he did not find it very interesting. I said, "How would you translate it?" Two days later he brought me the following: Mushroom does not know that leaf is sticking on it.

Getting the idea, I made during the next three years the following: That that's unknown brings mushroom and leaf together. And the one I prefer: What leaf? What mushroom?

Since syntax is not present in the original, one is able to use Basho's poem in as many ways as one discovers (c.f., Buckminster

Fuller: Given the choice between fixity and flexibility, choose flexibility).

The chants to be heard in London on May 22, 1972 (with David Tudor's *Rainforest*), three recorded, one performed live, are improvised on fixed texts. These texts are my most recent attempts to free English from syntax. They are letter-syllable-word-phrase-sentence mixes obtained by subjecting all the remarks by Henry David Thoreau about music, silence and sounds he heard that are indexed in the Dover publication of *The Journal*, edited by Bradford Torrey and Francis H. Allen (N.Y. 1962), to a series of *I Ching* chance operations. The personal pronoun was varied according to such operations and the phrasing which corresponds to changes of typography in the printed version (a new book published by Wesleyan University Press, 1973) was likewise determined. The title is the first syllable of the word music followed by the second syllable of the name Thoreau.

P.S.   We must
            find something else to do than art:
    we are going to China.   We hope our visit
                will leave no traces.

Song Books: Vols. I and II (1970): Solos for voice. The solos may be used by one or more singers. Any number of solos in any order and any superimposition may be used. Superimposition is sometimes possible, since some are not songs, but are directives for theatrical activity (which, on the other hand, may include voice production). A given solo may recur in a given performance. Specific directions when necessary precede each solo. When such directions have already been given, they are not repeated, but reference is simply made to them. Each solo belongs to one of four categories: 1) song; 2) song using electronics*; 3) theater; 4) theater using electronics.* Each is relevant or irrelevant to the subject: "We connect Satie with Thoreau."

Given a total performance time-length, each singer may make a program that will fill it. Given two or more singers, each should make an independent program, not fitted or related in a predetermined way to anyone else's program. Any resultant silence in a program is not to be feared. Simply perform as you had intended to, before you knew what would happen. *Wireless throat microphones permit the amplification and transformation of vocal sounds. Contact microphones amplify non-vocal sounds, e.g. activities on a table or typewriter, etc.

Sixty-Two Mesostics Re Merce Cunningham (1971): Mesostic means row down the middle: in this case the name Merce or Cunningham (a given letter of the name does not occur between itself and the preceding letter of the name). No attempt should be made to clarify this structure in a performance.

A performance will include at least five separate mesostics (but may present all of them, though the complete work should be a full program: from one and one-half to three hours). According to the number of mesostics performed and according to the total time-length determined, space each in silence (e.g. in the case of the decision to perform all of them in a three-hour period, allot approximately three minutes to each mesostic plus its succeeding silence (exception: the last one); say, one takes twenty seconds then follow it with two minutes and forty seconds of silence; let a single mesostic plus its succeeding silence equal at least one and one-half minutes; a shortest performance will therefore be something less than seven and one-half minutes).

The texts are *I Ching* determined syllable and word mixes from *Changes: Notes on Choreography* by Merce Cunningham and from thirty-two other books chosen by him from his library. They have been instant-letterset using a gamut of about seven hundred and thirty different type faces or sizes. These type face and size differences may be used to suggest an improvised vocal line having any changes of intensity, quality, style, etc., not following any conventional rule. The words and syllables are not to be made clear: rather, attention is to be given each letter (though not separating it from the letter that follows; a given letter may be vocalized in many ways; do not search to establish any pronunciation rule).

Tempo is free, though (just as each mesostic has been letterset as a single visual event—letters touching both horizontally and vertically and dots of i's when necessary superimposed on letters above) each mesostic when performed should hold together: like a single cry, shout, or vocal event, not including in it longer silences than those necessary for breath (exception: punctuation marks at ends of lines), breathing, if necessary, taking place at the end of a word or syllable.

"Speaking without syntax, we notice that cadence, Dublinese or ministerial, takes over. (Looking out the rear-window.) Therefore we tried whispering. Encouraged we began to chant. (The singer was sick.) . . . . To raise language's temperature we not only remove syntax: we give each letter undivided attention setting it in unique face and size; *to read* becomes the verb *to sing*."

Etcetera (1) (1973) was written for the ballet by Merce Cunningham, *Un Jour ou Deux*. Twenty performing musicians were given two ways of performing, first as unconducted soloists, then as members of small conducted duets, trios, and quartets which they voluntarily formed. I wrote this first *Etcetera* when I was still living in the country at Stony Point. It is accompanied by a tape recording of the environment in which the music was written, sounds in the woods by a stream. *Etcetera 2* (1985) is for a full orchestra divided into four. It has the same intention, to give the musicians two ways of performing, but, in this case, first led by conductors, then free to leave the group, going to special stations where they play as soloists. There is also a tape recording, but of Sixth Avenue sounds, the sounds of New York City, where the music was written. The solos in *Etcetera 2* are indeterminately written. They are for one to five unspecified tones together with one short changing or not changing auxiliary tone; sixteen of each were written. There are seventeen events in each solo. Each is a kind of haiku.

Since in each orchestra, everyone is playing in rhythmic unison, notations are given which bring it about that they are not playing exactly together. Small changes in pitch frequently accompany these small deviations from beat. There is also no coordination between the orchestras. They are independent of one another. The common denominator between the determinate and indeterminate parts of this work is the characteristic of my work since 1952, nonintention. I compose by means of asking questions. The answers are given by means of *I Ching* chance operations, just as numbers, not as wisdom.

Empty Words (1973-78) is a large literary work in four parts which, when read in its entirety, starts during the evening, and terminates at dawn, with the sound of waking birds being heard. The text is derived from extracts of Thoreau's journal. Each part has an "introductory text." The introduction to Part IV reads:

"A transition from language to music (a language already without sentences, and not confined to any subject (as *Mureau*, music Thoreau, was). *Nothing has been worked on: a journal of circa two million words has been used to answer questions. Another reservoir?* Finnegans Wake. *Another?* Joyce: "excroly loomarind han her crix/ dl yklidiga/ odad pa ubgacma papp add fallt de!/ thur aght uonnon.""

Languages becoming musics, musics becoming theatres; performances; metamorphoses (stills from what are actually movies). At first face-to-face; finally sitting with one's back to the audience (sitting *with* the audience), everyone facing the same vision. Sideways, sideways."

Part IV is approximately 2½ hours in total duration, which we divide over two evenings.

Etudes Australes I, II, and VIII (1974): The title of these etudes begun in January 1974 for Grete Sultan comes from *Atlas Australis*, a book of star maps printed in six colors (blue, green, orange, red, yellow, violet), published in Czechoslovakia. In order to write one of the 32 two-page pieces, I begin by placing a transparent grid over a particular one of the 24 maps. *Etude I* is derived from Maps XXIV and XXIII; *Etude II* from Map XXII; *Etude VIII* from Map XVI. (I am at present — December 1974 — writing the 26th.) The width of the grid (approximately 9½ inches) corresponds to the width of the music paper designed in collaboration with Carlo Carnevali. The vertical distance apart of the parallel lines ($^1/_{16}$ of an inch) was settled upon after experimentation. Smaller spaces did not seem to give sufficient room for distinguishing between the 12 tones of the octave, while greater spaces permitted the tracing of such a large number of stars that the resulting music, it seemed to me, would be consistently dense and possibly unplayable. In addition to the narrow grid, I decided to distinguish between the six colors, so that though at times all stars might be traced, at other times only certain of them would be.

I also made use of the *I Ching*, not as the book of wisdom it is, but as a means of answering questions through chance operations in relation to the number 64. Thus, having placed the transparent grid over the star map (eight of its 16 spaces for the right hand, eight for the left), I ask which stars I am to trace and how many. Numbers 1-9 give blue and green; 10-18 orange and red; 19-27 yellow and violet; 28-37 blue, green, orange and red; 38-46 blue, green, yellow and violet; 47-55 orange, red, yellow and violet; 56-64 all stars. Formerly I tossed three coins six times to get a number or numbers. In 1969 Ed Kobrin at the University of Illinois programmed the *I Ching* for me, so that now I refer to a printout. I have made tables relating all the numbers less than 64 to 64. When this tracing is finished for both hands, I translate the points in space into musical notation (the 12 tones), and then distribute these tones into the available octaves by means of chance operations.

As this distribution into different octaves takes place, I keep track of which tones of the three lower octaves are utilized, and, if all of them are, which was the last to be introduced. I then change the octave

of this last tone so that for each single etude at least one tone remains unplayed. This unplayed tone is held down (by wedge or tape) throughout
a single etude, producing a tonal drone of harmonics that arise as the
other tones are played. For *Etude I* this unplayed tone is the lowest A;
for *II* it is an interval, the lowest C and the C an octave above; for *VIII*
it is the aggregate: the lowest A (and continuing up the keyboard from
there), F, G#, A, and D. These five tones are *sostenuto* throughout.

I then ask whether a given note is a single tone or whether it is to
give rise to an interval, triad, quatrad, or quintad. In *Etude I* only the
number 64 brings the intervals, triads, etc. into operation. For *Etude II*
both 63 and 64 yield intervals, etc. For the 32nd etude (yet to be
written) 32 numbers (33-64) will yield tone-aggregates.

It was when it was not clear to me how to write this music that I
decided to begin again from the beginning, that is to go back to Grete
Sultan herself. Sitting beside her at the piano, I asked her to place her
hands on the keys. I began to imagine duets for her two hands, each
doing its own work unassisted by the other. I then went home and
made tables, as exhaustively as I could, of what a single hand unassisted by the other can do. I was surprised to find 546 quintads, 520
quatrads, 81 triads, and 28 intervals (all within the interval of a ninth).
Thus, by means of chance operations I am able to introduce harmonies
into a music which is not based on harmony but rather on the uniqueness of each sound, of each combination of sounds.

Neither tempo nor dynamics have been notated. Time proportions
are given (just as maps give proportional distances) but these are sometimes so complex that the music cannot be read with certainty (there
being four staves, two for each hand, for each system); and sometimes
(beginning with the ninth etude) the music cannot even be notated in
the space allotted to it. In such a circumstance a beam with stems gives
the rhythm and a letter, A, B, C, etc. refers to an Appendix where the
notes themselves are clearly written. By the time I needed to think of
having an appendix Grete Sultan was already at work on the pieces she
plays this evening. She had already told me that they could not be
played with any fluency unless they were memorized. Thus, introducing an appendix did not seem unreasonable.

Sometimes in the course of an etude the next tone to be played can
be reached without releasing the first. The first, notated as a white
note, is then held, giving rise in some cases to transient harmonies
which supplement the continual drone mentioned above. This principle of holding a tone while playing others is introduced whenever
practical. A notation conventionally referring to the pedal appears

practical. A notation conventionally referring to the pedal appears whenever a tone is held through more than one successive tone.

However, through the use of the star maps and the *I Ching*, the hands more often than not are leaping, widely leaping here and there through the keyboard territories open to them. The territory of the left hand extends from the lowest A to the C above the treble clef. The territory of the right hand extends from the highest C to the A of the first space of the bass clef. Even these boundaries, due to chance operations, are not respected, and sometimes the awkwardness resulting from the crossing of hands (and arms) has seemed in the course of this work excessive. I then am reminded of Arnold Schoenberg who said (when he was told that some violin music he had written was unplayable except by a violinst having six fingers), "Then someone will grow a sixth finger!"

When I wrote the *Sonatas and Interludes* it was with Maro Ajemian in mind. David Tudor was in my mind when I wrote the *Music of Changes*. Without Grete Sultan in mind, her quiet, indomitable strength, her devotion to the piano (which I also love), her discipline, her determination to transform music from paper into life, I would not have embarked on this project. Now of course I am delighted that I did.

Score (40 Drawings by Thoreau) and 23 Parts (for any instrument and/or voices): Twelve Haiku followed by a Recording of the Dawn at Stony Point, New York, August 6, 1974 (1974): My father, an inventor, used to say that he did his best work when he was sound asleep. How to write this music was mostly figured out toward dawn, sometimes before, sometimes after, dozing off. I wanted it to be written so that its parts could be performed on any instruments, Occidental or Oriental, or by use of the voice. That's why there are no notes, no sharps or flats, no staffs—just the drawings by Thoreau, always surrounded by space (which becomes silent). In the parts, the Drawings have been fragmented so that they read from left to right.

Branches (1976): In 1975 when I was on tour with the Cunningham Dance Company in Arizona, Charles Moulton, one of the dancers, brought a dry piece of cactus from the desert and, placing it near my ear, plucked one of the spines. Since then, in a piece called *Child of Tree*, composed to accompany *Solo*, an eight-minute dance by Merce Cunningham, I have always used cacti along with other plant materials, amplified by means of cartridge-like attachments constructed by John Fullemann. As an accompaniment for the longer Cunningham events, I composed *Branches*, a series of variations of *Child of Tree*, strung together on a string of silence. After a performance in Kyoto, Japanese friends said this music was botanical music.

Quartets I-VIII (for 24 Instruments) (1976): The Quartets are subtractions: I from *Lift up your Heads, O ye Gates* (Jacob French); II from *The Lord Descended*; III from *Old North* (both by William Billings); IV from *New York* (Andrew Law); V from *Heath*; VI from Judea (both by William Billings); VII from *Greenwich* (Andrew Law); VIII from *The Lord is Ris'n* (William Billings).

The 24 instruments are: Fl., 2 Obs., Cl., 2 Bns., 2 Hns., 5 Vns. I, 4 Vns. II, 3 Vlas., 3 Vc., Cb.

The score sounds as written. The *parts* for Cl., Hn. and Cb. are transposed.

Let players of the same instruments (e.g. violinists) sit as far apart from one another as possible rather than close together as usual.

The grace notes in IV and VII are to be played on the beat. *p* in a string part = *pp* in a woodwind part = *ppp* in a part for horn.

Renga with Apartment House 1776 (1976): Haiku, waka, and renga are Japanese poetic structures. Haiku is 5-7-5 syllables; waka is haiku plus 7-7; renga is a linking of at least thirty-six wakas. Renga was often written by a group of poets. Each would write a line and then pass it on to his neighbor who would write the second. His neighbor would write the third. Etc. Each line was as far-reaching, as distant from the preceding line as the poet's imagination could take it. The finished renga was a social act.

The score of *Renga* is graphic: three hundred and sixty-one drawings by Henry David Thoreau disposed in a space corresponding to thirty-six wakas. Vertical space gives relative pitch within limits determined by the performer himself. Horizontal space gives conducted time. Which of Thoreau's drawings were used, their sequence, reappearance, superimposition, and placement, were all determined by *I Ching* chance operations. Seventy-eight different parts were then written. They are the original drawings literally taken apart so that they read, as music conventionally does in the West, from left to right. Which instrument is to play which part is not specified, nor is any instrument named. But the parts have been colored, some in two, some in three colors, suggesting changes from one instrument to another or to the voice, or from one way to another of playing a single instrument. This absence of specification permits the use of instruments from other cultures and times, from 18th-century America, for instance; and the actual sound of the piece cannot be imagined until it is actually performed. The number of instruments playing a particular drawing and how loudly the drawings are to be played were also *I Ching* chance-determined. The use of drawings rather than conventional musical notations leads towards sounds that change quality and pitch in their course, as sounds in folk, popular, and oriental musics often do. They are also part of an attempt (as is the use of chance operations rather than personal choices) to free the sounds from the tastes and memories of the performers and the composer.

Apartment House 1776 is performed by twenty-four members of the orchestra and four solo vocalists. The title refers to the fact that many things happen concurrently rather than one at a time. The twenty-four musicians make four quartets (each with an assistant time-beater), and four soloists: a drummer, a string player, a fife or flute player, and a keyboard player. The *Marches* are authentic military drumming transcribed into modern notation from Benjamin Clarke's *Drum Book of 1797* by James Barnes. The other pieces are subtractions from music one might have heard at the time of the American Revolution and they are conventionally notated.

Which pieces from the past were to be varied was the result of *I Ching* chance operations as were in different ways the several composing means used. Not all of the forty-four *Harmonies*, fourteen *Tunes*, and two *Imitations* are used in a single performance. Each quartet and each soloist makes a program from the available materials. This program (except in the case of the drummer who plays only briefly) is roughly one-third the total time. And the total time is given by the conductor, who may change his tempo and introduce silences at the ends of most of the lines.

The four solo vocalists (whose programs are a little longer than one-third the total time) represent the peoples living here two hundred years ago: Helen Schneyer, the Protestants; Nico Castel, the Sephardim; Swift Eagle, the American Indians; and Jeanne Lee, the Negro Slaves. The songs they sing are their own (they have not been composed by me). And they are authentic, whether learned through notation, oral tradition, or racial feeling. If all four singers are not available for all performances in person, they are to be represented by recordings of their voices, each having its own channel.

Renga with *Apartment House 1776* is material for a musical happening. *Renga* is a score and parts for seventy-eight musicians. *Apartment House 1776* is a body of material (sixty-four pieces, any number of which may be performed in any sequence and any superimpositions) for the rest of the orchestra (say, twenty-four musicians) and four Voices (Protestant, Sephardic, American Indian, and Negro) representing the peoples living here two hundred years ago.

The seventy-eight who play *Renga* act on the suggestions of graphic notation. In western tradition, tones are musical when they are fixed with respect to their characteristics. In folk and oriental traditions, tones are musical when they change pitch and quality in their course. Graphic notation suggests such changes.

The parts for *Renga* are some in two, some in three colors, suggesting two or three different ways of playing a single instrument, or one or two changes from one instrument to another or to the voice. No instruments are specified, so that those from other cultures and times may be used together with conventional orchestral instruments, particularly instruments from 18th-century America if such are available through special collections or instrument makers. A score and sample parts (one in two colors; one in three) are enclosed.

By being conducted, *Renga* is given its time-length. Since the conductor may introduce silences at the ends of most of the lines and since his changing tempi are his own, he must first of all attempt to know fairly closely how long *Renga* is when he conducts it. (It is probably something in the neighborhood of thirty minutes.) Then he must decide whether *Apartment House 1776* is to begin before or after *Renga* and which of these pieces is the first to end. Then he will be able to tell the four singers and the twenty-four musicians of *Apartment House 1776* how long their programs which they themselves make are to be; and he will be able to establish means for them to know when to begin and when to conclude their performances (perhaps large clocks visible to all).

The programs of the musicians and singers performing *Apartment House 1776* are a fraction (the singers 2/5, the musicians 1/3) of the total time-length. These fractions may be diminished if the conductor so chooses.

Inlets (1977) was made to accompany the dance of the same title by Merce Cunningham. It was first performed in Seattle, September of this year. It requires the amplification of gurgles obtained by three musicians tipping conch shells of graduated sizes which have been partially filled with water. The music also includes a recording of pine cones on fire, and, at a point post-central in the time, a single tone from a conch shell used as a trumpet is heard.

Chorales (1978) are derived from posthumous chorales of Erik Satie. They became microtonal by the use of a music staff giving equal space to each chromatic tone. This staff was placed over the conventional staff of the printed music of Satie and tracing of the notes was made. This became a *Solo for Voice* in *Song Books I, II*. At the suggestion of Paul Zukofsky it was then arranged for solo violin.

A Dip in the Lake: Ten Quicksteps, Sixty-two Waltzes, and Fifty-six Marches for Chicago and Vicinity (1978): A work for

listener, performer and/or recorder scored for two places, three places and four places with the idea of two-step, waltzes and marches. The concept is to go to the places and either listen to, perform at and/or make a recording of the sounds and therefore possibly connect with the life of the city.

Etudes Boreales for Cello Solo and for Piano Solo I-IV (1978):

In the writings of Erik Satie, somewhere, I don't know just where, I read that music notation is nothing but points and lines. That was written sometime in the first quarter of this century. I was reading it in the third quarter, roughly fifty years later. In the late forties, proportional notation came about as a result of making music directly on magnetic tape. Space on the page was equal to time: therefore the lines which had been used in music notation were unnecessary. All that music notation needed were points: they would make clear what notes were to be played; where they were on the page would indicate *when* they were to be played. I had already written *Music for Piano 1, 2,* and *3–84* which uses no lines; but at the time I am recalling I was in the Center for Advanced Studies at Wesleyan University in Middletown, Connecticut. I had just accepted a commission from the Montreal Festivals Society to write a piece for orchestra. As usual I didn't know what it would be, and I was sitting there wondering what form it would take. I had seen that the university had a telescope; it was just up the hill. Before I knew it I was on my way to it. I asked them when I got there whether they had a library. They had a very good one. I browsed rather quickly. What I was looking for were points, points that were stars in the books that would become notes in my music. The photographic maps were useless, but I found a number of other maps that were simplistic, published in Czechoslovakia, that were nothing but points of various sizes and colors. I chose one of these, *Atlas Eclipticalis*, borrowed it and began my piece for orchestra which has the same title.

In 1964 I went around the world with the Cunningham Dance Company. When we came to Prague we were paid but were told that the money we received had no value except in Prague. I used what I was given to buy books about mushrooms and maps of the stars. *Atlas Eclipticalis* maps the great circle around the Sun, *Atlas Australis* the southern sky, *Borealis* the northern. I have these and others.

In the last twenty years I have used these books to write a great deal of music, not all of my music, but some of it. The most recent one (1978) is the one here recorded by Frances-Marie Uitti and Michael Pugliese, *Etudes Boreales I-IV* for Cello Solo and for Piano Solo. Originally it was written for Jack and the late Jeanne Kirstein. Jeanne Kirstein was a great pianist and a vivacious and energetic person. But what I wrote needed the experience of a percussionist. For her the music was impossible to play. Some compromise in her case, possibly the omission of some of the events, something had to give. I never heard what she or Jack Kirstein did with the *Etudes*. I came to the conclusion that they were unplayable.

I had become interested in writing difficult music, etudes, because of the world situation which often seems to many of us hopeless. I thought that were a musician to give the example in public of doing the impossible that it would inspire someone who was struck by that performance to change the world, to improve it, following, for example, the clearly outlined projects of Buckminster Fuller. That has not happened but I remain optimistic and continue to write music, which is, after all, a social art—it is not finished even when other people play it; it requires listeners too, and among them even sometimes the composer. Thus pieces of music can be taken as models for human behavior, not only proving the possibility of doing the impossible, but showing too, in a work performed by more than one person, the practicality of anarchy. In the United States in the 19th Century there were many communities of anarchists. In the face of the growth of large cities and mechanical technology, however, these anarchist communities were unable to continue. Now, with the shift from mechanical to electronic technology, there is hope for anarchists. Anarchy is now practical. We have extended the central nervous system (Marshall McLuhan); the world is an individual mind which does not need to be psychoanalyzed, it just needs to be clearheaded, not divided (as it now is schizophrenically) into nations, not involved with government or governments, just equipped with utilities.

Though there is no score for the two solos (*Etudes Boreales*), they fit together by being played in the same amount of time. Their relation is like that of the music and dance in the theatre of Merce Cunningham. Through circumstances both solos were recorded separately. Uitti and Pugliese have not yet played together in concert. But I have jumped ahead of the story I am telling.

It was Frans van Rossum, when he was living in a town outside of Amsterdam, directing an important music center, who told me of Uitti and took me to hear her play my impossible etudes. Her playing delighted and encouraged me. What I was doing was not utterly hopeless. The next thing I knew, Nils Vigeland, director of the Bowery Ensemble, told me Michael Pugliese would play the piano solos in a concert having to do with my seventieth birthday in Washington, D.C. Excellent as his performance was, I was not utterly pleased. I said something to Pugliese that made clear to him the work that he had yet to do. After a month or so he invited me to come up to the Manhattan School to hear him. His performance was magnificent. The *Etudes Boreales* for Piano Solo (in memoriam Jeanne Kirstein) are now dedicated to Michael Pugliese. Even though his mastery of them makes it clear that they are not piano solos (they are percussion pieces), I have kept the title the way it was originally, so that the revolutionary intention remains underlined.

What distinguishes these etudes from the *Etudes Australes* for piano are the noises, the use of beaters, and the use of general categories in the notation rather than specific determinations. Dynamics are given in the *Etudes Boreales*, not in the *Etudes Australes*. The doors that open on unexplored territory and of course the territory itself to be explored are in each set of pieces different.

And the Cello solos differ from the *Freeman Etudes* for solo violin (begun several years before the *Etudes Boreales* and not yet finished). The *Freeman Etudes* are written constantly in the total range of the instrument, whereas the range within which the *Etudes Boreales* is written is constantly changing. Sometimes it is narrow, sometimes very wide; never is it total, though it might have been. These pieces, like virtually all of my work since the late forties, early fifties, are nonintentional. They were written by shifting my responsibility from making choices to asking questions. The questions were answered by means of *I Ching* chance operations. Following my studies with Suzuki Daisetz in the philosophy of Zen Buddhism, I have used in all my work, whether literary, graphic, or musical, *I Ching* chance operations in order to free my mind (ego) from its likes and dislikes, trusting that this use was comparable to sitting crosslegged, and in agreement with my teacher that what Zen wants is that mind not cut itself off from Mind but let Mind flow through it.

I am a poor historian and did not keep a detailed record of what the questions were that I asked in writing these pieces. The questions asked for the cello pieces were of course different than those asked for the piano pieces. In both cases however the differences in color of the stars on a map allowed me to ask at the beginning, "Am I to trace the position of those that are blue or green, red or orange, violet or yellow, blue or green and red or orange, blue or green and violet or yellow, red or orange and violet or yellow, or all of them?" There were seven answers, that is, to this first question. And the answer given by the *I Ching* a number between 1 and 64, would be read in relation to the table relating 7 and 64; 1 = 1-9; 2 = 10-18; 3 = 19-27; 4 = 28-37; 5 = 38-46; 6 = 47-55; 7 = 56-64. Say it was 23: I would then trace the positions of the violet and the yellow stars, the third group. "How many of them are to be traced?" was the next question. That answer was taken as given, a number between 1 and 64. Once the place or time of an event was established, its nature had to be determined, its pitch in a changing range in the case of the cello pieces, its place on the map of the piano (on the keyboard, on the strings, or on the structure) in the case of the piano pieces, whether it was in legato or detache in the case of the cello pieces, played on what with what in the case of the piano pieces. The last question asked had to do with amplitude. These included crescendi and diminuendi for the cello but not for the piano. All of the questions had to do with process; none of them with structure (the division of the whole into parts). Just as it had been decided to write for cello and piano, it had been decided in advance to use two pages for each piece, each page having six systems. This followed without any change the composition of both the *Freeman Etudes* and the *Etudes Australes*.

ON NAM JUNE PAIK'S
ZEN FOR FILM (1962-64) (1968)

Cage's first appreciation of the Korean-born composer/video artist Nam June Paik appeared in Cage's book A Year From Monday *(1967). The second, reproduced below, appeared initially in* Cinema Now, *a catalogue published by the University of Cincinnati in 1968; the third, also here, was first published in German translation by the Kunsthaus in Zurich. Here it appears in its original English for the first time.*

On the nature of silence: Well now, you know that I've written a piece called *4'33"*, which has no sounds of my own making in it, and that Robert Rauschenberg has made paintings which have no images on them — they're simply canvases, white canvases, with no images on them — and Nam June Paik, the Korean composer, has made an hour-long film which has no images on it. Now, offhand, you might say that all three actions are the same. But they're quite different.

The Rauschenberg paintings, in my opinion, as I've expressed it, become airports for particles of dust and shadows that are in the environment.

My piece, *4'33"*, becomes in performance the sounds of the environment.

Now, in the music, the sounds of the environment remain, so to speak, where they are, whereas in the case of the Rauschenberg painting the dust and the shadows, the changes in light and so forth, don't remain where they are but come to the painting. In the case of the Nam June Paik film, which has no images on it, the room is darkened, the film is projected, and what you see is the dust that has collected on the film. I think that's somewhat similar to the case of the Rauschenberg painting, though the focus is more intense. **The nature of the environment is more on the film,** different from the dust and shadows that are the environment falling on the painting, and thus less free.

ART AND TECHNOLOGY (1969)

The following text was found among Cage's papers. He has no recollection of whom it was written for or where it might have appeared, even though the photocopy is marked "Copyright ©1969 by John Cage."

(They) bring people together (world people), people and their energies and the world's material resources, energies and facilities together in a way that welcomes the stranger and discovery and takes advantage of synergy, an energy greater than the sum of the several energies had they not been brought together . . . not just inside our heads, but outside of them in the world where our central nervous system (electronics) effectively now is.

Everything happens at once (a different music).

Art's in process of coming into its own: life. Life includes technology.

The purpose of art is not separate from the purpose of technology.

Do not imagine there aren't many things to do. We need for instance an utterly wireless technology. Just as Fuller domes (dome within dome, translucent, plants between) will give impression of living in no home at all (outdoors), so all technology must move toward the way things were before man began changing them: identification with nature in her manner of operation, complete mystery.

Introduce disorder.

Sounds passing through circumstances.

Invade areas where nothing's definite (areas—micro and macro— adjacent the one we know in). It won't sound like music — serial or electronic. It'll sound like what we hear when we're not hearing *music*, just hearing whatever we happen to be. But to accomplish this our technological means must be constantly changing.

Bewildering and productive of joy.

Are we an audience for computer art? The answer's not No; it's Yes. (A computer that turns us into artists.)

What'll art become? A family reunion? If so, let's have it with people in the round, each individual free to lend his attention wherever he will. Meeting house.

Composer, who no longer arranges sounds in a piece, simply

111

facilitates an enterprise. Using a telephone, he locates materials, services, raises money to pay for them.

Art and TV are no longer two different things. They're equally tedious . . . TV's vibrating field's shaken our arts to pieces. No use to pick them up. Get with it . . . . Art's socialized. It isn't someone saying something, but people doing things, giving everyone (including those involved) the opportunity to have experiences they would not otherwise have had . . . . Sounds everywhere. Our concerts celebrate the fact concerts are no longer necessary.

Tried conversation (engineers and artists). Found it didn't work. At the last minute, our profound differences (different attitudes toward time?) threatened performance. What changed matters, made conversation possible, produced cooperation, reinstated one's desire for continuity, etc., were *things*, dumb inanimate things (once in our hands they generated thought, speech, action).

We do what no one else does. Economy. (We do not believe in "human nature.") We are nouveaux-riches. Beyond that, we are criminals. There, outside the law, we tell the truth. For this reason, we exploit technology. Circumstances determine our actions.

Computers're bringing about a situation that's like the invention of harmony. Sub-routines are like chords. No one would think of keeping a chord to himself. You'd give it to anyone who wanted it. You'd welcome alterations of it. Sub-routines are altered by a single punch. We're getting music made by man himself: not just one man.

Art's (Technology's) self-(world-)alteration.

PREFACE TO *NOTATIONS* (1969)

The following text appeared only on the jacket-flaps to the hardbound edition of Cage's anthology of contemporary music notation; it was not included in the paperback.

The reading or memorizing of something written in order to play music is an Occidental practice. In the Orient, music by tradition is transmitted from person to person. Teachers of music require that students put no reliance on written material.

Western notations brought about the preservation of "music," but in doing so encouraged the development not only of standards of composition and performance, but also of an enjoyment of music that was more or less independent of its sound, placing qualities of its organization and expressivity above sound itself.

Furthermore, as the permissions to reprint in this book testify, music, through becoming property, elevated its composers above other musicians, and an art by nature ephemeral became in practice political.

In any case, until recently, notation was the unquestioned path to the experience of music.

At the present time, however, and throughout the world, not only most popular music but much so-called serious music is produced without recourse to notations. This is in large part the effect of a change from print to electronic technology. One may nowadays repeat music not only by means of printed notes but by means of sound recordings, disc or tape. One may also compose new music by these same recording means, and by other means: the activation of electric and electronic sound-systems, the programming of computer output of actual sounds, etc. In addition to technological changes, or without employing such changes, one may change one's mind, experiencing, in the case of theatre (happenings, performance pieces), sounds as the musical effect of actions as they may be perceived in the course of daily life. In none of these cases does notation stand between musician and music nor between music and listener.

Asked to write about notation, André Jolivet made the following remark: "One hundred and fifty years ago, western musical writing acquired such flexibility, such precision, that music was permitted to become the only true international language."

François Dufrêne, replying to a request for a manuscript, wrote as follows: "I am not in a situation to give you any kind of score, since the spirit in which I work involves the systematic rejection of all notation ... I 'note' furthermore that a score could only come about after the fact, and because of this loses from my point of view all significance."

This book, then, by means of manuscript pages (sometimes showing how a page might leave its composer's hand in its working form, sometimes how it looked in its working form as he used it, sometimes finished work), shows the spectrum in the twentieth century which extends from the continuing dependence on notation to its renunciation.

POLITICAL/SOCIAL ENDS? (1969)

Question: Have you, or has anyone ever used your music for political or social ends?

I am interested in social ends but not in political ends, because politics deals with power, and society deals with numbers of individuals; and I'm interested both in single individuals and large numbers or medium numbers or any kinds of numbers of individuals. In other words, I'm interested in society, not for purposes of power, but for purposes of cooperation and enjoyment.

The best___ form   of gov. ern _ ment

is no   gov _ _ ern _ ment   at   all.

"Solo for Voice 35" (from *Song Books*)

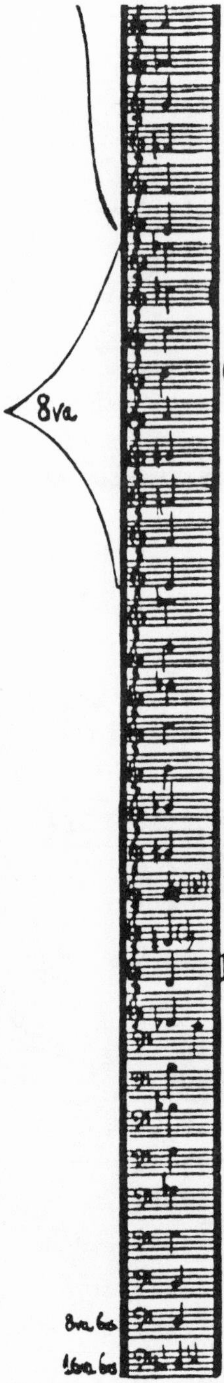

			MED. BOLT	2-3	2 3/8*
			SCREW	2-3	2 1/4*
			SCREW	2-3	3 3/4*
			SCREW	2-3	2 15/16*
SCREW	1-2	3/4*	FURN. BOLT + 2 NUTS	2-3	2 1/8*
			SCREW	2-3	1 13/16*
			FURNITURE BOLT	2-3	1 7/8
			SCREW	2-3	1 15/16
			SCREW	2-3	1 1/16
(DAMPER TO BRIDGE = 4 5/16; ADJUST ACCORDINGLY)			MED. BOLT	2-3	3 3/4
			SCREW	2-3	4 9/16
RUBBER	1-2-3	4 1/2	FURNITURE BOLT	2-3	1 1/4
			SCREW	2-3	1 3/4
			SCREW	2-3	2 5/16
RUBBER	1-2-3	5 3/4			
RUBBER	1-2-3	6 1/2	FURN. BOLT + NUT	2-3	6 7/8
			FURNITURE BOLT	2-3	2 9/16
RUBBER	1-2-3	3 5/8			
			BOLT	2-3	7 1/8
			BOLT	2-3	2
SCREW	1-2	10	SCREW	2-3	1
(PLASTIC (see G))	1-2-3	2 5/16			
PLASTIC (OVER 1 UNDER 2-3)	1-2-3	2 7/8			
(PLASTIC (see D))	1-2-3	4 1/4			
PLASTIC (OVER 1 - UNDER 2-3)	1-2-3	4 3/8			
BOLT	1-2	15 1/2	BOLT	2-3	14/16
BOLT	1-2	14 1/2	BOLT	2-3	7/8
BOLT	1-2	14 3/4	BOLT	2-3	9/16
RUBBER	1-2-3	9 1/2	MED. BOLT	2-3	10 1/8
SCREW	1-2	5 7/8	LG. BOLT	2-3	5 7/8
BOLT	1-2	7 3/8	MED. BOLT	2-3	2 1/4
LONG BOLT	1-2	8 3/4	LG BOLT	2-3	3 1/4
			BOLT	2-3	14/16
SCREW + RUBBER	1-2	4 7/16			
ERASER (OVER D UNDER C & E) AM. PENCIL CO. #346	1	6 3/4			

*MEASURE FROM BRIDGE.

Table of Preparations for *Sonatas and Interludes* (1946-48)

FOREWORD TO
THE WELL-PREPARED PIANO (1973)

> The total desired result has been achieved if, on completion of the preparation, one may play the pertinent keys without sensing that he is playing a piano or even a "prepared piano." An instrument having convincingly its own special characteristic, not even suggesting those of a piano, must be the result.
>
> **John Cage,** Preface to *Amores* (1943)

In his preface to Richard Bunger's booklet The Well-Prepared Piano, *Cage recalls his earliest notorious invention.*

In the late thirties I was employed as accompanist for the classes in modern dance at the Cornish School in Seattle, Washington. These classes were taught by Bonnie Bird who had been a member of Martha Graham's Company. Among her pupils was an extraordinary dancer, Syvilla Fort, later an associate in New York City of Katherine Dunham. Three or four days before she was to perform her *Bacchanale*, Syvilla asked me to write music for it. I agreed.

At that time I had two ways of composing: for piano or orchestral instruments I wrote twelve-tone music (I had studied with Adolph Weiss and Arnold Schoenberg); I also wrote music for percussion ensembles: pieces for three, four or six players.

The Cornish Theatre in which Syvilla Fort was to perform had no space in the wings. There was also no pit. There was, however, a piano at one side in front of the stage. I couldn't use percussion instruments for Syvilla's dance, though, suggesting Africa, they would have been suitable; they would have left too little room for her to perform. I was obliged to write a piano piece.

I spent a day or so conscientiously trying to find an African twelve-tone row. I had no luck. I decided that what was wrong was not me but the piano. I decided to change it.

Besides studying with Weiss and Schoenberg, I had also studied with Henry Cowell. I had often heard him play a grand piano, changing its sound by plucking and muting the strings with fingers and hands. I particularly loved to hear him play *The Banshee*. To do this, Henry Cowell first depressed the pedal with a wedge at the back (or asked an assistant, sometimes myself, to sit at the keyboard and hold the pedal down), and then, standing at the back of the piano, he produced the music by lengthwise friction on the bass strings with his fingers or fingernails, and by crosswise sweeping of the bass strings with the palms of his hands. In another piece he used a darning egg, moving it lengthwise along the strings while trilling, as I recall, on the keyboard; this produced a glissando of harmonics.

Having decided to change the sound of the piano in order to make a music suitable for Syvilla Fort's *Bacchanale*, I went to the kitchen, got a pie plate, brought it into the living room and placed it on the piano strings. I played a few keys. The piano sounds had been changed, but the pie plate bounced around due to the vibrations, and, after a while, some of the sounds that had been changed no longer were. I tried something smaller, nails between the strings. They slipped down between and lengthwise along the strings. It dawned on me that screws or bolts would stay in position. They did. And I was delighted with the sounds they produced. I noticed the difference obtained by use of the *una corda* so well-described in this book *The Well-Prepared Piano (1973)* by Richard Bunger. I wrote the *Bacchanale* quickly and with the excitement continual discovery provided.

I did not immediately write another piece for the "prepared piano." It was later in the early forties in New York City, due to the difficulties of organizing a percussion ensemble outside a school situation, that I began writing for a time almost exclusively for the prepared piano.

For Robert Fizdale and Arthur Gold I wrote two works for two prepared pianos, *Three Dances* and *A Book of Music*. These, together with *The Perilous Night* which I played, made a program at the New School in New York. There were five pianos on the stage, each prepared differently. There were only fifty people in the audience, but among them was Virgil Thomson who wrote a review for *The Herald-Tribune* which was enthusiastic about both the music and the performances. It was the first performance anywhere by Fizdale and Gold. I later revised the *Three Dances* for Maro Ajemian and William Masselos.

It was in the late forties while writing the *Concerto for Prepared Piano* and *Chamber Orchestra* that I received a telephone call from a pianist who had performed *The Perilous Night* on tour in South America. He asked me to come to his studio and hear him play. I did.

His preparation of the piano was so poor that I wished at the time that I had never written the music.

Many years later while on tour in the southeastern U.S. with the Merce Cunningham Dance Company, Richard Bunger asked me to listen to his performance of *The Perilous Night*. I tried to get out of what I thought would be an ordeal. I said I was too busy. However, Richard Bunger persevered. When I finally heard him play, I was amazed to discover that he loved and understood the music and that he had prepared the piano beautifully.

When I first placed objects between piano strings, it was with the desire to possess sounds (to be able to repeat them). But, as the music left my home and went from piano to piano and from pianist to pianist, it became clear that not only are two pianists essentially different from one another, but two pianos are not the same either. Instead of the possibility of repetition, we are faced in life with the unique qualities and characteristics of each occasion.

The prepared piano, impressions I had from the work of artist friends, study of Zen Buddhism, ramblings in fields and forests looking for mushrooms, all led me to the enjoyment of things as they come, as they happen, rather than as they are possessed or kept or forced to be.

And so my work since the early fifties has been increasingly indeterminate. There are two prepared piano pieces of this character, *34'46.776" for a Pianist* and *31'57.9864" for a Pianist*. They may be played alone or together and with or without parts *for a Stringplayer*, *a Percussionist*, and *a Speaker*. In these timelength piano pieces (or "whistle pieces" as David Tudor and I came to call them, since, to produce auxiliary noises called for in the scores, we had used whistles, our hands being busy at the keyboards) objects are added and subtracted from an initial piano preparation during the actual performance. Interesting notations for such circumstances are provided by Richard Bunger in this book.

PREFATORY NOTE TO COWELL'S
QUARTET ROMANTIC AND
QUARTET EUPHOMETRIC (1974)

This text began as a memo to C.F. Peters, Inc., which was publishing a score by Cage's sometime teacher, Henry Cowell. It seems appropriate to publish Cage's original handwriting along with Tennessee Jerry Hunt's transcription.

Nowadays when things happen so quickly that many of them escape notice, we are apt when we see attached to them dates such as these Cowell pieces have (1915-1916) — we are apt to subtract from our attention anything like urgency. We are not so concerned with the aging of things as we are with their distant quality.

But the liveliness of music 1974 has rich American causes. A prime cause is the music of Henry Cowell. And all the other causes for his musical interests know no boundaries, could be summed up by saying Henry Cowell the man. This means not only the music of Ives, Ruggles, Varèse, etc., but the research in laboratories and the machines that were made that made the twentieth-century the American one.

Advances in technology were paralleled by advances in imagination and vision. Often there did not come together at all. (The inventor of musical instruments, electronic ones capable of doing anything, who refused to permit the use of his machine for anything but consonance. My father's airplane engine that was so powerful the plane it was in flew to pieces without leaving the earth. These quartets (by Henry Cowell written when they were impossible to perform.) How we move from something we have in mind to something we can do without being thrown out of our sense of poetry. The Impossible is the Possible. These pieces are published. They've been performed (if the one with the difficult rhythms hasn't been, it shortly will be, either by real live musicians or by someone who supplies a computer with the necessary information). And how do they sound? As Cowell sixty years ago knew they would; warm and rich.

The twain have met (Read the newspapers): we live in a global *village. This music is up-to-the-minute: it is occidental and oriental at one and the same time.*

John Cage

Nowadays, when things happen so quickly that many of them escape notice, we are apt when we see attached to them dates such as these Cowell pieces have (1915-1916) — we are apt to subtract from our attention anything like urgency. We are not so concerned with the aging of things as we are with their instant quality.

But the liveliness of music 1974 has rich American causes. A prime cause is the music of Henry Cowell. And all the other causes for his musical interests had no boundaries, could be summed up by saying Henry Cowell the man. That means not only the music of Ives, Ruggles, Varèse, etc., but the research in laboratories and the machines that were made that made the Twentieth Century the American one.

Advances in technology were paralleled by advances in imagination and vision. Often these did not come together at all: (The inventor of musical instruments, electronic ones capable of doing anything, who refused to permit the use of his machine for anything but consonance. My father's airplane engine was so powerful, the plane it was in flew to pieces without leaving the earth; these quartets by Henry Cowell, written when they were impossible to perform). Now we move from something we have in mind to something we can do without being thrown out of our sense of poetry. The Impossible is the Possible. These pieces are published. They've been performed (if the one with the difficult rhythms hasn't been, it shortly will be either by real live musicians or by someone who supplies a computer with the necessary information). And how do they sound? As Cowell sixty years ago knew they would: warm and rich.

The twain have met (Read the newspapers). We live in a global village. This music is up to the minute: it is occidental and oriental at one and the same time.

FROM *CONTEMPORARY MUSIC CATALOGUE (C.F. PETERS) (1975)*

Shortly I'll be writing again (this time for orchestra). What will it be? I don't know. As usual I want to keep from interrupting the silence that's already here. "Bubbles on the surface of silence." That's how Thoreau describes sounds, that way or nearly that way.

Shortly I'll be writing again (this time for orchestra). What will it be?... I don't know. As usual I want to keep from interrupting the silence that's already here. "Bubbles on the surface of silence." That's how Thoreau described sounds, that way or nearly that way.

John Cage

7 OUT OF 23 (1977)

This initial mesostic interpretation of James Joyce's Finnegans Wake
differs considerably from Cage's later reworkings of Joyce's texts.

Joh joseph's   366
beAuty
Mouth, sing mim.   367
look at lokman! whatbEtween
the cupgirlS and the platterboys.

Juke
dOne it.
in his perrY boat
the old thalassoCrats
of invisiblE empores,

as the Just
hAs bid to jab the punch
of quaraM
on thE mug of truth.
k.c. jowlS, they're sodden in the secret.

with the atlas Jacket. brights,
brOwnie
eYes
in bluesaCkin
shoEings.

Jiff exby rode,   369
Adding the tout
last Mannarks
makEth man
when wandShift winneth womans:

Jeremy   370
trOuvas or kepin o'keepers,
anY old howe and any old then
Courcy
dE courcy and gilligan-goll.

Jeremy yopp,
frAncist
de looMis, hardy smith
and sEquin pettit
followed by the Snug saloon seanad of our café
béranger. the scenictutors.

Jameseslane. begetting a wife 373
which begame his niece by pOuring
her Youngthings into skintighs.
it Crops out
in your flEsh. 374

Just press
this cold brAnd against your brow
for a Mow. cainfully!
thE
Sinus the curse. that's it.

and kick kick
kickkillykick for the house that Juke built! 375
wait till they send yOu to sleep, scowpow!
then old hunphYdunphyville'll be blasted to bumboards
and it's all us rangers you'll be faCing
in thE box before the twelfth correctional.

Just
hold hAnd,
richMond
rovEr!
Scrum around, our side!

sporting the insides of a rhutian Jhanaral and little mrs ex-skaerer-sissers
is bribing the halfpricers tO
praY
in berkness Cirrchus
clouthsEs.

Jik. 376
sAuss.
aunt as unclish aMs
thEy make oom.
not to looSe's gone

and a good Jump,
pOwell!
drink and hurrY.
all of your own Club too.
with thE fistful of burryberries were for the
massus for to feed you living in dying.

feeling the Jitters?
you'll be As tight as trivett
diaMindwaiting.
what a magnificEnt
geSture you will show us this gallus day.

mr Justinian
jOhnston-johnson.
help, help, hurraY!
Cut it down,
matEs, look slippy!

379   rubyJuby. phook!
no wonder, pipes As kirles, that he sthings like a rheinbok.
one bed night he had the delysiuMs
that thEy
were all queenS mobbing him.

it Just gegs
Our goad. he'll be the deaf of us,
pappappoppopcuddle, samblind daiYrudder.
none of you, Cock icy!
you kEep that henayearn and hev
fortycantle glim lookbehinder.

380   for the Jolly
good reAson that he was
the whiloM joky old top
that wEnt before him
in the taharan dynaSty,

381   he Just went heeltapping
thrOugh the winespilth
and weevilY
popCorks
that wEre kneedeep round his own right

his most exuberant maJesty king roderick o'conor
but, Arrah
bedaMnbut,
hE
finaliSed by lowering his woolly throat

382   more that halibut oil or Jesuits tea, as a fall back,
Of several different quantities
and qualities i should saY,
horihistoriCold
and fathEr

he Just slumped to throne.
so sAiled the stout ship *nansy hans*.
froM liff away.
for nattEnlaender.
aS who has come returns.

If, on the other hand, one were to start at the beginning:

3   wroth with twone nathandJoe. rot
                 A peck
           of pa's Malt
           had jhEm
                 or Shen entailed at such short notice

               the pftJschute
                   Of finnegan, erse solid man,
        that the humptYhillhead of humself
          is at the knoCk out
             in thE park

or at the end:

626   my lips went livid for from the Joy
                of feAr.
                 like alMost now. how? how you said
           how you'd givE me
             the keyS of me heart.

627   Just a whisk brisk sly spry spink
        spank sprint Of a thing
              i pitY your oldself i was used to.
           a Cloud.
           in peacE

or make a cyclic return:

627   Just
                   A
                   May i
                   bE wrong!
                   for She'll be sweet for you as i was sweet
                       when i came down out of me mother.

3   Jhem
                   Or shen brewed by arclight
         and rorY end
        through all Christian
          minstrElsy.

IF THERE ISN'T ANY, WHY DO YOU WEAR THEM? (1977)

These mesostic poems were written with words not by James Joyce (or another writer) but from Cage's own head, and they resemble other short poems of his, including one reproduced later, in being based upon incidents or occasions in his own life.

it doeSn't stand to reason
tHat
i cOuld
havE
loSt them;

Someone
must Have
run Off
with thEm
by miStake.

perhapS
i left tHem
Outdoors,
thE way i do
the keyS

(it waS raining). no.
tHat's
nOt
what happEned.
i muSt have been in japan.

that'S it!
that explains everytHing!
what I have tO do is get
somE
new oneS.

NOTES ON COMPOSITIONS IV (1979-86)

Most of the following notes on Cage's own compositions come from the printed matter accompanying discs recording their performances.

Concerto Grosso for 4 TV Sets and 12 Radios (1979), First Installation: In 1969 at the University of California, Davis, I arranged an event called 33⅓ which consisted of an auditorium with eight sound systems, the sound sources being recordings played on playbacks. Each playback had a technical assistant who did not himself play the records but who was available in case a member of the "audience" had difficulty in doing so. For the audience was the performers. Without them nothing was heard. This piece is in that "tradition." It is assumed, however, that everyone knows how to "play" a television set and how to "play" a radio.

Litany for the Whale (1980): Recitation and thirty-two responses for two voices without vibrato. W = wou as in would; H = hu as in hut; A = ah; L = ll as in will; E = e as in under. A "word" is sung in one breath but pronouncing each letter separately and giving more or less equal time ($\musEighthNote$ = 72) to each letter except the last (or only) letter of a word which is to be held longer than the others. Let there be a short silence after each response. The first singer sings the recitation. The singer follows with the first response (the second singer that is). A short silence and the recitation. The first singer then sings the second response, waits and then sings the recitation, etcetera, quietly, without dynamic changes.

Dance/4 Orchestras (1982): The orchestras are separated from one another and placed at different points with respect to the audience. They are not to be grouped together on a stage at one end of the auditorium. They may be placed in lobbies or adjoining hallways, the doors between them and the audience left open.

Each two facing pages of score last at least two and one-half minutes. They may last longer. They may be conducted at a steady tempo of any speed from extremely slow to extremely fast, or at one which ritards or accelerates. In the latter case, the conductor must make the change in tempo very gradual so that it continues to get slower or faster throughout the period of time devoted to the two facing pages. Each conductor is to begin conducting at any time during the first minute (each conductor works independently of the others, with respect particularly to his beginnings and his tempo). The number of seconds for the time bracket between pairs of pages is given in a box at the upper end of the second page. The conductor may begin the next pair of pages at any time during the given time bracket, provided the total time length required has been reached.

Each two facing pages consist of a section or sections to be repeated. At the beginning of each section is an arrow and at the end of each section there is a repeat sign. When there are two or more such sections the arrows at the beginnings are differently oriented: ←, ↖, ↑, ↗, and →. These correspond to signals to be given by the conductor with his left arm and hand. At each repeat sign the orchestra returns to whichever section the conductor indicates. If none is indicated, the orchestra and conductor continue to the next section. At the end of the last one, a signal must be given unless the two and one-half minutes required have passed.

In the case of extremely high or low sounds notated *mp–ppp* for the winds and brass, the player is to observe the dynamic faithfully, attempt the pitch conscientiously, and accept with equanimity whatever sound that results.

Where there are notes connected by stems, tone production is notated above and amplitude is notated below. These notations apply to all the tones connected by the stem.

Improvisation IV (1982): For three cassette players using machines equipped with a device designed by John Fullemann which allows one to change the playback speed from seven o'clock (slow) to twelve o'clock (normal) to five o'clock (fast). For *Fielding Sixes* there are three identical sets of twelve cassettes of Irish traditional music: six are Matt Molloy on flute; six are Paddy Glackin, fiddle. This improvisation may use other material than Irish traditional music, material suitable for the accompaniment of another dance, or material suitable to be heard independently of the dance. In the latter case, an agreement as to time-length among the players should be made.

Ryoanji: Solos for Oboe, Flute, Contrabass, Voice, Trombone with Percussion or Orchestral Obbligato (1983-85): In recent

years I have made a number of works, some of them graphic, some musical, all having the Japanese word *Ryoanji* or a reference to it, in the title. These began in 1982 when I was asked by Andre Dimanche to design a cover for Pierre Lartigue's translation into French of my

Mushroom Book. This is a part of his series of fifteen books called Editions Ryoan-ji, all of which are paperbacked with a paper that reminds one of raked sand. My suggestion for the cover of my book that I draw around fifteen stones (fifteen is the number of stones in the Ryoanji garden in Kyoto) placed at *I Ching*-determined points on a grid the size of the cover plus the flaps was accepted.

In January of 1983 when I went to the Crown Point Press to make etchings I took the same fifteen stones with me, but soon found that what can be done with pencil on paper cannot be done with needle on copper. The mystery produced by pencils disappeared, reappearing only on copper when the number of stones was multiplied ($225:15 \times 15$; $3375:15 \times 15 \times 15$).

That summer I began a series of drawings which continues even now, having titles such as 3R/5, or R/12. R is Ryoanji or 15 and the number below the line is the number of different pencils (between 6B and 9H) used to make the drawing. At some point that year an oboist in Baltimore, James Ostryniec, began writing a number of letters asking me to compose some solos for him to play in Japan. I kept putting him off. Eventually he came to visit bringing both his oboe and several textbooks about playing the instrument. I was amazed to see that one of the books began with the division of the octave not into seven or twelve tones but into twenty-four. Students of oboe playing must make special efforts to keep from sliding up or down while playing a single tone. I told Ostryniec that I would write some music for him.

Paper was prepared that had two rectangular systems. Using two such sheets I made a "garden" of sounds, tracing parts of the perimeters of the same stones I had used for the drawings and etchings. I was writing a music of *glissandi*. Where, through the use of chance operations, more lines than one were drawn in the same vertical space, I distinguished between sound systems, taking four as a maximum (loudspeakers around an audience; prerecorded tapes). For the accompaniment I turned my attention to the raked sand. I made a percussion part having a single complex of unspecified sounds played in unison, five icti chance-distributed in meters of twelve, thirteen, fourteen or fifteen. I didn't want the mind to be able to analyze rhythmic patterns. I dedicated this work to Michael Pugliese because he was the first to discover a way to play my *Etudes Boreales* which I had thought were too difficult to play literally, that is, to play all of the notes that had been written.

These were the first pieces in a series that continues: flute solos for Robert Aitken, songs for Isabelle Ganz, pieces for double bass and voice for Joelle Leandre for whom I also made (enjoying a Commande d'Etat from the French Ministry of Culture) an orchestral version of the percussion accompaniment. I am about to write trombone pieces for James Fulkerson. Inclined as I am to listen to as many environmental sounds as there are I look forward to hearing these solos together, providing the space in which they are heard is large enough to accommodate several "gardens," i.e. multiples of four sound systems.

All of them are eight in number, except the songs for Isabelle Ganz which are nine. The ranges within which the *glissandi* play are sometimes wide, sometimes narrow. The texts are variations of lettristic *Haikus* (Letters from the seventeen chapters of *Finnegans Wake* which I had written earlier that year). I kept the letters of the original *Haikus* but using chance operations made vowel additions to them. Thus *dlyr, l, f, p r* (*k* the first part of the first *Haiku*) became *dya ayl-y rya, eul fio pie air ki*. A silence of an undetermined length takes place after each solo. The accompaniment continues. It also begins almost a minute before the first solo and does not end until slightly less than a minute after the last one.

Thirty Pieces for String Quartet (1983) takes its title from the work for five orchestras written in 1981. Just as that was a coincidence of chamber orchestras, so this is a coincidence of solos. There is no relationship of the four parts fixed in a score. Each solo is either microtonal, tonal, or chromatic or presents these differences in pairs; or presents all of them in succession. Each begins at any time within a forty-five second period and ends at any given time within another forty-five second period that overlaps the first by fifteen seconds. Thus a given piece may be played as fast as possible or it may be drawn out to a maximum length of seventy-five seconds. The work is dedicated to the Kronos Quartet resident in San Francisco. Its flexibility of structure makes it a music that is, so to speak, earthquake-proof.

Music For _____ (1984-87): Parts for voice and instruments without score (no fixed relation), title to be completed by adding to *Music For _____*, the number of players performing.

Each part is a sequence of "pieces" and "interludes." Each "piece" is written on two systems. It begins and ends at any time within the time-brackets given. It is made up of one or the other or of both of two kinds of music: a) a single held tone *p*, preceded and followed by silence, repeated any number of times, and b) a number of tones in proportional notation (space = time), not to be repeated, characterized by a variety of pitches, dynamics, timbres and durations within a limited range. Beamed notes are to be played as *legato* as possible. Each "interlude" (five, ten, or fifteen seconds in total duration) is to be played freely with respect to dynamics and the durations of single notes, normally with respect to timbre, but within the time length given, and following the phrasing given.

The part for flute makes use of fingerings given by Robert Dick in his book *The Other Flute*, that for clarinet of those given by Phillip Rehfeldt in his *New Directions for Clarinet*. I am grateful to Richard Samarotto for editing this part.

♪ , ♪ indicate mircrotonal pitch inflections up or down. M is muted (with hand or cloth). o = harmonic.

In the trumpet part, the numbers are of mutes chosen by the player. Unnumbered tones are open. The part for horn sounds a perfect fifth lower than written whether in bass or treble clef. Asterisks above notes in the part for trombones indicate special sounds to be determined by the trombonist. They can be any alterations of pitch and/or timbre the player chooses to introduce.

To make the single held tones on the piano, remove the lid; place fishing line or a bundle of horsehair tied at both ends (obtainable new or used in violin shops) around the string or strings of the key notated. With the piano pedal down, holding the line or bundle taut and up, one end in each hand, set the string in vibration by pulling the material back and forth. The material may be lightly rosined. The speed of "bowing" can vary in the middle and low register but should be fast in the high register.

Each percussionist has fifty instruments of his own choice. Of these, some are not used: for the first percussionist 1–6 and 50; for the second percussionist 1 and 46; for the third percussionist 1, 3, 4, 5, 20, and 50; for the fourth percussionist 1 and 50. Each must be able to produce held tones on the various instruments; for the first percussionist: 9, 11, 12, 17, 18, 19, 21, 22, 27, 32, 33, 37, 39 and 41; for the second percussionist: 4, 6, 12, 14, 15, 16, 20, 21, 24, 29, 44, 48, 49, 50; for the third percussionist: 2, 6, 10, 17, 24, 26, 27, 29, 34, 38, 41, 42, 43, 46 and 48; for the fourth percussionist: 3, 4, 6, 10, 20, 24, 26, 29, 31, 34, 36, 39, 45 and 49 (these are the single held tones *p* mentioned above). Percussion sounds given notated durations in proportional notations may be performed L.V. (where the instrument resounds) or intermittently XXXX (where the instrument does not resound). Asterisks above notes indicate special sounds produced, for example, by using some other beater than the usual one. If a pitched instrument (e.g. vibraphone, glockenspiel, etc.) is used as one of the fifty, use only one of its tones. Or use two tones that are widely separated in pitch as two of fifty.

The string parts follow the notation of the *Freeman Etudes* for violin.

Each player should prepare his part by himself and learn to play it with his own chronometer. There should be no joint rehearsal until all the parts have been carefully prepared. They are then to be played as though from different points in time. The players may sit anywhere within the auditorium with respect to the audience and to each other.

Each part begins (has its own 0'00") at any time within the boxed time-bracket given at its beginning. Played in its entirety the work will last thirty minutes. If desired, performances of shorter lengths may be given, each player independently of the others choosing an uninterrupted sequence of pieces and interludes the length of which is approximately that of the agreed upon time.

Music for Five (1984): One way or another, let orchestras aspire to the state of chamber musicians, or be led to that state—the love of music—no matter what difficulties lie between it and musicians. Not a job but a way of life.

Project: Beginning with chamber music to approach (instrument by instrument), musician by musician, the condition of orchestra. No conductor (*Music For _____*). (*From the program of the IGNM Weltmusiktage '87.*)

Mirakus² (1984): To be sung without vibrato, as in folk singing. The lines of the music should be sung as lines of poetry, with a space of time between each that seems right to the singer. Whether this should be short, longer, or very long is suggested by the numbers after each line, 1, 2, 3, and 4.

These texts are derived from *Marcel Duchamp, Notes (1983)* by Alexina S. Duchamp and Paul Matisse with their kind permission. The same *I Ching*-determined collection of notes was used as was used for *Mirage Verbal*. These texts, however, are not a "writing through." They use the MESOLIST computer program (which follows the Mink rule) in conjunction with *I* (a program by Andrew Culver which simulates the *I Ching* coin oracle and relates the numbers 1–64 to any other numbers 1–262, 144). They are called *Mirakus* in reference to "Mirage Verbal" and *haikus* (these are short texts).

Selkus[2] (1984): There are a total of thirteen songs. These texts are derived from *Marcel Duchamp, Notes*. They are called *Selkus* in reference to *"Marchand du Sel"* and *haikus*.

Nowth Upon Nacht (1984): *For the singer*: If you sing this song sing it without break after singing *The Wonderful Widow of Eighteen Springs (1942)*. *For the pianist*: The lid which covers the keys is opened and struck against the piano structure, pedal down. Then hold it back from the structure in preparation for the second attacks.

Eight Whiskus (1984): Chris Mann (Launching Place 3139 Australia) sent me an untitled text which begins as follows: "whistlin is did be puckrin up th gob n blowin thru a ol a brownie sod th box n I seen a compo front up n stack on a blue a bit of a spoon th doodlers hump arguin by buying up all buns n juice crack a fudge a droopie go th roy n late th light. . . ."

Using MESOLIST, eight mesostics were written on the first three words of Chris Mann's text. In contrast to my *Writing Through a Text by Chris Mann*, these eight mesostics are short poems (cf. *haiku*). Therefore I call them *Whiskus*. All lines follow the Mink rule for a pure (100%) mesostic, that is, between two capitalized letters neither of the two appears. The last line of the first *Whisku* is an exception.

Sonnekus[2] (1985): To be sung without vibrato as in folk singing as a part of *The First Meeting of the Satie Society the Socie Satiety*. The lines of the music should be sung as lines of poetry, with a space of time between each that seems right to the singer, except when a line is followed by a slur in which case one continues metrically. The theatrical character of the performance is to suggest (not heavily) both church and cabaret. The singer will make a program including silences of any lengths (and changes of dress) that presents all nine of these songs in the auditorium space. Elsewhere with accompaniment any cabaret songs by Satie may be performed (at a distance from the audience). There shall be no repetitions of songs. The texts are derived from the first book of Moses, *Genesis*. The texts are called *Sonnekus* in reference to Satie's title *Sonneries de la Rose + Croix*.

ASLSP (1985): The title is an abbreviation of "as slow as possible." It also refers to "Soft morning city! Lsp!" the first exclamation in the last paragraph of *Finnegans Wake* (James Joyce).

There are eight pieces, any one of which must be omitted and any one of which must be repeated. The repetition may be placed anywhere (even before its appearance in the suite) but otherwise the order of the pieces as written shall be maintained.

Neither tempo nor dynamics have been notated. Time proportions are given (just as maps give proportional distances). Accidentals apply only to those pitches they directly precede.

Each hand plays its own part and is not to be assisted by the other. A diamond-shaped note indicates a note to be depressed without sounding. All the notes have stems. The stem gives the point in time of the single note, interval or aggregate. Where there is insufficient horizontal space, the stems are splayed to accommodate the noteheads. A closed notehead tied to an open notehead indicates the end of a sustained sound. Sustained sounds are also notated sometimes with straight line-extentions.

In a performance a correspondence between space and time should be realized so that the music "sounds" as it "looks."

But What About the Noise of Crumpling Paper Which He Used to Do in Order to Paint the Series of "Papiers Froisses" or Tearing Up Paper to Make "Papiers Dechires?" Arp Was Stimulated by Water (Sea, Lake, and Flowing Waters Like Rivers), Forests

In celebration of the work of Jean Arp on the occasion of the centenary of his birth (1985): Note: Ten parts any number of which between three and ten may be used to make a performance of any desired time-length (any number of repetitions may be made). Each player uses at least two (preferably more) only slightly resonant instruments of different materials (wood, metal, and glass, for example, not metal, metal and wood) played in unison (+). Very slow, but without conductor, each player following his own beat (. = a "quarter note" rest). The parts should be given some life by means of slight but not obvious changes of dynamics. The open circles (o) are water (pouring, bubbling, etc.), paper (crumpling, tearing, being caused to vibrate like a thundersheet), or not easily identified sounds suggestive of events in nature, all for durations even longer than those notated (repeated circles) though never overlapping a unison in the same part. The half circles opening first to the right (( ) and then closing to the left ( )) are also such sounds, but cut in half, i.e. sounded twice and always for the same length of time. Repeated half circles are also durations that may be exceeded, providing unisons are not overlapped and both halves are equal. The parts have been composed so that a single player can play both the unisons and the circles; however performing each part with two players is preferable. The players may be stationed around the audience, or within it in case the audience is not seated, or they can be on stage, but not close together. The title is from a response to my letter to her by Greta Ströh.

Each player will play their part twice, but as each player keeps their own time, the second half of the work will change in terms of when things occur relative to the other parts — i.e. this work is *not* temporally replicable in the way that *Ten* (1991) is.

Etcetera 2/4 Orchestras (1986):

Since, in each orchestra, everyone is playing (A) in rhythmic unison, care is taken not to play exactly together. Arrow-like notations ⟵ , and ⟶ , indicate very slightly before and very slightly after the beat. Their absence means the tone should be played more on the beat than not. The conductor's function will be to keep the beat in the air, so to speak, not to bring it down to earth. These deviations should be microrhythmic. Microtonal pitch glissandi are analagous to the notations given ♪ , ♪ , ♪ , ♪ , ♪ , ♪ . The pitch range used for these glissandi should be very small. Each orchestra begins more or less at the same time but not following a signal given by one conductor. The time in minutes and seconds is given for each "event" on a page where space equals time.

There are two players at each desk of each orchestra (with the exception of the harpist, the pianist, and the four percussion players). One of the two may leave at any time, going to one of eight stations (four with microphone reserved for strings and bassoons at the front of the stage; four at the back of the stage on elevated platforms without microphones) where he plays one solo from the materials B2, B3, B4, or B5, after which he returns to his desk, learning from the player who did not leave where he is in the conducted music. The harpist, pianist, and the four percussion players play their solos (B1) at any time but without changing position on the stage. Each must use a watch in order to know, when he returns to the conducted part, where he is. The second trombonist and one of the cellists (since they do not share their parts with another) must also use watches when they return from solos (B2–B5) in order to know where they are.

Percussion instruments are described as beater/instrument, e.g. wood/metal, meaning a metal instrument played with a wooden beater: Avoiding the flexatone, choose instruments with which sliding tones can be produced (e.g. pedal tympani, water gong, etc.). Also avoid the use of instruments which are "representational" (the sounds of which are understood rather than experienced). ● = unison with another percussion instrument (not sliding).

MUSHROOMS (1979)

they are found in Moss.
Under bark,
on Stumps,
on the sides of patHs in the woods,
near stReams,
arOund trees,
in the spring in Old orchards,
in the autuMn
among fallen leaveS,

at any tiMe,
even while eating a picnic lUnch,
or croSsing a bridge,
or driving along a Highway,
or going to the supeRmarket,
O
lOoking out the window,
or coMing home,
or viSiting friends (providing you live in
the country).

soMe are edible:
the matsUtake,
ruSsula virescens,
some Hydnums,
the moRel, the chantarelle,
and the lepiOtas:
prOcera,
aMericana,
and *rachode*S, the honey, and lots of others.

and soMe are deadly.
yoU
muSt not eat
tHe amanitas.
Red
Or
Orange tubes. (*piperatus* is o.k. cooked.)
avoid any hebeloMa
and all the entolomaS.

soMetimes none seem to be growing.
bUt look for them anyway:
you might be Surprised.
the masked tricHoloma was found
on the edge of the deseRt,
and during a drOught
clitOcybe
Monadelpha (old name)
waS found in quantity

in oklahoMa.
yoU
muStn't
eat any of tHem
Raw except *fistulina*
hepatica which is deliciOus
uncOoked.
it tastes like leMon even though
itS

nicknaMe is the beefsteak.
strangely enoUgh,
caeSarea
is served fresH
in the best italian Restaurants in italy,
nOt
cOoked at all,
even though it's an aManita.
rubeScens is also edible.

if you're interested find soMeone
who will introdUce you
Say to one or two species at a time
(books won't Help).
when you know one like a fRiend,
recOgnizing it
in all its variatiOns,
you'll have becoMe fairly certain before dinner
that you're not about to commit Suicide

or kill your coMpanions.
some prodUce
viSions. it is said of two elderly ladies
in tHe midwest that they thought
they saw small automobiles being dRiven
upside-dOwn
acrOss the ceiling
of the rooM
in which they had juSt finished eating.

one of theM (not one of the ladies) is said
by the bUddha   to have been eaten
juSt
before He died. that may have been
a way of saying he enteRed nirvana
Or it may simply mean
that he died a natural death. whO knows?
see My
Story about this in *silence*.

no Matter how many years
yoU've hunted them,
you'll alwayS welcome
tHe
next oppoRtunity
tO
lOok
for theM.
it'S hard to explain,

but More
prodUctive
of pleaSure
tHan cooking
oR even eating them
is just the experience Of finding
any One
of theM, no matter which.
it iS always a sudden

refreshMent,
reassUrance,
Surprise,
deligHt,
thRill,
push in the right directiOn,
inspiratiOn,
Moment you'll never forget, and on
a continuing enveloping myStery.   top of that

soMe people don't feel this way
aboUt them.
thoreau didn't, for inStance.
He found them
moRe
Often
than nOt disgusting.
he never ate theM. but in 1856 (9/1)
even he admired their colorS (*Journal* IX: 50-51).

in recent decades their old latin naMes have been changed.
the new Unfamiliar
oneS are difficult to learn.
some of tHem have also been
foRced
tO leave their genera
and mOve into new ones. there's even
a ruMor
that along with fernS, and lichen, algae, etc.

they'll be separated froM the rest of creation
and pUt in a kingdom
by themSelves.
all of tHis is an attempt
to stRaighten
Out
Our understanding of these plants,
which perhaps
are not plants at all. so far they've Managed to remain
juSt as mysterious as they ever were.

MUSIC AND PARTICULARLY SILENCE
IN THE WORK OF
JACKSON MAC LOW (1980)

Even in his late sixties, Cage was writing the kind of extended critical appreciation (from Paper Air, *II/3, 1980) that he had done decades before, in this case extending a contribution to* Vort, *III/2 (1975).*

Jackson Mac Low's training in music began when he was four years old. He studied piano and harmony at the Chicago Musical College until he was eight. He then continued these studies, adding violin lessons, at the Northwestern University School of Music, graduating from its Preparatory Department in 1936 when he was 14. He then stopped taking music lessons because high school work left him insufficient time for practice. Since then in New York he has studied piano intermittently, for one year with Shirley Gabis (1943-44), for four years with Grete Sultan (1953-56), and, since 1976, with breaks now and then, with Franz Kamin. He studied composition and sight singing with Erich Katz (1948-49) at the Manhattan School of Music, and recorder with Tui St. George Tucker (1950-54) with whom he also discussed composition. He frequently attended my classes in experimental composition at the New School (1957-60) providing the class with most of the examples of work presented in it. Subsequently he attended the same classes when they were continued in his own home by Richard Maxfield.

Like everyone in the public school system (classes in reading and writing), Mac Low was trained to become a poet. It is remarkable that when he was younger he never made musical settings of his own poems, choosing instead something from the Bible or texts by Blake, Whitman, or Conrad, for example. There is a *Rilke Motet* and music for Auden's *Age of Anxiety* as presented by the Living Theatre in the '50s. By 1961 however, he established methods for reading his *Asymmetries* (poems of which the words, punctuation, typography, and spacing of words on the page have been determined by certain kinds of chance operations) which bring his music and poetry into such a close relation that a performer, who can, may change from reading a poem to performing as a musician, the letters of the language having been coded by Mac Low in relation to all or nearly all of the twelve tones so that words either remain words or become tone rows.

Much of his early music has been lost. Much of what is extant is unfinished. One might say these unfinished pieces fell into silence, for otherwise they did not include any. Those of the thirties, forties, and early fifties, whether finished or not, are engaged in continuous contrapuntal procedures, tonal or modal, uninterrupted musical developments, or, towards the end of this period, inventions using twelve-tone rows. They did not stop until their work was finished. In the middle fifties, however, silence was sometimes introduced between phrases of finished pieces as in Nos. II, III, and IV of *Four Pianissimo Preludes* (1955), and the *Piano Piece* of March 20, 1956. In No. 2 of *Three Essays in an Intervallic Series*, for piano, there are passages of silence divided into equal lengths (e.g. 8/16, 20/16, 12/16, 22/16, 19/16, 5/16) to be articulated at the bar lines by rapping lightly with the fingertips alternately of the right and left hands on the piano structure below the keys. And in the second of the *3 Haikus* silence is used to express two of both the first five "syllables" and the following seven, and three of the concluding five.

Silence is part and parcel of *Piece for Recorder* (1961). (Though in *F#*, written at about the same time, any break in the sound due to any cause ends the piece. Any further playing of F# is a second performance.) *Piece for Recorder* is for any number of performers. Each proceeds from any parenthesized number-group in a Fingering Score to any other, reading either from left to right or vice-versa to realize an Event Score which relates quantity (many, few, one, or none of these fingerings) with duration (long, short). Thus NS is none short, a short silence, and NL a long one. In producing a short event, performers *silently* finger through a number-group until they blow the recorder. Furthermore, between events silences of any duration may (but need not) occur. Though 97 fingerings are given and 102 events, the score includes directions for composing further fingerings and events making use of a random digit table. The end of this composition is not envisaged by the composer.

The basic method for reading *Asymmetries* (1961) with respect to silence is as follows: "blank spaces before, after, and between words or parts of words, between lines of words and before poems are rendered as silences equal in duration to the time it would take to read aloud the words printed anywhere above or below them." In other words, the page is a typescript having on each line an equal number of spaces, some of them completely empty, others partly empty but including words or parts of words. All empty spaces are silence. In addition to the basic method there are six others, so that words, tones, and silences are either alone, in pairs, or all three together. The basic method is the pair of words and silences. When all three are together, tones are used to realize right-marginal space, and during whole lines of silence, a performer is either silent, or, "not too often," continues the tone from the line above. He is silent during left-marginal space. In the pair, tones and silences, a performer plays tones during right-marginal spaces, is silent during left-marginal spaces and words, and is silent or prolongs tones from the preceding line during whole empty lines. On the 4th of August 1961 an 8th method was described replacing silence with whisperings of any of the words printed above or below the spaces. And on Dec. 15, 1969 a 9th method is described, developed over nine years of performance, in which silence is not measured but is indeterminate in length. The notation, to cite Busoni, begins to no longer stand between poet-musician and music-poetry. Tones are also indeterminate in length. Only the word-strings remain themselves. This ninth method followed indeterminate *Asymmetries* (1961), in which the words are provided by the performer himself, either by following MacLow's compositional chance-operational method or by freely improvising. The performer however is advised to think three times before rejecting chance operations in favor of free improvisation, for in the latter case the perfomer is at the beck and call of his likes and dislikes and his notions of what is effective, meaningful, etc.

In June 1961 MacLow wrote *Thanks II* in which any break or pause in sound production is followed by a silence of any length, but at least one minute. In *Pitches* (also entitled *Harpsichord Piece for George Maciunas* in the case where it is a harpsichord solo rather than a piece for any number of performers using any instruments) the process of composing takes place silently during the performance. After composing one event the performer is silent for any length of time before composing a second.

In *Chamber Music for Barney Childs* (May 1963) three to eight note-groups having each three to eight notes are composed by the conductor using chance operations before a performance. During a performance following the conductor's signals the performers improvise using note-groups from among those composed, chosen sometimes by themselves, sometimes by the conductor, freely introducing silence between notes, and falling silent whenever the conductor signals to do so. The signal for the end of a performance is always preceded by the signal for silence.

In 1966 a program of electronic music, electronic poetry, and live simultaneities by Jackson Mac Low, Max Neuhaus, and James Tenney was given at Town Hall in New York City. Printed in the program is A *Little Sermon on the Performance of Simultaneities*. There are seven admonitions (the 7th is a repetition of the first). Five of the six different statements propose silence. "1) Listen! Listen! Listen! 2) Leave plenty of silence. 3) Don't do something just to be doing something. 4) Only do something when you have something you really want to do after observing and listening intensely to everything in the performance and its environment. 5) Don't be afraid to shut up for awhile. Something really good will seem all the better if you do it after being still. 6) Be open. Try to interact freely with other performers and the audience."

Heavens (1974-75) is a simultaneity for three to eighteen reader-musicians with slide projections. Relevant statements (relevant to the heavens) collected by participants or obtained from Mac Low are used as material to be read or as instrumental or vocal parts, A C D E F G being natural tones, B being B flat, H being B natural, S being E flat. All other letters are either disregarded when thought of as musical notation or used to cue silences of any duration. Participants are advised to listen closely to the total situation making choices in accordance with its moment-to-moment character. Tact should be used so that tones produced will not drown out words.

In *Homage to Leona Bleiweiss* (1976) each player's part consists of alternate segments of silence and of improvisation using only the notes of the given note-groups or their corresponding words. The length of silences (which may be prolonged past their minimal durations whenever performers feel that they and the total situation are not ready for the next event) and the determination of which word-note-group is to be used is composed during the performance unhurriedly and silently by means of playing cards drawn from a shuffled deck. A code is given in the score for interpreting these.

Mac Low has written many gathas since 1961 on quadrille paper, many of the squares filled with letters, others left empty. A performer moves freely from any square to any of the eight adjacent squares pronouncing the letters or sounding them, interpreting empty squares as silence. These silences "ought often to be prolonged until one feels one can add positively to the total situation. Since so much depends upon the performer's choices during performance, awareness, sensitivity, tact, courtesy and inspiration must be one's guides, and one must listen silently for quite a while before adding something new to the situation." This statement appears both in the directions given for performing the *1 Milarepa Gatha* (Oct.1976) and the *WBAI Vocabulary Crossword Gatha* (March 1977). And nearly the same words appear in the performance instructions for *Musicwords (for Phill Niblock)* (Dec.'77-May'78). Further, MacLow writes, "While egoistic overpowering of the total sound should never take place, virtuosity is strongly encouraged when exercised with as much consciousness as possible of its place in the total aural situation. One must be both inventive and sensitive at all times. As with my other simultaneities, the most important "rules" are "Listen" and "Relate." This last statement appeared earlier in the directions for the *Homage to Leona Bleiweiss*.

In the instructions for *A Notated Vocabulary for Eve Rosenthal* (May 1978) this direction first appears: "After each few minutes of improvisation, the performer must fall silent and listen attentively for at least fifteen seconds before resuming improvisation." It is underlined and the other admonitions quoted above are repeated. Somewhat abbreviated the same advice appears in the performance instructions for *A Vocabulary for Pete Rose*, and in *A Vocabulary for Custer LaRue*.

A Vocabulary for Annie Brigitte Gilles-Tardos was exhibited at the Poetry Room of the Sound Show at Project Studios One in Long Island City (Queens), New York from Sept. 30 to Nov. 18, 1979. In April 1980 it was performed as a solo by MacLow himself in the course of the 12th International Festival of Sound Poetry at Washington Square Church in New York City. The performance includes the exhibition of the vocabulary itself and, like earlier works, is an alternation of speaking or musically improvising and falling silent. The silences are here described as "at least fifteen seconds, at most a minute or so." Though they embody no essentially new material for one acquainted with MacLow's earlier indeterminate work, the performance directions (Jan. 20, 1980) for this *Vocabulary* constitute the most complete and precise description of the methods for realizing one of MacLow's performance works. Where other directions are one or two pages long, these are seven and a half. In the same spirit and also in this year, MacLow has revised and extended the *Methods for Reading and Performing Asymmetries 1-260*. The earlier text was two or three pages, whereas the recent one which supercedes it is over twelve. Where, earlier, MacLow had used the term "total aural situation" asking for concentrated attention to it, he now describes this and how one should act with respect to it very beautifully: "This 'whole' can be represented by concentric spheres: the inmost is that of the individual performer; next, that of the whole performance group; next, that of the larger social group including audience as well as performers; next, that of the performance space, including room acoustics, electronics, etc.; and finally, the larger spaces within which the performance space is situated: the rest of the building, the surrounding streets, neighborhood, city (or rural area) etc., all of which may affect significantly the aggregate of sounds heard by each individual at each moment. The spheres are best conceived as transparent and interpenetrating — not static shells but concentric ripples travelling simultaneously out from and in toward each center." And from page 7: "*Asymmetries* may be performed in this way with live or recorded sounds of any kind (sound continua other than *Asymmetries*...environmental sounds of any kind)."

Mac Low's work, it seems to me, is that of an idealist—or religious-anarchist. Like other such anarchists, he finds through experience the necessity to make laws ("No jumping up and down on the beds!"), but this paradox in which he finds himself does not distract him from his ethical purpose. Sometimes as recently, he leaves the group and returns to the solo circumstance, and because of his sensitivity, devotion, and long experience, gives a beautiful performance. He intends this, I believe, as an example, particularly to those who have not yet freed themselves of themselves. I think that his work conduces to an extension of family, to a religious spirit in which one feels there is nothing to which one is not related (George Herbert Meade, also from Chicago). This is the experience of silence. All of Mac Low's work is moving towards a single work, always the most recent one. It was necessary for him to turn away from the interesting and difficult 3 *Essays in an Intervallic Series* though they were written using chance operations and in response to original questions. He had to reach the recent *Tardos Vocabulary*. In the case of the *Essays*: "Player chooses the highest speed at which he can play all three essays *exactly*." In the case of the recent work, everything is by its nature exact since it was not precisely determined to begin with. Concern has moved from the work to include the world and the people in it, those performing and those listening, the audience. The audience completes the work (Duchamp), makes the paradox, brings us back to a concern with what they have done, the work itself in its many forms. And this leads the artist directly to the work which he has not yet composed. Etcetera. There is never any silence.

MORE ON PAIK (1982)

I have known Nam June Paik for more than twenty-five years. Though I wrote the text for the 1965 Bonino Gallery exhibition of his first TV works, I have never stated explicitly what I think of his musical work. Since Paik has frequently referred to our meeting as a turning point in his life and work, and since this panel is part of a major recognition of that life and work, it seems incumbent on me now to draw lines as clearly as I can between us, showing what I do in my work, what he does in his, and what area, if any, there is in which we are equally at home.

I find myself wanting to say that I have never thought of Nam June Paik as a composer. But that would not be true. Formerly I was the only musician for the dance programs given by Merce Cunningham. Then there was David Tudor also, and somewhat later Gordon Mumma, three of us. When Merce Cunningham began to multiply the number of his performances by programming *Events*, Tudor, Mumma, and I decided to open the Company programs to music provided by other composers. We would do this because the Cunningham dancers were trained to support themselves on their own two feet, not on the music. We believed that any other music than ours, providing it interested us, could go with the dance without disturbing it. Twice we have been proved wrong. Once with the music of Charlemagne Palestine which consisted in large part of a recital of his thoughts while defecating, thoughts about how uncomfortable it was for him not only to move his bowels but to have his music (which he did not play) in a situation which was not a planned collaboration. And once with the music of Christian Wolff which consisted of overtly political songs. Our way of choosing composers was this. Each of us made a list of five. We then found names repeated from one list to another. Finally we voted. In this way Nam June Paik was invited to accompany two *Events* in the Westbeth Studio given by Merce Cunningham and Dance Company. Shigeko Kubota sat beside Paik who played just a few notes on the piano (it seems to me these notes were a quote from the literature) and then placed his head on the keyboard giving the impression of someone filled with sorrow. This was an excerpt from his *Etude for Pianoforte*. Afterwards Shigeko told Merce: "Your dance beautiful! Nam June's music Ugh! Ugh! Ugh!" For the second evening Paik played a recording of the *Verklaerte Nacht* at a speed much slower than normal. Afterwards, smiling, he said, "Now we know Schoenberg great composer."

It is frequently noted that Paik was trained as a musician at the University of Tokyo, having written his thesis on the work of Arnold Schoenberg; and that among his early compositions, all of them conventionally notated, there are Korean folk music flavored pieces, serial melodies for solo violin, and a nonserial *String Quartet*. I know of no performances of these works. They seem to have been abandoned by the composer except for documentary or exhibition purposes.

I first met Nam June Paik in 1958 in Germany. I had been invited to teach and lecture at Darmstadt. I had more than twenty years earlier studied with Arnold Schoenberg for two years free of charge having promised him in return to devote my life to music. I could argue that I have been faithful to my promise. Concerned to find a better reason for writing music than the one I had been taught, that was to have something to say and say it, I had embarked on a study of oriental philosophy, finally attending for two years the classes in the philosophy of Zen Buddhism given at Columbia University by Daisetz Suzuki. In one of his lectures he drew an oval on the blackboard, placing two parallel lines half way up the left-hand side. He said, This is the structure of the Mind. The two parallel lines are the ego. The ego has the capacity through its likes and dislikes to cut itself off from its experience whether that comes to it from above, the world of relativity, through the sense perceptions, or from below, the absolute, through the collective unconscious and the dreams. Or, instead of cutting itself off from it, the ego has the capacity to flow with its experience, and that is, Suzuki said, what Zen wants. Having earlier taken as true the reason for writing music given me by Gita Sarabhai from her teacher in India, that is to sober and quiet the mind thus making it susceptible to divine influences, I then, in response to Suzuki's lecture, determined to go out rather than in, to use chance operations as a discipline in my music, a discipline equal I trusted to sitting crosslegged, having faith that the Mind's structure was indeed oval (continuous upon itself), that my writing of music would be as a result not self-expression but self-alteration. I had been practicing the discipline of chance operations for ten years before I met Paik. One or two years later I found myself in Cologne attending a performance by him of his *Etude for Pianoforte*. Behind Paik as he performed was an open window, floor to ceiling. His actions were such we wouldn't have been surprised had he thrown himself five floors down to the street. When at the end he left the room through the packed audience, everybody, all of us, sat paralyzed with fear, utterly silent, for what seemed an eternity. No one budged. We were stunned. Finally the telephone rang. "It was Paik," Mary Bauermeister said, "calling to say the performance is over."

I determined to think twice before attending another performance by Nam June Paik. In the course of my studies of Indian philosphy, I had become aware of the nine permanent emotions of aesthetic tradition. The rasas. The four black, sorrow, fear, anger, disgust; the four white, the heroic, the wondrous, mirth and the erotic; finally, the one without color, in the center, towards which any work of art should conduce, tranquility. The *Etude for Pianoforte* was definitely black, a mixing of sorrow, anger and fear, and these three separate from tranquility.

Some years later in New York, Paik invited Merce Cunningham and me to Canal Street to see his *Zen for Film*. An hour-long film without images. "The mind is like a mirror; it collects dust; the problem is to remove the dust." "Where is the mirror? Where is the dust?" In this case the dust is on the lens of the projector and on the blank developed film itself. There is never nothing to see.

Here, we are both together and separate. My *4'33"*, the silent piece, is Nam June's *Zen for Film*. The difference is that his silence was not sounds but something to see. His life is devoted, it seems to me, not to sounds, but to objects. He is a performance artist and a sculptor. He activates, timeifies, sculpture with video. As an extraordinary performance artist, Paik is concerned with the emotional impact of his work on the audience. Left to himself he accumulates and recycles a personal iconography not unlike a similar development in the work of Marcel Duchamp and Jasper Johns.

From a concentration on the black rasas in *Etude for Pianoforte* Paik moved through the colorlessness of tranquility exemplified by *Zen for Film* to the concentration on the white rasas of the present exhibition. The result is a delightful and amazing spectacle. As Cathy Kerr said, Cheerful. As Lise Friedman said, Exuberant! As Ray Gallon said, "Isn't it wonderful?" *Fish Flies on Sky*, those completing the work comfortably reclined below it. Or *TV Garden*. "I could hardly tear myself away." The moment I got off the elevator on the fourth floor I began smiling. I didn't stop until I left the building. A charming lady asked me whether I was John Cage. Admitted I was. "You must feel very close to this." I replied: No closer than you; we are both on Madison Avenue. We were looking at *V-yramid*. Paik has shown us both sides of the coin, but as Suzuki said in response to the question "Why do you say death one day and life the next?", in Zen there's not much difference between the two.

In Zen they say: Men are men and mountains are mountains before studying Zen. While studying Zen things become confused. After studying Zen men are men and mountains are mountains. Asked what the difference is before and after, Suzuki said, No difference, just the feet are a little off the ground. Paik's involvement with sex, introducing it into music does not conduce towards sounds being sounds. It only confuses matters. I am sure that his performance with Charlotte Moorman of my *26'1.1499" for a String Player* is not faithful to the notation, that the liberties taken are in favor of actions rather than sound events in time. I am thinking of the point where Paik, stripped to the waist, imitates a 'cello, his back being bowed by Charlotte Moorman.

Once Virgil Thomson told me that his mother after hearing my prepared piano for the first time, said, "It's very nice, but I would never have thought of doing it myself." A similar remark could be made about many of Paik's pieces, the *Serenade for Alison*, for instance, in which nylon panties, black lace panties, and blood-stained panties in the course of a strip tease are stuffed into the mouths of a music critic, the second music critic, and the worst music critic, and the *Chronicle of a Beautiful Paintress* which is a list of the months and the flags which are to be stained "with your monthly blood." But one would have to say instead of "very nice," "Shocking! and I would never have thought of doing it . . ." or "It's disgusting, etc."

The *Danger Music for Dick Higgins* ("Creep into the Vagina of a Living Whale") is pure fiction, not music, not danger, at all. That is to say, never to take place. The *Young Penis Symphony* is another matter. What with society's changed manners and the popularity of the present exhibition both with critics and art lovers, we can expect many performances, say two years ahead of Paik's schedule, "Expected World Premiere around 1984 A.D." Referring to one of the performances, however, a person will say, I saw it, not I heard it.

Likewise Paik's prepared piano *Klavier Integral* is in a museum, not in a concert hall. It is to be seen rather than heard.

His *Symphony No. 5*, dealing as it does with days, weeks, years, centuries, mega-years, is also not music but fiction.

In fact the most musical of Paik's works are those for which he has given no performance directions, for which the accompanist is simply the sounds of the environment. I am thinking of the ones which are just sculpture, *TV Chair*, *TV Buddha*, for instance.

FOR DON GILLESPIE (1983)

in the middle of the night before the full flower moon 5/25/83

```
     we were com  P  aring

         not  E  s   the bridge'n'i

fireworks?!  flo  T  illa?!

         cak  E  ?!

  spectacula  R  but ephemeral

  what'll la  S  t're my books!
```

for Don Gillespie, gratefully, John Cage

159

MUSIC AND ART (1985)

Just as Cage has composed music entirely with "found" sounds, he has written essays (in this case an exhibition preface) entirely with "found" texts.

"J'écrivais, à ce moment-là, le *Fils de Etoiles*—sur un texte de Joséphin Peladan; & j'expliquais, à Debussy, le besoin pour nous Français de se dégager de l'aventure Wagner, laquelle ne répondait pas à mes aspirations naturelles. Et lui faises-je remarquer que je n'étais nullement antiwagnérien, mais que nous devions avoir une musique à nous—sans choucroute, si possible.

"Pourquoi ne pas se servir des moyens représentatifs que nous exposaient Claude Monet, Cézanne, Toulouse-Lautrec, etc.? Pourquoi ne pas transposer musicalement ces moyens? Rien de plus simple. Ne sont-ce pas des expressions?

"Là était la source d'un départ profitable à des expériences fécondes en réalisations quaisures—fructueuses, même...."

Erik Satie, towards the end of an article, *Claude Debussy*

"Un'avvertenza sullo spartito del *Socrate* segnala l'affinità tra la purezza di questa musica e la purezza del disegno di Ingres. Si vede che l'autore della nota confondeva Ingres con Puvis de Chavannes."

Alberto Savinio, in the course of an article, *Erik Satie*

"The musical composition written by Albert Savinio should be called New Music rather than Modern Music. Savinio has devoted himself to finding the place of music among the modern arts. He does not try to express in music either a state of consciousness or an image. His music is not harmonious or even harmonized, but DISHARMONIOUS. Its structure is based on drawing. His musical drawings are, most of them, very rapid and DANSANTS, and belong to the most discordant styles, for this composer thinks that a sincere and truthful musical work must have in its formation the greatest variety of musics — ALL THAT WHICH ONE HEARS — ...."

Editorial, from "291" no. 2, New York—February 1915

"The critical fortune of Savinio as composer was almost zero: he was also writer (of novels and essays), painter and playwright. His versatility, under the preventable accusé to be dilettantism, has paradoxically provided to devaluate his work...

"In 1905 with his mother and his brother, the painter Giorgio de Chirico (Alberto Savinio is in fact a pseudonym of Andrea de Chirico) moved to Munich, where he wanted to perfect his knowledge of composition under the guide of Max Reger. But. . .

"In Paris he met Picasso, the cubist painters, Picabia; he became a friend of Cocteau and Apollinaire, who made every possible effort to make known his and his brother's work. His talent . . . suddenly came out as the musical equivalent of the more advanced experiences in poetry (Apollinaire) and in painting (Giorgio de Chirico) of that period. . . .

"The presence, in the same painting, of two perspective systems which contradict themselves, realized by de Chirico, is analogous to the musical DISHARMONY of Savinio which consists in the DE-COMPOSITION of a melodic line in two dissonant tonalities. That implies the end of an old concept of a universe dominated by absolute reference systems and it also excludes the research of new and relative reference systems."

Michele Porzio *[via Battistotti Sassi 29, Milano]*, Short introduction
to Alberto Savinio and his music, letter to the author

"Le non-sens se tient en prodigieux équilibre. Il est l'expression du sentiment naturel et supérieur—vrai partout—qui a des racines dans la terre et qui s'exhausse au-delà du septieme ciel.

"Cést là que flotte la musique."

Albert Savinio, "Donnez-moi l'anathème, chose lascive," in *291*, no. 4,
New York, 1915

Savinio did not compose anymore from 1915 until 1947, except for a short parenthesis in which he composed the *Ballata delle Stagioni* and the *Morte di Niobe*, which was written in 1913 in a version for three pianos, orchestrated in the style of *Les Noces* of Stravinsky in 1925 and represented at the Teatro dell'Arte of Rome directed by Luigi Pirandello.

In 1926 he came back to Paris and his interests turned to painting. As painter he became very successful and while he was in Paris he closed a friendship with André Breton and the surrealists (although we do know that he always defended Cocteau against the polemics of the surrealists).

I end with a short quotation by André Breton:

"The whole modern mythology, still in formation, has its roots in two works, almost indivisible in the spirit: the ones of Alberto Savinio and Giorgio de Chirico." **Michele Porzio**, ibid.

"SCULPTURE MUSICALE"

"Sons durant et partant de différents points et formant une sculpture sonore qui dure."

Marcel Duchamp, *La Mariée Mise à Nu Par Ses Célibataires, Même*

"One way to write music: Study Duchamp."   **The author**

"The musical notes taken out of a hat." (Duchamp: *Erratum Musical)*
                                             The author

A moving freight train, cars passing below a note-giving funnel, each car representing a different octave so that a scale nonrepetitive from one to another results, upon which new melodies may be composed or improvised (Duchamp: *La Mariée Mise à Nu par ses Célibataires même 1913 Erratum Musical.)*

                                             The author

"Etant donnes: 1. La Chute d'eau/2. Le Gaz d'éclairage"

"Mixed media assemblage, approximately 242.5 cm high, 177.3 cm wide, 124.5 cm deep, and including: an old wooden door, black velvet, bricks, wooden table, leather stretched over an armature of metal and other material to form a female nude, human hair, gas lamp (*bec Auer* type), twigs, aluminum, iron, glass, painted glass, ground glass, linoleum, cotton, light bulb, fluorescent light, spotlight, electric motor, etc.

". . . Duchamp's written instructions as embodied in a practical manual entitled *Approximation démontable, exécutèe entre 1946 et 1966 à New York.* Duchamp also added that *Par approximation j'entends une marge d'ad libitum dans le démontage et remontage. . . .* This manual includes thirty-five pages of notes and diagrams and one hundred sixteen photos (made by Duchamp) showing in detail the fifteen different stages of the mounting operations."

Arturo Schwarz, *The Complete Works of Marcel Duchamp*

Duchamp's *Approximation démontable* is a score for a performance, like his other musical works, seminal. "You were doing the year I was born what I am doing now." (Conversation with Duchamp in Venice circa 1959) "I must have been fifty years ahead of my time."

                                             The author

WRITING THROUGH *HOWL* (1986)

For Allen Ginsberg on his Sixtieth Birthday

Writing for the first time through *Howl*:

I   sAw
themseLves
    Looking for
hipstErs

starry dyNamo

    hiGh sat
    theIr
heaveN

    Saw
    puBlishing
    odEs on
    Rooms

listeninG to the terror

    beArds returning through
    Laredo

    beLt
for nEw york
    iN
druGs
    wIth
alcohol aNd
ballS

    Blind
in thE mind
towaRd
illuminatinG
    dAwns
    bLinking
    Light

    thE
    wiNter
    liGht

endless rIde

    broNx
wheelS
    Brought

thEm
    wRacked
    liGht of zoo
    sAnk
    Light
continuousLy
    musEum to
brooklyN
    bridGe

    platonIc
    dowN
    State
and eyeBall
    wholE
    Recall

    niGhts
    brilliAnt eyes
    Leaving
    traiL of
    picturE
    atlaNtic

    Go and
    lIt

    sNow
farmS
    Bop
    thE
    vibRated
seekinG

    visionAry
    onLy
supernaturaL
    Ecstasy
    iN
streetliGht

    spanIard
    aNd
    taSk

But
thE
dungaRees and
chicaGo
coAst

incomprehensibLe
capitaLism
distributEd
iN
deliGht

polIcecars
No
pederaSty
By
thosE
the sailoRs
the eveninGs
And the
pubLic
freeLy
comE

wouNd
Golden
ecstatIc
aNd
Sweetheart
tremBling

thE
Red
flashinG
bArns

Lake
coLorado
hEro
cocksmaN

Gaunt
waItresses
loNely petticoat
eSpecially
Blood
on thE snowbank docks
foR
floodliGht

&
obLivion
Lamb
stEw
romaNce
bridGe
to buIld
oN
Sixth
By
orangE
cRates
of theoloGy
And
Lofty
animaLs
hEart
&
veGetable
threw theIr
eterNity
outSide of
Blasts
thE
iRon
intelliGent
hAppened

the ghostLy
fiLthy
criEd
daNced

German
whIskey
aNd
earS
Blast
thE
hotRod-
liGht

And
untiL
souL
crashEd
miNds
Golden
realIty
saNg
Sweet

haBit or
thE

oR
accusinG
rAdio
Left
saLad

thE
graNite
wiG
foetId halls
aNd
Solitude-
Book
thE
dooR
hanGer
And
hopefuL
carL
you arE

Not safe
i am
throuGh
the Icy
suddeN
flaSh of
viBrating
planE

dReamt
imaGes
juxtAposed
souL
2 visuaL
imagEs
aNd
toGether
wIth
aeterNa
deuS

madman Bum
and angEl

Rose
Ghostly
jAzz
in the goLdhorn shadow

eLi
Eli
sabacthaNi

II   Good
theIr skulls
aNd
Solitude

Boys
armiEs
paRks
judGer of men

And
moLoch
buiLdings
arE
stoNe of
Governments
            moloch
Is
moNey
whoSe
canniBal
whosE
aRe
lonG
endless johovAhs

moLoch whose
moLoch
whosE
aNd

sexless hydroGen moloch
Is
loNely
cockSucker
without a Body

mE
my natuRal
liGht
streAming out of
moLoch

moLoch
industriEs
graNite cocks
Gone down
rIver
aNd
flood highS

III   Bronx
scrEam

you'Re
losinG the
the Abyss
in rockLand
souL

diE
iN
all toGether

I'm
rocklaNd
that coughS
out of the coma By
airplanEs
Roof
anGelic bombs

illuminAtes

itseLf
eternaL war is
victory forgEt your
uNderwear

hiGhway
cross amerIca

the westerN
Footnote   iS
holy

everyBody's holy

angEl
soul aRe holy

anGels
in the insAne
hoLy

the
hoLy
thE
saxophoNe
diGs

los
Is los
New
San

the eyeBall

thE
chaRity
intelliGent

Writing for the second time through *Howl*:

I   mAdness
coLd-water
fLats

thE
braiNs
throuGh
wIth
aNd
academieS
Burning
monEy

maRijuana
niGht

After
endLess
cLoud
hE
motioNless
Green
joyrIde

suN

aShcan

Brain
drainEd of
bRilliance

niGht

submArine
fLoated
Lost

thE
wiNdowsills

ambiGuous
cIty
easterN
heartS

Boxcars
rackEting
towaRd
niGht

telepAthy

instinctiveLy
angeLs who
angEls who
iN
throuGh
amerIca
eterNity

So
the f.B.i.
sExy
daRk skin
passinG out
Arms
whiLe
of Los
thEm
dowN

roseGardens
cemeterIes
semeN
turkiSh
Bath
whEn
with a swoRd
nothinG but
Ass
Loom who

aLong
thE
aNd

down
Gyzym of
sunrIse
uNder
Stolen
Backyards

rickEty
Rows on mountaintops

upliftinGs

soLipsisms of
suicidaL dramas

thE
baNks of
diGested
rIvers
aNd
muSic
Borsht
drEaming
puRe
kinGdom who
meAt

Looking for
aLarm

fEll
oN
Gave up

antIque
aNd
madiSon
By
thE
dRunken
who sanG
in despAir

Leaped
nostaLgic

finishEd
iNto
hiGhways

hall-
crosscouNtry

          Seventytwo   cities
came Back
waitEd   moLoch whose
  bRooded   oiL
waitinG for   stonE
  heAds   aNd
                          moloch who friGhtened
  bLues   whom I
  aLcatraz
  mExico   skeletoN
mouNt   capitalS
or Grave   Backs lifting moloch

sanIty   thE
  &   miRacles
lecturerS on   Gone
  loBotomy   epiphAnies
  givEn   Loves the
concRete   rocks of time reaL
and finGers
                                       thE
  the wArds of   dowN to the river
  piLgrim state's
  rockLand's and   **III**   lauGh
  thE
  iN the   thIs
cataloG the   rocklaNd
  tIme   writerS
  &   Bang
  Space
verBs   thE
and sEt   immoRtal
                                   unGodly
pooR   An
and intelliGent
  And   rockLand
the souL to   souL
  Lamma   thE
                                   iN
saxophonE cry
                                   huG and
  dowN to the   kIss
                                   uNited
                                   uS
II   judGment
              moloch   Footnote   Bum's as holy as
  Is   thE
  teN   aRe
armieS   anGeles
  tomB
whosE   frAncisco
  stReets   hoLy
  foG
smokestAcks   hoLy
                                   tangiErs

                                       istaNbul holy

Writing for the third time through *Howl*:

I
            stArving
            fLoating
    contempLating jazz

    who barEd
            uNder
            liGht

        theIr
          aNd
        got buSted

          puBic
    who atE
            fiRe

            niGht
        dreAms with
            Lightning
        worLd
    of timE

          wiNe
    borouGhs of
        traffIc
            aNd
            Shuddering
            Bickford's

          thE
          cRack of
    jumpinG
          escApes off
            bLeak furnished
            raiLroad

    grandfathEr
          plotiNus
        throuGh
            Idaho
        wheN baltimore
    impulSe
    followed the Brilliant
            thE
            fiReplace
    with biG
            pAcifist
          hoLes

            aLamos
            thE
            islaNd
                Grass

            theIr
            bloNde
            loSt
            loveBoys
            thE
            thRee

    a packaGe
              A
            fLoor
            eLuding
            thE
            sNatches
        throuGh
          myrIad
                Night-
          carS
        the craB

            thE
            stReets
            couGhed
            flAme

    tubercuLar
            Lung
            thE
            uNder
        thouGht
          crIed
        burNed
          verSe &
    taxicaBs
            rEality

            bRooklyn
            neGroes
            bArefoot
            bLoody
            goLgotha
    who drovE
          to fiNd
        throuGh

theIr
aNd
heartS

    who
   Buddha
locomotivE
   naRcissus
& a hunG
 potAto
subsequentLy
 insuLin
  mEtrasol
occupatioNal
   Greystone's
 wIth
 beNch
realmS of love

But
littlE
you'Re
jumpinG
sensAtion
you speechLess

   Lamma
thE
owN

II breakthrouGhs

the rIver
dowN

III   yearS animal
   Body

its pilgrimagE

   cRoss in
lonG
islAnd
  Living
in rockLand
arE
thousaNd

cottaGe
  nIght
Footnote the toNgue
iS
  Burroughs
thE
maRijuana
anGeles

peoriA
hoLy

hoLy

timE
iN

Writing for the fourth time through *Howl*:

  nAked
the eL and
 angeLs
who passEd
  uNiversities

traGedy among the
theIr

draNk
paradiSe
  Backyard
thE
  Rooftops
kinG

chAined
themseLves
hoLy
thE
 Noise of
throuGh

fIre
mooN
 Screaming

Boxcars
studiEd
cRoss
thouGht

mAd
gLeamed
okLahoma
thE
wiNter
ciGarette

theIr
Narcotic
pamphletS
naked and tremBling
thE
shReiked with
committinG
And
howLed
genitaLs and
bE
iN
ciGarettes
wIth
cuNt
laSt
But
thE
giRls in empty lots &
hunGover
tokAy
stumbLed

apartment cLiff-
thE
hudsoN
Gas
edItors or were
ruN
abSolute
Birmingham
hE
jouRneyed
tanGiers
pAcific
bLack
woodLawn
thE
daisychaiN

Gaps
wIth
coNform to
hiS
Band

thE
foR love into

II   filth

uGliness
And
chiLdren

oLd
thE
prisoN
lauGhter

rIver they saw

III

carl solomoN
muSt feel
tomB
mad comradEs
ouR
niGht
And
Let
rockLand
wE
owN

Footnote   Grandfathers
hIpsters
&
drumS

lamB of
thE
cRazy
anGel in moloch

holy the seA

hoLy
hoLy
thE
visioNs

Writing for the fifth time through *Howl*:

I   drAgging
        cooL
        schoLars of
        thE
        &
     throuGh

        wIth
        aNd
        of

          Shuddering
          viBrations
          thE
          fRom

   listeninG to

   from pArk to
       Leaving
       Lava
       poEtry
       iN
       Gas-
    sordId movies
       oN
       Sudden
       Bottom

       thE
     pushcaRts
      niGht

    tortillAs
      pLunged
      cLocks
      thEir
        Next
     bridGe
     thIs
     aNd

        Soup
        to Boys
        thE
        juRy
     demandinG
          And
          eLectricity
        onLy
        onE
        iN
       throuGh
        tIme

       dowN here
        to Say

II   Brains
        scrEaming

       staiRways
     sobbinG in
  moloch

     the heAvy
      moLoch

      moLoch
      thE
    crossboNe

  where we are Great
III   typewrIter
      rocklaNd
      haS

Footnote holy the Bop
     apocalypsE

       stReets

Writing for the sixth time through *Howl*:

I   At
bLake-
hoteLs
dEath
iNcomparable

hydroGen
empIre
aNd
memorieS and
Boxcars

poE

st. john of the
stReets

midniGht
rAin

Lounged

aLso
brokE
dowN

Great
wartIme
mooN
headS
Bad
thE
daRkness
stanzas of Gibberish

An egg

successiveLy
growing oLd

thEir
oN

forGotten
& fIretrucks

Not
over the Street

truly Bald

thE
dReam
flunG
And
Last
Last

thE
iN
thouGht
mIght
aNd
clotheS of

II   Blood
arE
bReast

is a smokinG
A
bLind

moLoch
whosE
staNd

III   a straiGhtjacket
I'm
oN
iS
JazzBands
thE
Rebellion

Writing for the seventh time through *Howl*:

I dAwn   skeLetons
   Leaping   wiLd
dusks of brookLyn   thEir
         kNees

  battEry
   oN II
  ciGarettes III   Game
  theIr   wIth
who loNed   catatoNic
  viSionary   Should
  aBout
volcanoEs Footnote aByss
  shoRts
        hE
weepinG   bRilliant
  And   . . .

Writing for the eighth time through *Howl*:

I An   toBacco
  poLes   hazE of
  untiL   squaRe
  thE   cookinG
  iN
throuGh   intoxicAtion
  It
        Let
  oN   saintLy
 Smalltown   sEraphim
      atlaNtic

Writing for the ninth time through *Howl*:

  Angry
  soLidities
 battaLion
  thE
  aNd

TOKYO LECTURE AND THREE
MESOSTICS (1986)

*The following texts were given as a lecture in Tokyo on 5 December, 1986 at
the new Suntory Hall. I had been asked to speak about my life and work. On
the 8th of December a concert was given of works chosen by me. The program
was* Exercises 24 & 25 *by Christian Wolff,* Socrate *by Erik Satie,* Symphony
Op. 21 *by Anton Webern, and my own* Etcetera 2/4 Orchestras. *The* Songs for
C.W. *first appeared in* ex tempore 3, no. 2.

The first time I saw the *I Ching* was in the San Francisco Public
Library circa 1936. Lou Harrison introduced me to it. I did not use it
at that time in any way other than to glance at it. Later in 1950
Christian Wolff gave me the Bollingen two-volume edition of the
English translation by Cary F. Baynes of Richard Wilhelm's German
translation with the introduction by C.G. Jung. This time I was struck
immediately by the possibility of using the *I Ching* as a means for
answering questions that had to do with numbers. There were, it seems
to me, two reasons for my being so immediately struck.

The first was that I had heard a lecture by Daisetz Suzuki, with
whom I was studying the philosophy of Zen Buddhism, on the structure of the Mind. He had gone to the blackboard and had drawn an
oval shape. Halfway up the left-hand side he put two parallel lines. He
said the top of the oval was the world of relativity, the bottom was the
Absolute, what Eckhart called the Ground. The two parallel lines were
the ego or mind (with a little m). The whole drawing was the structure
of the Mind. He then said that the ego had the capacity to cut itself off
from its experiences whether they come from the world of relativity
through the sense perceptions or from the Absolute through the
dreams. Or it could free itself from its likes and dislikes, taste and
memory, and flow with Mind with a capital M. Suzuki said that this
latter choice was what Zen wanted. I then decided not to give up the
writing of music and discipline my ego by sitting cross-legged but to
find a means of writing music as strict with respect to my ego as sitting
cross-legged.

I chose the Magic Square as a means of changing my responsibility from that of making choices to that of making moves on a chart

that had not numbers but sounds on it. Two other composers did likewise at the same time (the idea was in the air): one of them was
Wyschnegradsky in Paris. So that when Christian Wolff brought me
the *I Ching* with its square of 64 hexagrams I was immediately struck
and quickly outlined the composing means for the *Music of Changes*.
My responsibility had become the asking of questions. I was able to
relate any number of answers to the 64 numbers of the *I Ching*.

I became free by means of the *I Ching* from the notion of 2
(relationship). Or you could say I saw that all things *are* related. We
don't have to bring about relationships.

I use the *I Ching* whenever I am engaged in an activity which is
free of goal-seeking, pleasure giving, or discriminating between good
and evil. That is to say, when writing poetry or music, or when making
graphic works. But I do not use it when crossing a street, playing a
game of chess, making love, or working in the field of world improvement. I also use the *I Ching* as a book of wisdom, but infrequently, and
not as often as formerly.

The way the *I Ching* works as a computer musically is to tell me
for instance how many sound events take place in what length of time,
at what points in time, on which instruments, having what loudnesses,
etc. And in my writing it lets me continue, in a variety of ways, my
search for a means which comes from ideas but is not about them but
nevertheless produces them free of my intentions.

To repeat, the *I Ching* is a discipline of the ego. It facilitates self-
alteration and weakens self-expression. I never compose without it:
even when I follow other "metal balls" (rolling ahead of me on the path
I am taking) such as maps of the stars in the space outside of us, or
imperfections in the paper upon which I happen to be writing (how
many spots? how many stars? etcetera).

At one point during my last visit to Japan (invited then as now by
Toru Takemitsu), I gave a lecture called "Composition in Retrospect."
It appears in my last book from Wesleyan University Press called *X*.
Since *X*, "Mushrooms et Variationes" was published by Burning Books
in Oakland, California as part of a collection of texts by six composers
called *The Guests Go In To Supper*. And *The First Meeting of the
Satie Society*, a collection of materials conceived as presents to Eric
Satie from me, Henry David Thoreau, Marcel Duchamp, Marshall
McLuhan, Chris Mann, and James Joyce, can now be accessed on the
ArtCom Electronic Network carried by the Whole Earth 'Lectronic
Link, San Francisco. "Composition in Retrospect" has 112 short

sections on what seemed to me in 1981 to be the principles of my musical works from their beginnings in the early thirties to more recent times. The first sections were mesostics on the words Method, Structure, and Intention (my intention being, of course, nonintention). The next three were on the word Discipline, discipline conceived as a means of sobering and quieting the mind, freeing that mind from its likes and dislikes, taste and memory, making it subject to the Mind outside it. The following six sections were on Notation, Indeterminacy, Interpenetration, Imitation, Devotion, and Circumstances. This was the history of a mind that had changed, from, among other things, a concern with structure to a concern with process; from a whole having parts to something not characterized by a beginning, middle, or ending. Five years or so have passed. If I were to continue "Composition in Retrospect" what would be the words for the new sections? Thinking of my *Thirty Pieces for Five Orchestras*, the *Thirty Pieces for String Quartet*, and the *Music For_____*, a work in progress for the rest of my life (which began as *Music for Six* but this next year will have fourteen parts), I would make a new section on the word Structure or the words Flexible Structure. Parts, no score, periods of time that can vary in length, a music, you might say, that is earthquake-proof. And then thinking of the percussion accompaniment for *Ryoanji*, the conducted orchestral parts of *Etcetera 2/4 Orchestra*, and the percussion piece in memoriam Jean Arp, I would make a new section on the word Experience or Nonunderstanding, for I have become devoted to tempi so slow that they cannot be heard or felt as tempi. There should also be a section on the word Contingency. I am thinking of *Inlets*, and even, also the numbering rather than naming of percussion instruments in *Music For_____*, making the connection between cause and effect inoperative. Surely there should be a section on the word Inconsistency. This characterizes both *Etcetera* and *Etcetera 2/4 Orchestras*. In the earlier piece the musicians begin playing as soloists, but move in an ambience of country sounds if they wish to stations where they will be conducted when those stations are filled. The present *Etcetera* begins with the musicians being conducted, but in an ambience of urban sound. They may move whenever they wish to stations where they are soloists, providing those stations are not already filled. The opposites coexisting. And the other day I finished a new piece called *Hymnkus*. It is made up of the solos of *Etcetera 2* all reduced to the same eight-note chromatic range and repeated as are the

verses of hymns but at slightly different speeds. Perhaps this will be like
A *Collection of Rocks.*

In 1982 I was asked by André Dimanche to design a cover for
Pierre Lartigue's translation of my *Mushroom Book.* This is a part of
his series of 15 books called Editions Ryoan-ji, all of which are paperbacked with a paper that reminds one of raked sand. My suggestion for
the cover of my book that I draw around 15 stones (15 is the number of
stones in the Ryoan-ji garden in Kyoto) placed at *I Ching*-determined
points on a grid the size of the cover plus the flaps was accepted.

In January of 1983 when I went to the Crown Point Press to make
etchings I took the same 15 stones with me, but soon found that what
can be done with pencil on paper cannot be done with needle
on copper. The mystery produced by pencils disappeared, reappearing only on copper when the number of stones was multiplied
(225:15 × 15; 3375:15 × 15 × 15).

I have had for some years a large indoor garden in New York. I was
encouraged by a 20 × 20 foot pyramidal skylight and 11 large windows
on the east and south. There are now over 200 plants of various kinds
and in among them I have placed rocks large and small brought by me
from my tours or brought sometimes in a car from the New River in
Virginia by Ray Kass or from the Duke Forest in North Carolina by
Irwin Kremen, after I had chosen them *in situ.* Though when I was
younger I couldn't live with sculpture, now I find that I love the
immobility and calm of a stone in place.

Outside the 11 windows are the noises of Sixth Avenue. They
continue all night. I have found a way of translating burglar alarms (a
constant unchanging insistent sound in New York) into Brancusi-like
images while I am sleeping. This has led me to find pleasure not only as
long as I long have in the unpredictable ever-changing sounds of
metropolitan traffic, but also in the immobile never-stopping sounds
associated with modern convenience and comfort (the refrigerator, the
humidifier, the computer, feedback, etc.).

Picking up *Salt Seller: The Writings of Marcel Duchamp,* I read:
"Musical Sculpture: Sounds lasting and leaving from different places
and forming a sounding sculpture which lasts." That is what I mean
A *Collection of Rocks* [1984] to be. It is for Marcel Duchamp that we
never forget him who, as he said, must have been fifty years ahead of
his time.

There are 15 rocks. Each is made up of three, four, or five sounds.

There are 65 points in the performing space. There are 22 different sound-producing groups of musicians, each group divided into two parts so that a tone can be made to last, the second group spelling the first when the first is losing its breath. There are no conductors, each group has two chronometers. Each group performs three times from three different points in space. The piece lasts 20 minutes. Versions may be performed which last for a longer time (1½, 2, 2½, 3 times as long as the present version). The musicians must move in order to play from a different position. The audience is free to move about. We are back in the world of traffic, at home, that is to say, in our own time.

Is this another section? And what is the word for it? Sculpture? Immobility? Technology?

My paying attention to slow tempi began, I think, with the accompaniment for the solos called *Ryoanji*, sometimes performed as a percussion solo, sometimes by a chamber orchestra. What I did was, given a metronome reading of 60, to establish a series of measures having 12 to 15 beats, only five of which would be heard. Finding this direction fascinating I decided in *Etcetera 2/4 Orchestras* to go further: Increase the measure lengths from 12 to 15 beats to measure lengths from 27 to 36 beats, keeping the number 5 as the number of beats that would be heard in a single measure. I also changed the space between single beats from 60 to 5 for the first orchestra, 5¾ for the fourth orchestra, 7½ for the second orchestra and 10 for the third orchestra. Had I kept my notations conventional the conductors would have been obliged to count at a metronome reading of 60 up to 12 between beats for the first orchestra, 11 for the fourth, 8 for the second and 6 for the third. I decided to simplify the notation and make it chronometric rather than conventionally musical.

The solos of *Etcetera 2/4 Orchestras* are indeterminate. They consist of one to five repeated tones and another auxiliary tone which may but need not be repeated. I give only the voice leading. The musicians have been asked to choose their own tones but to remember them rather than writing them down. Each solo has 17 events in proportional notation, space suggesting time, but on unspecified time.

I had the idea for this work for quite a while before I was able to write it. I knew that a musician would begin by being conducted, would leave that circumstance in order to play a solo. How would he know where he was in his part when he came back to the group he had left? Then in Ljubljana after a performance in Zagreb of *A Collection of*

Rocks it occurred to me one morning that there could be a music stand shared by two players. If one of them left to play a solo, the second one could remain until the other returned being able as a result to point out to him where he was in the part. It was this practical idea that got me started writing. As time went on I no longer needed that initiating idea, for the notation became chronometric. But it wasn't chronometric to begin with.

I would like to finish this talk by reading my first autoku and then my most recent one and, finally, *Songs for C.W.*, since the program on Monday includes Christian Wolff's *Exercises 24 & 25* for orchestra. I wrote these mesostics by establishing for each letter of the name a gamut of six full and six empty words and then asking the question, which of the twelve is to be used? An autoku is a mesostic limited to its own words: the string upon which it is written provides all of the wing words that go off to the left or the right. In this case it is in French and the words are those by Marcel Duchamp cited above. My most recent autoku is on a sentence in *Silence* from my "Lecture on Nothing": I have nothing to say and I am saying it and that is poetry as I need it.

SCULPTURE MUSICALE

sons durant et partant de differents points et formant
une sculpture sonore qui dure
— **Marcel Duchamp**
New York City, August 1985

This is a 50% mesostic,* the words of which are limited to the words
upon which it is written. A program made by Andrew Culver extended
the number of characters in a search string for MESOLIST (a program
by Jim Rosenberg) to any length; this extended MESOLIST was used to
list the available words which were then subjected to IC (a program by
Andrew Culver simulating the coin oracle of the *I Ching*). For several
letters there were no words: the *p* of *sculpture*; the *l* of *musicale*; the *o*
of *sons*; the *s* of *points*; the *m* of *formant*; the *p* again of *sculpture*; the
o of *sonore*; and the *q* of *qui*. Spaces between lines take the place of
the missing letters. There are also spaces between words. This printing
is for three "voices," each having its own typeface.

* In a 50% mesostic the second letter of the mesostic does not appear between itself
and the first letter. In a 100% mesostic neither the first nor the second letter appears
between the first and second letters.

pointS et formant
musiCale
qUi
musicaLe

parTant de
mUsicale sons
sons duRant
sculpturE

points et forMant
scUlpture
Sonore
quI
sCulpture
durAnt

musicalE

muSicale

sculpture soNore
pointS et formant

et partant De differents points

qUi
sculptuRe
musicAle
musicale soNs
parTant

musicalE
eT

et formant sculPture
musicAle
une sculptuRe
de differenTs points et
musicAle
soNore qui
qui dure sculpTure

Durant
diffErents

sons Durant
poInts et
points et Formant
Formant
qui durE
duRant
sonorE
uNe
sculpTure
Sons durant

sculPture
sOns
musIcale
sculpture soNore
sculpTure
poıntS
unE
eT partant de

de diFferents
pOints
une sculptuRe sonore

musicAle
soNore
duranT

mUsicale
et formaNt
sculpturE

Sonore qui dure
musiCale sons
et formant Une
musicaLe

poinTs et formant
mUsicale

duRant
unE
une Sculpture

duraNt
pOints
foRmant
Et formant

dUre sculpture
quI

De
formant Une
et foRmant
qui durE

LECTURE ON NOTHING

This is a 50% mesostic, the words of which are limited to the words upon which it is written (taken from the "Lecture on Nothing" in *Silence*, p. 109). For several letters there were no words: the *v* of *have*; the *p* and the *r* of *poetry*.

<pre>
        that Is poetry as
          notHing to
            And

    and that is poEtry as
          it aNd that
            tO say

          poeTry as
            tHat
          as I
            i Need
      nothinG
            iT and that
            tO
            aS

          thAt is
      poetrY
        to sAy

            Nothing to
          anD
            Is
          thAt

          i aM
            iS
          thAt is
        to saY
</pre>

```
      that Is poetry as
       notHing to
       And

      as  I
       aNd
   am sayinG
   say and I
         iT
       thAt is

         Nothing to
      anD

         iT and
      notHing

         hAve
         iT
          I
         aS

         tO say
    i havE
    and That

         saYing it
    i hAve
         Say and
         It

   sayiNg it
   i havE
       poEtry
       anD
       as I
         That
```

```
                    I have nothing to say
          and I am saying it        and that is
       poetry              as I need it
```

SONGS FOR C.W.

For Christian Wolff

Istanbul, Montpellier
July 1985

C   aCross
               Hope
            gReet we
     deeplIer

               Simply
               Turn
               It
         to plAy it

         it souNds

               When
         i lOve

         we Leap

   and ever aFter

        ever Fine

H   musiC
               Hums

      longeR and
      movIng
               Service

               Turns round
      socIety

              A society
   deeply iNterested

         just With
      pianO

         gLad
      good Fortune
         Find

R   aCt
            Humanity

      we aRe
       chIldren

   we make Sound

    you eaT

   he drInks

        A
long welcomiNg

        Winter
        lOve

   never Late
     iF
     aFter

I   Continue
         tHis
         Rattle
    and pIano
       Sound

make inexacT
      musIc
        After
music's souNd

       Winter
    pianO
never Light

   oFten
   or Few

S

musiC's
tHin
and Rattles
sIlent

gave uS land
and wiTh land
rIver

flute After flute
tromboNe if

Where
chOice
is musicaL

choice aFter
iF

T

Causing us
to Hope

fRee
cookIng

muSic
to be eaTen

It's
Apple
violiN

Western
chOice

Loud
Face

land Fire

I

        aCt
         Have
        oR

      denatIon
        uS

       righT
        lIke
        lAugh

  this theN
      vieW

      chOice
space musicaL

        Few
    to be Far

A

        Continue
       tHese

     conveRse

     socIety
      Service

  food and eaTen

    we lIsten
   long After hours
completely iNterested

   space Write
     lOve

it is musicaL

    we Find
  and then aFter

N and then Continue
wHist
we gReet

musIcal
Service

iT and
drInk

plAy music
souNds

Write
relatiOns
gLad
Fortune
whether Few

W   Cymbals
witH
oR

you lIft
Space
and righT
o lIsten

sound A
tromboNe

West's
bOat
Lute
aFter
Find

O

Cause
wHose
tRavel

pIano
Space

eaT
lIke
Apple
eNgraved

you in West
and Operate

Loud
Face
eye Far

L

politiCs
witHout
Repeat

socIety
and Spring
wiTh
Is
All
bright whiteNed

We
lOve
Land eye

you Few and
Fire

F

Cause
witHout
Rattle

hummIing
Sound

plaTe
and socIety
plAy
iN plate

Write and read
Oh
bright Leap

Fact
iF loves

F

ACross
tHis land
aRe sun
and actIon
Severed
aT
drInk
plAy
souNd

When and read
sOund is
Leg

Few
and Find

NOTES ON COMPOSITIONS V (1987-92)

Most of the following notes on Cage's own compositions come from the printed matter accompanying concert performances.

Essay (1987): is short for *Writings through the Essay: On the Duty of Civil Disobedience* (Henry David Thoreau). There are eighteen of them. They are mesostics (like an acrostic but having the string of letters down the middle rather than down the edge; a given letter does not occur between it and the preceding letter of the string) on Erik Satie's title *Messe des Pauvres*. Thoreau said, "The best thing a man can do for his culture when he is rich is to endeavor to carry out those schemes which he entertained when he was poor." Satie was known as Monsieur le Pauvre. He had no interest in saving money. He preferred something he could use, a handkerchief, a watch, an umbrella, and these he bought not singly but in quantity. All of the words that are used in a single writing through are removed from the source text for a subsequent writing through. Thus the series of writings through tends towards shorter and shorter texts. The series was continued until the nineteenth, which being incomplete, brought it to an end. It is one part of a collection of materials, some of them musical, most of them literary, called *The First Meeting of the Satie Society*.

 Essay was made in two forms, one unstratified, and one stratified. For both forms readings giving nine seconds to each stanza of all eighteen writings through were superimposed. For the unstratified form the voice pitch was kept constant by compressing or expanding a single writing through to a common chance-determined timelength, 16'49". (The timelengths varied from 36" to 20'42".) For the stratified form (14'04") the different writings through were broadcast by chance operations to points in a two-octave range of which the center was the pitch of the unstratified form. For both forms each reading was given its own stereophonic position. This was accomplished at The Center for Computer Music at Brooklyn College of the City University of New York, directed by Charles Dodge. Programming, which involved the optimization for extreme elongation of Paul Lansky's software for the analysis and synthesis of vocal material, was done by the technical director Kenneth Worthy, and the work was carried out by him, Frances White and Victor Friedberg. The original voice recording was done at Synesthetics Inc. with the assistance of Paul Zinman.

Essay was included in "Documenta 8," an international art exhibition held in Kassel, Germany in 1987. The work, with the added element of light, has been reconfigured for the Wexner Performance Space. The sound installation for the Wexner Center uses 36 loudspeakers placed around the perimeter of the overhead grid. Thirty-six auto-reverse cassette decks are used to make a performance that continues without repetition for the full duration of the installation. The 50 lights change intensity slowly but continuously over each eight-hour day, starting each day at a different point. Six chairs are positioned in new locations and directions each day. The lighting and chair placements were composed according to chance operations; the installation was carried out by Andrew Culver.

The material from *Essay* was also used to accompany *Points in Space*, a dance by Merce Cunningham. Since the computer program separated vowels and consonants, it was possible to make *Voiceless Essay* without any vowels, just the noise-like consonants of the four writings through (IV, IX, XV and XVI), the last which follows.

Man will
useEful
man will not Submit
to leaSt
throughout thE
worlD

hE who
himSelf entirely

Put through
And
with retUrn

priVate feelings
foR
thE
proportion aS

The structure of the music is analogous to that of the dance, having the same number of parts, but their lengths, being chance determined, are different.

Two (1987): Each part has ten time-brackets, nine which are flexible with respect to beginning and ending, and one, the eighth, which is fixed. No sound is to be repeated within a bracket. In the piano part each ictus in a single staff is to be played in the order given, but can be played in any relation to the sounds in the other staff. Some notes are held from one ictus to the next. A tone in parentheses is not to be played if it is already sounding. One hand may assist the other.

Five Stone Wind (1988): The dance by Merce Cunningham called *Five Stone* was performed first in Berlin and lasted about 30 minutes. Later, the same year (1988) it was presented in Avignon as *Five Stone Wind*. It then lasted nearly an hour. Using chance operations I composed a framework of time-brackets with flexible beginnings and endings for three players, one who did not begin playing until after 30 minutes (Takehisa Kosugi). I did not in any way give details to David Tudor or Kosugi for the realization of their parts. However, for Michael Pugliese's part I made specific plans with him for the use of the clay drums within particular brackets and the subsequent alternation of these plans for performances on tour. These included, in addition to the playing means mentioned in the notes by Pugliese, the use or not while improvising of electronic feedback produced by moving the drum closer to the microphone.

Twenty-Three (1988): The piece is not to be conducted. Each player has his own chronometer which he starts at his own time neither immediately nor long after the tuning of the instruments. Most of the time-brackets are flexible with respect to beginning and ending. Exceptionally, one in a given part, which lasts thirty seconds, is fixed.

Play *col legno tratto* holding and turning the fairly loose-haired bow with the fingers, not turning the sound on or off as one does an electric light, but brushing it into existence as in oriental calligraphy where the ink (the "sound") is not always seen, or, if so, is streaked with its absence, or changes of intensity.

101 (1988): Thoreau said, "The best form of government is no government at all and that is the form we'll have when we are ready for it." This piece rightly or wrongly, assumes we are ready for it. Though we don't have them, we need utilities: good air, good water, good homes, good food, transportation, clothing, communication, etc., including intelligence. But we don't need government: the struggle for power between nations, the protection of the rich from the poor, the deprivation of the poor, and the demoralization of both the poor and the rich, the ruination of the environment by means of government's collaboration with the military and the corporate.

A performance of music can be a metaphor for society. In this music there is no conductor. There is no score. The parts are written in flexible time-brackets. You may use a stopwatch, or you may find an ordinary watch will do. Or you may use your own "built-in" sense of time. This twelve-minute piece is not complicated. It opens with a ragged burst of high, loud sound from the brass and all of the woodwinds except the flutes and clarinets. At the same time the sound of strings playing *col legno* and *mezzo-piano* begins. Now and then it is accompanied by *pianissimo* events from the flutes and clarinets that one is not always sure he has actually heard. Other percussion events take place sporadically: two soft timpani rolls, seven anklung events, four low contrabass marimba events, twelve bowed piano events, and a single whirring bullroarer intensified sometimes by one, two or three other bullroarers joining in.

Towards the end, but not at the end, actually but approximately between 9'00" and 10'15" from the inexact beginning, the brass and all the woodwinds except the flutes and clarinets are heard *fortissimo* and in their highest range, a second and last time, falling apart, so to speak, rather than holding together as a group. The strings, flutes and clarinets and the percussion continue, and less after a minute or so stop playing, each at his own time.

Throughout there is another kind of music being played on the piano and on the harp. It is *mezzo-forte*, more articulate. It stands out like a duet or two solos, and though we hear them, we hear everything else too and not in the background.

The piece is not to be conducted, though the conductor will coach the orchestra at rehearsals. Each player has his own chronometer (which does not beep) which starts at his own time neither immediately nor long after the tuning of the instruments. Most of the time-brackets are flexible with respect to beginning and ending. Exceptionally, one in a given part, which lasts thirty seconds, is fixed. No sound is to be repeated within a bracket.

For the Piccolo, Double Reeds and Brass: Play as loud as possible. One breath only. The quality of tone should be "ragged" or imperfect, that is, not turned on or off as one does an electric light, but brushed into existence as in oriental calligraphy where the ink (the sound) is not always seen, or if so, is streaked with white (silence).

For the Flutes and Clarinets: Play very softly. Use unconventional fingerings so that the sound as described above is full of uncontrolled changes.

For the Strings: Play with a completely loose bow, slowly rolling it from a normal position to a fully *col legno* position and back again. The sound should be more like a frictional percussion sound than like a sustained one, full of uncontrolled changes of frequency, tone quality and silence in the manner described above for the winds and brass.

For the Harp and Piano (played from the keyboard): Each ictus in a single staff is to be played in the order given, but can be played in any relation to the sounds in the other staff. Some notes are held from one ictus to the next. A tone in parentheses is not to be played if it is already sounding. One hand may assist the other.

Two² (1989): This piece is in response to a conversation in Leningrad with Sofia Gubaidulina. "There is an inner clock." It is also a *renga* (36 × 5·7·5·7·7). Quiet but equally, no tones inaudible, damper pedals down throughout.

Though the order of the tones within a measure is to be observed by each pianist, the relation of each to the other is completely free. Do not begin the next measure until the previous one is finished by both pianists. Pauses between the *renga* units without release of pedals.

A *renga* is a Japanese five-line verse form with a foot count of 5, 7, 5, 7, 7 syllables. Note that each line of music in *Two²* consists of five bars, each bar being the equivalent of one poetic foot. Each vertical note collection within a bar = 1 syllable. A note collection can consist of from one to many notes. [Cage's titles for his fifty "Number Pieces" (1987-92) indicate (1) the number of players required; and (2) the chronological order of composition. Thus, *Two²* is the second piece written for two players.]

Four (1989): The players sit in the conventional relation to each other. There are three five-minute sections, A–C each having flexible time-brackets and one which is fixed; these are notated from 0'00" to 5'00". There are four parts (1–4). The two violinists then exchange their parts with the other two players either as 1 with 3 and 2 with 4, or 1 with 4 and 2 with 3. After resetting their chronometers they play section B again.

If the performance is to last twenty minutes, all players play sections A and C without pause between. Players 1 and 2 then exchange their parts with players 3 and 4 in either way and play A and C again.

If the performance is complete, ABC, with the repetition it will last thirty minutes.

Scottish Circus (1990) Select pieces of Scottish traditional music for the instruments and voices of the group. This should be done independently by each player or singer without regard for the speed, key, mood, type of piece (e.g., Jig, Reel, Lament, Lullaby, Gaelic Song, etc.) of the pieces chosen by the other players.

Enter the hall one by one, playing while walking. If the instrument is not portable (as in the case of the small harp), walk to it and begin playing. Where possible, move freely around the hall while playing. When singing, do not accompany yourself with an instrument; sing regardless of what the other players or singers are doing.

The performance should last for approximately thirty minutes. However, each player or singer should take three breaks, with each break consisting of approximately five minutes of silence. These silences should be chosen independently by each performer without regard to the occurrence of silences among the others. That is, each performer plays for approximately half of the total performance time.

When nearing the end of the performance, gradually leave the hall or performance space one by one.

Try to measure the durations that occur during the piece instinctively, without reference to watches or clocks, using the body-clock's natural perception of time.

One[8] (1991): Fifty-three flexible time-brackets with single sounds produced on 1, 2, 3, or 4 strings. Durations, dynamics and bow positions are free.

The total duration is 43′30″. The cellist uses a modern "curved bow," with a high arch, and with a lever worked by the right hand thumb. The lever allows the bow hair tension to change, thereby allowing for either melodic (single string), or polyphonic (sustained multiple string) playing.

Two[5] (1991): The microtonal playing on the trombone is notated so that there are six steps each semitone.

Any changes of dynamics (*pp* and thereabouts for both instruments) should be, like changes in breath, as imperceptible as possible. The piano should sound absent-minded, without regularity or presence. If there is at some point a very short sound on the trombone it can be extremely loud, inexplicable.

A time-bracket piece lasting forty minutes.

Two[5] (1991): The microtonal playing on the trombone is notated so that there are six steps each semitone.

Any changes of dynamics (*pp* and thereabouts for both instruments) should be, like changes in breath, as imperceptible as possible. The piano should sound absent-minded, without regularity or presence. If there is at some point a very short sound on the trombone it can be extremely loud, inexplicable.

A time-bracket piece lasting forty minutes.

Four[4] (1991): Single percussion sounds in flexible time-brackets. Since the beginning periods and ending periods overlap, a sound can be long, medium in length, short or very short. Very long sounds should not be loud unless nothing else is either actually or potentially happening. In the case that a sound is alone amplitude is completely free. Where such periods exist is to be learned in rehearsal, so that when the performance is given all the players know when they are free with respect to the amplitude. The piece is 72' (CD length). Whenever there is no activity, simply listen, as listeners to the finished recording will, hearing the sounds wherever they are."

Two[3] for Sho and Five Conch Shells (1991): Ten pieces of different lengths having ten flexible time-brackets to be played without accompaniment, or with amplified conch shells containing water and tipped so as to produce audible bubbles. The shells are numbered by the player. He tries to obtain the number of bubbles given by the superscript within the time period given. If one is not forthcoming he remains in silence. Either three parts of *One*[9] with or without *Two*[3] may be played with *108*. If more than one of these ten pieces is played, two chronometers will be needed by each player.

Ten (1991): Single tones or any number of them in flexible time-brackets. The time-brackets overlap (the sounds may be long or short, rapidly played or slower).

For the percussion: instruments are numbered but not specified. In choosing an instrument try it both for short and for long sounds (within which long sounds individual attacks are not heard).

For the piano: the single low strings may be normally plucked; the higher strings will need a plectrum. Numbered parts of the piano construction (bars and box) are not specified but are chosen by the pianist. The keyboard aggregates may be sounded together, partly sustained unsounded by pedal (as in *Winter Music*), or entirely sustained by pedal and sounded by manual *gliss.* on strings as in the piano music of Henry Cowell.

All other instruments play microtonally.

Phrasing, use of silence, articulation is free. But only play the tones that are written once. Search with them for melisma, florid song. When durations or phrases are long, keep the amplitude low. Short sounds can be of any amplitude.

Total duration = 30′00″.

103 (1991) is an orchestral work. Like the film [*One*[11] (1992)], it is ninety minutes long. It is divided into seventeen parts. The lengths of the seventeen parts are the same for the strings and the percussion. The woodwinds and the brass follow another plan. The shots of the cameraman still another. Following chance operations, the number of wind instruments changes for each of the seventeen parts. Thus, the density of *103* varies from the solo trombone of Section Eleven, to the tutti of Section Five and the near tuttis of Sections One, Eight, Thirteen, Fourteen, and Sixteen.

While they are playing, the musicians should be attentive to what they are doing, listening, that is, to each sound s/he makes, how it begins, continues, and ends. *103* is not the expression of feelings or ideas on my part. I have wanted the sounds to be free of my intentions so that they are just sounds, themselves. The performance is not conducted; video displays give the time. During rehearsals, the conductor guides the musicians in their work.

108 for Large Orchestra (1991): To be played with or without *One*[8] for violoncello solo. Single tones (a single breath, a single bow, or the simulation of such [circular breathing, imperceptible bow changes]) within flexible time-brackets. The beginnings and endings overlap; thus the tones may be short or long or in between provided they do not end until the ending time begins. If the durations are medium or long, let the dynamics be on the soft and very soft side, particularly in the case of the woodwinds, brass, and sustained percussion sounds; if the durations are short or very short, the dynamics may be loud. Dynamics may change in the course of the sound (*dim. cresc.* or combinations of these, *espress.*).

The piece begins in silence (1′30″). It is followed by a period of activity (12′30″). Silence occurs (4′00″) and activity follows that

(14'30"). Again a silence (2'00"), then brief activity (30"), and a long silence (4'00"). Finally, 3'00" of activity and an ending in silence (1'30"). During the silences, in the case of a cello concerto, the violoncello is heard. A video monitor gives the four necessary clocks; each starting minus ten seconds before 0'00". The piece may be played with or without the soloist. It is called *One*^{8} and *108* with the cellist, simply *108* when the orchestra plays alone (*One*^{8} may also be played without the orchestra). In either case, the monitor is used. There is no conductor, though he guides the players in periods of preparation before performance.

The percussion instruments are distinguished from one another but not named. They should all be very resonant and are bowed or played with a tremolo such that individual attacks are not noticeable. Suitable instruments are like the following: Chinese and Turkish cymbals, Japanese temple gongs, thundersheets, bass marimba tones, and Balinese gongs (upside down and on pads). Very short percussion sounds must, of course, be struck.

Europera 5 (1991): **Staging:** Plot a grid of 64 areas and mark it with tape on the floor of the performance area. Place the stick-on numbers in the upper left corner of each grid square so that they can be read from the perspective of the performers. The size of the squares can range from 60 cm. to 100 cm. depending on the space available. The form of the grid can be an 8 by 8 square, or can be elongated symmetrically to fit a wide and shallow stage, or can be varied in other symmetrical ways, or in an asymmetrical way if the performance space is very curiously shaped, the design resulting not from choice but as a result or outcome of the space.

All instruments and furniture are positioned on the grid, except two of the chairs on which the singers may sit between arias, which are placed to the side or upstage of the grid. The singers move to new positions for each aria (positions given in the singers' parts). The positions of the piano, television, and tables — sound, light, and victrola, each with lamp and chair — are fixed, but are newly determined for each venue according to chance operations. . . . The radio is offstage, sounding from a distance. . . . Some latitude is required in positioning the piano.

The videotape shows a digital clock running from −0:30:00 to 1:30:00. It functions as a conductor. The monitors are placed downstage or in the F.O.H. light position, or wherever they are useful. It does not matter if the audience can see them or their image."

Performance: The performance is run by the light performer since he controls the VCR. When all is ready he pushes the *play* button. After a small pre-arranged amount of countdown time passes, the performance begins at 0:00:00. It ends at exactly 1:00:00. The light performer blacks the lights and video, and anyone still making sounds stops.

Whenever more than one player is making sound, one is heard clearly, and the others are distant (the pianist is shadow playing, the other singer is offstage). *Truckera* [the tape] is often no more than barely audible: at its loudest it is slightly ominous; at its quietest, its presence is in doubt. The radio is distant. The victrola has its own loudness.

Visually, the work is calm. The seated players should be still when not quietly active. The singers move to their positions without haste. There is no relation between the character of an aria and that of a singer's actions or walk to and from the aria's stage position. If time permits, the singers should arrive in position well before beginning to sing, and linger after ending.

Twenty-Six, Twenty-Eight and Twenty-Nine (1991): These pieces may be played alone, either two together, or all three at once. In either of the latter cases, the longer or longest piece shall begin and close the performance, the shorter one starting within the period of time that is its difference of length. Thus, if all three play together, *Twenty-Nine* will begin, *Twenty-Six* will begin anytime within three minutes and *Twenty-Eight* will begin anytime within one minute. The first Viola will start the video clock for *Twenty-Nine*, the first flute for *Twenty-Eight*, the first violin for *Twenty-Six*.

Single tones in flexible time-brackets (single bows or breaths, long or short) played only once.

One[11] (1992) is a film without subject. There is light but no persons, no things, no ideas about repetition and variation. it is meaningless activity which is nonetheless communicative, like light itself, escaping our attention as communication because it has no content. Light is, as McLuhan said, pure information, without any content to restrict its transforming and informing power. Chance operations were used with respect to the shots, black and white, taken in the FSM television studio in Munich by Van Carlson, Los Angeles cameraman. The producer and director was Henning Lohner. The executive producer was Peter Lohner. The light environment was designed and programmed by John Cage and Andrew Culver, as was the editing of the film, done in video format at Laser Edit East in NYC, with the help of Gary Sharin and Bernadine Colish. This edit was then transferred to the original 35mm film negative at ARRI, Munich.

Four[6] (1992): For any way of producing sounds (vocalization, singing, playing of an instrument or instruments, electronics, etc.). Choose twelve different sounds with fixed characteristics (amplitude, overtone structure, etc.). Play within the flexible time-brackets given. When the time-brackets are connected by a diagonal line, they are relatively close together. When performed as a solo, the first player's part is used and the piece is called *One*[7].

Seventy-Four (1992): Orchestral parts without score to be played with video clock without conductor. Single notes in flexible time-brackets. The first bracket is the time within which a tone may begin. The second bracket is the time within which the same tone may end. These brackets overlap. Therefore a single note can become a very short or a very long tone or one of any length in between.

The composition is a series of such tones in brackets played in a "unison" which is an arising of differences accompanied by another series of such but other and lower tones also played in such a "unison" of differences. Though the same pitches are played, the notes all have their own lengths— and further, their own amplitudes. They come from the same or different instruments. When they come from the same instruments, e.g. the violins, they may have different overtone structures, i.e. be bowed differently, etc. There should also be the usual imperfection of tuning perhaps slightly exaggerated so that the music is microtonal. *Vibrato*, differences of breathing, and special use of the lips can be present or absent. All these differences are to be expressed by each musician individually not as the result of plans made with others.

There are two "unisons" superimposed. Each has its own series of time-brackets. This is, however, in no sense a question of counterpoint.

for the Frankfurt/am/Main Städtische Oper

EUROPERA 1

John Cage

ORGAN (OPTIONAL)

0'00" ↔ 5'00"

Andante

5'00" ↔ 7'30"

Moderato

7'30" ↔ 8'00"

Andante moderato

STORIA DELL'OPERA (1987)

This letter, probably written in the spring of 1987, first appeared in the program book of the world premiere of Europeras 1 & 2, *1987.*

Here are my first ideas. Title: *Europera*. Empty stage (no curtains). On the back wall a changing collage of slides, changing here and there not allover change, scenes and closeups of opera performances both in color and black and white. In the stage space a changing collage of parts of sets (flats) from the repertoire they were performing. Jets of air here and there on the stage unpredictably blowing upwards (at least two hours). There will be no dropping or division into acts. Even when the audience first comes in, the entire stage will be visible with the changing slide show in operation and any necessary preparations by cast or crew visible. This is an oriental work made up of occidental materials. If there are any animals they shall from time to time make exits and entrances. This is all I have in mind to put on paper what I discussed with you in September and to send you the finished synopses, two for each of twelve different programs. The title is now *Europeras 1 & 2*. Their time lengths, respectively, will be one hour and thirty minutes (shorter by fifteen minutes than what we agreed upon) and forty-five minutes. I will use nineteen singers (s.col., s.lyr.col., s.lyr., s.lyr.spin., s.dram.; m-s.col., m-s.lyr., m-s.dram.; c.; t.lyr., t.buffo, t.lyr.spin, t.dram.; bar.lyr., bar.dram.; bs.-bar.; bs.lyr., bs.buffo, bs.profundo) divided into two separate groups, one for each opera. As soon as any one of these singers is under contract, please send me the name and address. I will then correspond with him or her, sending a list of the operas from which songs each singer, his stage positions, fixed or changing, being chance-determined, will perform independently of the others, assisted now and then and/or moved from place to place by dancers dressed in black as Japanese theatre assistants are, or sometimes appropriately as animals or trucks. Herewith I am sending you the images for the flats and slides for *Europeras 1 & 2*. The maximum number of images to be made from a single source is three (the minimum is one). These are distinguished on the xeroxes by pencil, red pen, and blue pen, where the final size is also given.

There are to be 18 flats and 18 rear-projection screens, 36 in all, having the following 18 dimensions (horizontal; vertical) in meters: 1×1, 2×2, 3×4, 4×3, 2×3, 3×2, 4×6, 6×4, 3×5, 5×3, 2×4, 4×2, 1×3, 3×1, 2×6, 6×2, 1×5, 5×1. The set of 18 flats will be hung and will have photographically blown-up images (are actually blank surfaces), they can receive projections as well (from the front). I have renounced the plan involving changes of weather effects (for I did not want a fixed centeredness); instead the decors will be a chance determined "garden of images" probably not less than three at a time, and not more than five, extending as far into the distance backstage as practical in view of other opera sets that will take up the space. In this rear space the set of eighteen rear-projection screens having the above sizes should be made as movable as possible from one position to another without the benefit of flying (e.g. easels, tracks, music, program notes, lights, costumes, decors, action). There is a maximum cast of nineteen singers who sing arias by dancers in dance practice clothes of their own choice though uniformly dark without white or light colors. The singers, whose costumes are from different times and often moved about, the woodwinds (2222), brass (2231), percussion and timpani, and strings (11111) are unconducted soloists. A taped collage of European opera is heard from time to time as though it were in the percussion section (a truck passing by). All of the instrumental musics may be done by someone else. Nothing "relates" to anything else except by coincidence, e.g. the lighting is independent of the action. Where necessary, flashlights are used. The decor is a changing list. If you sing anything from *Pelléas et Mélisande* , substitute a vocalise for Maeterlinck's words; they are not yet in the public domain. You would sing without accompaniment. Other arias may be being sung at the same time, and the musicians of the orchestra will be playing as soloists a part by singing in a situation where other things are happening, so the arias you choose to sing, nor will the action given you to perform be relevant either. Though the work is one that will take up not less than [20 OR 12] minutes not more than five. There are seven stage actions for each singer in "1" and all of these are used no matter how into a series by the assistants who keep putting the first one beyond the second. 5. Wearing tap dance shoes. *Tap dance shoes, both heel and toe.* 6. Knitting. *A large, strange, pieced-together, knitted but unfinished object* brought in in a large bag by assistants with yarn and needles. 7. Large flounder "swims" on stage. As it continues singer is revealed to have *singer of which singer is radius (body supports as invisible as possible).* 7. A jenny scaffold taken apart and erected again. *Materials and structural means.* Framed to resemble one of the flats.

Frame. Soprano lyric will be used that corresponds to the number of arias chosen to be sung. Also enclosed is a short opera and a letter and questionnaire to be sent to the singers as I learn who and where they are. We are still working on the lights and hope to learn much in Frankfurt about the lights in the house. We have distinguished these categories: wash, area, side stage, side backstage, individual specials, extants (use of those already focused for other operas). Each of these categories will have its own cue sheet, though these can be combined for the benefit of the light computer. We hope to bring an example of our cue sheets next week. We will also bring a flute in its final form. The instrumental music needs a good deal of information from the singers. For *Europera 1*, I need to know from Michal Shamir the timelength for "Elle a fui" (Hoffmann) and "Juliette's Waltz" (Romeo and Juliette). Then I need blanks filled out (20-30 minutes) from Harolyn Blackwell, Anny Schlemm, Seppo Ruohonen and Rodney Gilfrey. Finally I need a mezzo-soprano coloratura not yet named. For *Europera 2* I need to know from Valentin Jar his timelengths for Triquet (Onegin), *Steuermann* (Flying Dutchman), and *Am Stillen Herd* (Meistersinger). I also need a filled out blank (12–20 minutes) by William Cochran. Finally I need a soprano coloratura not yet named. Naturally I would like to have this information as soon as possible: I was promised it by the end of September! I cannot continue my work without it.

I guess that Gary [Bertini] and the Opera are not happy about the project and would willingly call it to a halt. I am myself not happy. I asked in August for information from the singers that I still do not completely have. Thus I cannot answer questions such as: call a halt to the project. In any case, I plan to complete the music so that it would be available for concert purposes. My time would not have been entirely wasted. There are other unresolved problems. One of the singers is not sure he wants to perform in the work: I'm expected to live away from home for at least two months while I do the work of direction, etc., bringing about meanwhile an almost insurmountable backlog of correspondence. No excerpt's to be repeated. Where there is insufficient time in the bracket to play all the material given exclamation points precede and follow the time bracket. In such cases the player gives priority to the bracket (stops if necessary in the course of an excerpt or starts at some point after the beginning). In a performance the musicians are independent of one another so that what happens happens by coincidence rather than by intention. Make a time schedule (a new one or not for each performance or whenever wishes) and then follow it strictly. Time the excerpts so that the relation of that time to that of the time bracket is known. Use a chronometer. Both silences and a lack of balance between parts are not to be found alarming. Max von Vequel Technical Director Frankfurt am Main Oper Städtische Bühnen Untermainanlage 11 D-6000 Frankfurt 1 Dear Max, We think you and your staff are doing beautiful work. Here are the references to your 17 questions of March 18, 1987:

1. See prop 153.5; 2. See prop 153.7; 3. See prop 191.1 and figure 13; 4. A real baby grand piano (normal height!); 5. See prop 105.4; 6. See prop 105.7 and figure 14. We now think that instead of having hooks the flounder should be moved by assistants who are inside of it. 7. See prop 152.4 Geissler tubes are neon lights; 8. See prop 151.3 and figure 15; 9. See prop 151.7 and figure 7. We don't know how to do this. 1. Please exchange costumes 154.4 and 154.5. 2. We would like to keep costume 254.5 as the one to be blown up like a balloon. Why not make it out of a sealed double layer of latex rubber so that air could be pumped in between the two layers? That way any costume design would work. 4. 191 is the mynah bird only (they wear their own dance practice clothes). Remember that the "ARIA" numbers refer to all activities for one aria, whether by S (singer), or A or AA (assistants), but that costumes are only involved when there is an S in the WHO column. Gilfry Schlemm October 1 Bodo Klaus Carlos Marie-Luise Rorholm Ruohonen October 2 Bodo Klaus Vesco Bavoni Shamir de Kanel October 6 Carlos Wendy David Marie-Luise Blackwell Glucksmann October 7 Bodo Klaus Coelho Hagenau October 8 Bavoni Andres Rosemary David Marie-Luise Blackwell Gamberoni October 9 Irene Gramatzki October 10 David Marie-Luise Gilfry Neubauer October 12 Bodo Klaus Irene Thomas Schlemm Jar October 13 Wendy Irene Thomas David Rorholm de Kanel October 14 Bodo Klaus Carlos Wendy Ruohonen Fox October 15 Vesco Andres Rosemary Irene Thomas Mueller Gamberoni October 16 Bavoni Andres Rosemary Irene Thomas David Marie-Luise Booth Glucksmann October 17 Card Workman. Instead of understudies, recordings (both those made by the absent singers and commercial ones, which to be used determined by chance operations) played on stage by assistant(s). Costumes on

costume forms including accessories and props brought in by assistants. During the intermission I want to add a movie (conceived by me, realized by Frank Scheffer, *The Complete Ring in 3'50"*) played continuously, not in the foyer but in the hall itself. Please let me know as soon as possible whether this is technically feasible. Assistants 1-6 should be athletes (wrestlers, gymnasts, weightlifters), 7-12, dancers. A variety of physical presences. The necessity of assistants at rehearsals even if during morning dance class time (a situation we avoided as much as possible). The rehearsal schedule: Please arrange as much time as possible for flats and lights in the theatre in September between the 15th and the end of the month. I assume that Bertini will prepare the orchestra in August. I would like to have several recordings made of each opera so that they could be used for rehearsal without the singers getting dependent on any one of them. Thanks for all the lighting charts; they make a great deal of work possible which we are doing now. We will not be needing any color gels other than those in your magazine. The changes to the use of the pipes are acceptable, however two mistakes in the image numbers on your plan were noted: Flat 36 should be Flat 37 (Hand 7), Flat 61 should be Flat 59 (Hand 24). Your letter made reference to acceptable frequencies for the radio which controls the zeppelin, but then none were included; so what are they? Is it sure that you will use your own radio (it must have four channels: rudder left/right, planes up/down, ballast release/gas release, propeller forward/reverse)? I don't know that you can use your own servo motors; they have to be a specific size and weight. Also, the smaller one is 11 feet and can lift about 18 oz. (0.5 kg), the bigger 13 feet, lifting 80 oz. (2.3 kg). So—which size?—is your radio 4 channels? —what frequencies?—will you try your own servos, or shall I get the "right" ones? Duchamp's goal: "The impossibility of transferring, from one like image to another, the memory imprint."

SYNOPSES (1988)

At the Frankfurt performances of Europera, *where separate programs were available for each performance, the synopses that follow here were distributed randomly, one per program, so that different members of the audience had different narratives to follow. After consultation with Mr. Cage, we print here all twelve alternative pairs of synopses. You may pick whichever takes your fancy.*

1

He, unhappy at her apparent indifference toward him, brings her captive to the Temple of the Holy Grail. Another man also loves her, accusing her of witchcraft. She expresses but a lifeless automaton who should have reported to jail for a minor offense. Disguising himself in exchange for his love, they are condemned as traitors. Conveniently, he flees to an inn on the Lithuanian border.

2

Exhausted, he is beset by his daughter who was once his wife. Her cousin, however, loves her; he resolves to be succored by her frequently. He is invited to utter the fearful renunciation. She, having already independently accepted, dies of fright. Another woman, his wife, calls her her new mentor, but he is convinced of her guilt. Her wish is granted by them and out steps the beautiful Queen. He threatens to tell how.

■

1

He, the nephew of a rich old bachelor, arouses him to obtain admittance to the palace, and, in return for safe passage, names him commander of the Holy Grail. Even her loving relatives feel a strange sympathy near his ship. First, he sounds the alarm, but she is tempted by the weaponless hero to hold him to a marriage contract. At the second alarm, he disguises himself after giving her wedding an unsuccessful attempt at a life of pleasure. She flees commanding a pardon for his bride, who has hidden herself to die with her hand on him.

2

She falls in love for reasons of state. He comes across her in search of adventure. At her birthday ball through rose-colored glasses he discusses plans to continue their search for a loan. In fact, he decided to join the governor who kills his friend. The two enemies wrest the sword from the tree, joining the protest against paying the fee. He assembles the court and tells his story. She manages to avoid being alone with him.

∎

1

The sensitive girl is planning the defense of the forest in the city protected for years by the young man she engages secretly. She, longing for him, deepens her despair, and is sent to marry his best friend. Soon his duty, however, utters the prophecy to lure him with the lawyer's child guarding them against background and antecedents he has signed. She dies. He has meanwhile bought his army contract by proclaiming himself her son. He is so young; this enables him to resist once again.

2

Dressed as an Irish princess, he gives birth; they plot to overthrow the French. He arranges to be kidnapped by her; rejuvenated, they desert: to him she has borne two children. He prays for help. Since they have decided she shall marry no one outside, he has himself crowned Emperor. She, told he is dead, begs him to look at her. First, before the young couple come to a climax, he agrees. Accidentally, she drowns them.

∎

1

He ignores the warnings at one of her brilliant supper parties when an astrologer arrives terrified by pangs of conscience. He brings the Oracle's word that their friends still refuse their friends. In despair, she seeks him to take a light from him. At the second alarm, he steps forward, confessing his love for her. She is unbeatable. His total innocence, sounded by his one-time friend, takes her off his hands. Her brief rage of jealousy in the end sets sail. In a golden coach, he commends her soul to heaven.

2

He, in love, is spurned as a suitor. He determines to learn the stories of his past in revenge. She waits. Two slaves discover her. Convinced she must ask the forbidden question, they meet. He gathers all his strength after the party breaks up, realizing he may never marry her. They finally convert him, swearing eternal friendship. He apologizes to her.

∎

1

He and she are betrothed when he hails her rigidly his. He also
promises his friend that she'll play up to him plotting revenge. The
gun accidentally fires reminding him of the Holy Spear. He offers
the giants his mother, and they are married. They play at cards in
his room despite her warning. Meanwhile he led her at the dwarf's
urging to repent, and then to find, to kill, and to take.

2

He has left her; she is accused by him and the populace, except the
innkeeper. He arranges for battle with the Moors. Killing the old
man, one condition is imposed: traditional hospitality. He, disguised
as a student, kills the governor. She flees. He kills the giant; she kills
herself. Her funeral cortege appears. Refusing to join her, he forgives
them, making a fool of himself. A strange hermit appears.

■

1

**She after a long life has fallen in his palace, and consequently
refuses plans to marry. He bemoans her absence. She asks for many
pranks and much confusion. It is love at first sight; however, he
expresses himself later and is banished. Their mood is suddenly
dead; she sends him away.**

2

**They are in love. Raised in a cave, he vows to reveal his identity,
thus freeing her to refuse his son's request. They tell him he is
invited to take holy order. Transforming himself into a monstrous
dragon, with the evil one's help they meet. Twenty-five years pass.
He repents. She manages to make him yield, but in the end remains
completely docile: she returns.**

■

1

*He is in a group of witches and plans to starve; she sells her expert
cardplayer; people pray for him to be awakened. Discovered, she
succeeds in making him meet only secretly with her. The wedding is
imposed: if he offers her younger sister her former sweetheart who
has rescued her, he cannot resist her gods. He steps forward and
they join, released from their vows. He, believing her to be
enlightened, reveals the virtues of her way, and suddenly plunders
the Temple with his last bullet. He is satisfied.*

2

He has promised his daughter active resistance; she lives disguised
as a sea captain. He curses his bride who has been adopted by a
band of gypsies. She feels a strange sympathy for his father. She
succumbs to him. They flee. She prevents him from meeting her in
the garden; he is furious; she is total innocence. He transforms
himself on his ship, which swiftly sets sail. Distraught, he orders,
forgives, sets fire to it.

■

1

She gains admittance to the palace. He accepts a commission to
outwit the two lovers. However, she kills him at her feet and assists
the lawyer who cannot resist her invitation to the palace, He tries
prayers, He displays a white dove and wins the hand of the
princess.

2

On a public bench, he falls in love; however, her father, an evil
magician, died, giving birth to him. He is in fact his son, her
delight. Soon his duty calls him away to guard them against danger
she quickly forgets. Though he renounces his vows, he accepts and
they are married. Face to face, the two can see no way out; in his
room, she flees when he obeys an inexplicable impulse. Desperately,
he asks her to run away with him. She appears half-crazed, makes
the sign of the cross, thereby destroying him and his castle.

■

1

*He falls deeply in love with a beautiful streetsinger who staggers
into the hut. He buys a love potion. Her candle goes out and
impressed by his wealth she decides to marry him on the spot. The
wound reveals that after three years he will have himself crowned
Emperor with the evil one's help in exchange for his love. At first
she flees; whereupon he gathers all his strength, becomes
passionately attached and begs a hermit's refuge.*

2

*She sells his soul to her father with the aim of improving his
impaired finances. Even her loving relatives are shocked. They
rescue him. He retires. She agrees. Torn, they, in shame, pardon all
conspirators. He agrees to marry her. She kills herself. He is chosen
the victor.*

■

1

She is the tragedy that has happened. He confides his love and he
says he is himself a father. He plots to marry no one. The victim
hides the stature of salvation if they rob her and the high priests,
but when she learns the ceremony is a fake she kills his friend,
who accepted his duplicity in vain since they had informed him of
his death. He kills her on the battlefield.

2

The villagers celebrate; an astrologer arrives lamenting the death
of his wife. She appears rejuvenated; she informs him that the gods
have taken pity on him: she loves him. His fears reach a climax:
her candle goes out. Doubtful of his love if he knows the truth, she
nevertheless enters the royal household intercepted by the King's
minister, who renounces his plan to rob her. She, in love with love,
is penniless. He asks her to run away with the King. She goes mad;
he, impressed, urges revenge.

■

1

He is happy with the court life and is in love with her; he ignores
her apparent indifference toward him. He meets with the Turks
a visiting knight who says to forget his stepmother and enlist his
help. Actually, he returns disguised as a monk on Christmas Eve.
She soon denounces him to his friend, each time they accept his
traveling companion. To circumvent discovery in his dark tomb,
she marries him; they are surprised to win.

2

He arouses her (they are about to be married): he threatens to
kill his mother. She expresses her delight; now his brother has
presumably been thrown into the flames. At her birthday ball, he is
very careful. After the bloody deed is done, she, remorseful, returns.
The two exchange ecstatic pledges. Nevertheless he is dying. He
offers his life to the gods.

■

■

1

*She is bored with most men; he is in love with her. He accepts a
preliminary trial hoping to find a way. She persuades him to give
her his life. He dies. Now in his dark tomb he goes to her rescue.
She reawakens his love early in the morning.*

2

*He lusts after her; she has died, his only hope of redemption. In his
despondency he maintains his reserve, accepts the bird. He fulfills
the second part of the witches' prophecy: They rescue him quickly.
He loses his power. He falls prey to another man's wife. Once more
he invokes Venus (he is first to admit it); in vain: her life is over. He
wishes; he refuses. Thoroughly embittered, he rails.*

■

TIME (ONE AUTOKU) (1988)

Sometime last year I was mugged. My watch and billfold were taken.
Time. Money. I get along I must say quite well without the watch, now
and then asking someone nearby what time it is. I do not trust in public
clocks.

I spent most of my life in the forties, fifties, sixties, and seventies as
a composer and dance accompanist, most of it with Merce Cunningham, not playing the piano for his classes, though I did that, but for
his performances with his company. When I was just beginning to
study composition I received a punitive, spontaneous lecture on the
importance of time for one who proposed devoting his life to music.
Richard Buhlig was angry with me because, having hitchhiked to see
him, I had arrived half an hour early, and, then, sent away, saved time
by returning some library books, thus ringing his doorbell the second
time half an hour late.

The result is that I am, if not always on time, generally a little bit
ahead. Sometimes I have a nightmare in which I set out for the theatre
where I am to perform but one thing and another comes between me
and my objective so that I never reach the theatre. That nightmare
recurs but infrequently.

When I first worked with modern dancers as a composer they
wanted the music to follow the dance because in classical ballet,
against which they were revolting, the dance had followed the music. I
found their likes and dislikes political and so I suggested agreement on
an empty time or rhythmic structure by both choreographer and composer. That suggestion was followed. We were able to work independently and anarchically together; everything always worked to our
satisfaction. This procedure did what tala had done through history for
Indian music, dance, and song, the time arts.

But in recent years, the last twenty-five, we have moved from an
interest in structure to an interest in process, away from the division of
a whole into parts and close to something without beginning, middle,
and end, something like weather. Before this change to process we
began to lose the sense of time as separate from space. We were using
both eyes and ears. Theatre. Space-time.

Now I am using time-brackets in my composition of music. It is like a process that includes structures, that can last any length of time, that can begin and end at any time within the time-bracket. I like the flexibility and, of course, if I am working with others, I like that our relationship is apolitical and anarchic.

Neither space nor time is substantially anything, but everything else in the world needs both of them. You could say space and time are the no things in between the things that are three-dimensional things. This is expressed from many points of view in a book of which my life could be described as an illustration: *Neti Neti* (Not this. Not that.) by L.C. Beckett. Or you could say there is no time exterior to any one of us. Each of us has his own time. Sitting in his class, I remember, out of nothing, Suzuki Daisetz saying "pure subjectivity," then, for a long time, not saying another word. Marshall McLuhan, in his *Understanding Media*, refers to Edward T. Hall's *The Silent Language* in which Hall discusses how

'Time Talks: American Accents,' contrasting our time-sense with that of the Hopi Indians. Time for them is not a uniform succession or duration, but a pluralism of many kinds of things co-existing. 'It is what happens when the corn matures or a sheep grows up. . . . It is the natural process that takes place while living substance acts out its life drama.' Therefore, as many kinds of time exist for them as there are kinds of life. This, also, is the kind of time-sense held by the modern physicist and scientist. They no longer try to contain events in time, but think of each thing as making its own time and its own space. Moreover, now that we live electrically in an instantaneous world, space and time interpenetrate each other totally in a space-time world. In the same way, the painter, since Cézanne, has recovered the plastic image by which all of the senses co-exist in a unified pattern. Each object and each set of objects engenders its own unique space by the relations it has among others visually or musically. When this awareness recurred in the Western world, it was denounced as the merging of all things in a flux. We now realize that this anxiety was a natural literary and visual response to the new nonvisual technology.

This lecture is not a lecture. It continues my search for ways of writing which come from ideas, are not about them, while at the same time inadvertently producing them. It is, in this case, three autokus, "Ku" I take from haiku. In your hands you have the three texts from which my autokus are derived. One is Jasper Johns' last response in an interview with Christian Geelhaar. The second is R. Buckminster

Fuller's "Now Hourglass" from his book *Synergetics 2: Further Explorations in the Geometry of Thinking*. This last [reproduced here] is the first paragraph in a text from my book called *A Year From Monday*, *"Rhythm, Etc."*

> There's virtually nothing to say about rhythm, for there's no time. We've yet to learn the rudiments, the useful means. But there's every reason to believe that this will happen and not over dead bodies. When I see everything that's to the left, I feel just as I do in front of something where there's no center of interest at all. Activity, busyness: — not of the one who made it (his intentions had moved down to next to nothing) — perhaps a speck of dust.
>
> **John Cage**, *A Year From Monday*,
> Wesleyan University Press (1963)

In all three texts, the word "time" appears. My mesostic texts made from them do not make ordinary sense. They make *nonsense*, which is taught as a serious subject in one of the Tokyo universities. An *autoku* uses its entire source as the string down the center of the mesostic, providing, at the same time, all the wing words. If you have questions about mesostics, strings, and wing words, I will respond to them later in detail. For the moment, if you find nonsense intolerable, think of my work as music, which is, Arnold Schoenberg used to say, a question of repetition and variation, variation itself being a form of repetition in which some things are changed and others not.

At the end of my reading I would like to engage twelve volunteers from among you to give a time-bracket performance using the text in mesostic form which [we] will read. It will be, I think, an interesting demonstration of how one can work with time in this day and age, and it will not be difficult for those who do it to do it.

RHYTHM, ETC.

Third Autoku

New York City
March 1988

To say
perHaps a
usEful means
foR
bodiEs when i
intereSt at
not oVer

tIme '
Reason '
The
bUt
At
to Learn the
feeL

just as
activitY
moved dowN
that's tO '
of dusT

wHere
tIme we've
aNd '
There's
say abOut rhythm
Speck

every reAson
rhYthm for ' there's
At
resemBles
his intentiOns had

activity ' bUsyness '
fronT of
oveR
made it His
everY reason '
virTually
Had '
the rudiMents 'the
oF
tO the ' left i feel ' just
eveRy
To '
rigHt
rudimEnts

the useful means but
viRtually nothing
timE we've yet to learn
the uSeful
meaNs
fOr
feel jusT as
belIeve

rhythM for
will happEn and '
moved doWn to '
to lEarn the
that's
actiVity
to thE right resembles
virtuallY nothing to
rEason
righT ' resembles
aT
nOt of
usefuL
to thE
thAt's to
theRe's

at all

activity busyNess
To
rigHt
rudimEnts
Resembles
dUst

moveD down to '
wIll happen and '
rhythM for
not ovEr
iN

had moved down To
uSeful means '
To
it His
timE
aboUt
hiS
lEarn
oF
bUsyness ' not of the

the right resembLes
rhythM for
not ovEr '
About
Not
where ' there'S no
Believe ' that this will
virtUally
The '
To
made it His

rEason
viRtually
yEt to learn
to Say '
yEt to learn the
there's Virtually
buysnEss not of the
Reason '
to saY about
leaRn

down to nExt to
thAt
there'S
nOt
all activity ' busyNess

down to nExt to
thAt
there'S
nOt
all activity ' busyNess
yeT '
fOr
But
happEn '
yet to Learn
thIs
thE '
Virtually
dEad
righT resembles
one wHo
every reAson
virTually
To learn
wHere there's no
I '
rhythm for' there'S
Who

tIme
to beLieve that this
feeL just as '
it His

All '
sPeck of
yEt to
Not over
interest At all activity
No center
as i Do '
froNt
tO next to nothing

resembles everyThing that's
center Of
actiVity

rEason to believe that
foR ' there's   this will
moveD down ' to
it his ' intEntions
All activity
i Do ' in
But
dOwn to next to nothing
perhaps a speck
Down to next to
everythIng

onE who made it
of the
one who made it hiS '
that this Will '
spEck

had moved dowN to next to
feel just as I do

everything that'S to
madE it his
to lEarn '
rudimEnts the useful means
but there's '
there's Virtually nothing
lEft i feel just as i do in
Rudiments
activitY

every reason To believe
intentions Had moved down to
next to
feel just as I do '
No
rudimenTs

it His
A ' speck
To nothing
we've
who made it hiS
no cenTer

the One who
reason To believe
wHo
mEans but there's '
Resembles
vIrtually
wHere
of dusT

about Rhythm for '
lEft
feel ' juSt as i do in front of
yEt

it his intentions had Moved down to next'
dead Bodies   the
rudiments the usefuL
yEt

nothing to Say
that this will happEn
Virtually nothing to
bodiEs when i
Reason to believe that
this will happen
all activitY
To
perHaps a speck of dust

over dead bodIes
of the oNe who made
rudimenTs
wHere there's no center
of interest
meAns
noThing

we've yet to learn
the uSeful means '
The
there's nO
righT resembles
made it His '
in front of somEthing
onE
For
To '
In
oF
thE

to thE right
to Learn
to say aboUt
that thiS will happen and
There's no center of
to leArn

dead bodieS
do In front of
moveD '
yet tO learn the
to belIeve that this will
Not
the leFt
the Rudiments the
Of
there's No
we've yeT
in frOnt
in Front of
everything that'S
Of '
rhythM '
spEck of
jusT as
wHen
belIeve that this
there's No
the riGht
that this Will
everytHing

no timE ' we've yet to
Right
thE
dusT '
one wHo

onE who
fRont
not of thE
meanS but there's
will happeN
mOved down
aCtivity '
lEft
dowN
righT '
onE who made it
Rudiments
mOved down
Front

to belIeve that this will
aNd
of someThing
that this will happEn and not
foR
thE
that'S
no cenTer of
no time
we've yet to leArn

rhyThm
And
Left i
to beLieve
will hAppen and
a speCk
of The
I see
had moVed
wIll
lefT i feel
everY reason
to Believe
there's virtUally
to See
all activitY busyness
aNd not
had movEd
of Something where
there'S every

oNe
tO believe
The rudiments the
whO
For
To next to
it His
busynEss
Of
everythiNg that's to
madE it
doWn to
that's to tHe
fOr there's '
there's no tiMe '
At
of Dust
thE left
bodIes when i see
jusT as i
wHen
I do
that'S to the
It his
there's No
righT
lEft
dowN
To the
this wIll
there's nO

yet to learN the
reaSon
wHere
yet to leArn
of Dust
no tiMe

dead bOdies ' when
actiVity
to thE
Down to
maDe it
bOdies

We've yet to
somethiNg where
buT
Of ' something where
Not of
to lEarn
There's every
nexT
nO time we've yet to
everythiNg
Of
To
wHen

bodIes
Next to
riGht
thE one
in fRont '
wHen
deAd
a sPeck of
there'S no
hAd
there'S
bodiEs when
no Center
tO believe
For there's no
had moveD
virtUally
Speck
i do in fronT

FIVE

PLAYER 1

John Cage

0'00" ⟷ 0'45"   0'30" ⟷ 1'15"

1'00" ⟷ 1'45"   1'30" ⟷ 2'15"

2'15"   2'45"

2'45" ⟷ 3'30"   3'15" ⟷ 4'00"

3'45" ⟷ 4'30"   4'15" ⟷ 5'00"

MARSHALL McLUHAN (1989)

At one of our meetings in the sixties, Marshall McLuhan suggested that I write some music using the ten thunderclaps of *Finnegans Wake*. They were a history, he said, of technology and they were the subject of a book by his son. I received a typescript of the book from Eric McLuhan and fully intended to make *Atlas Borealis* with *The Ten Thunderclaps*. It would have been for orchestra and chorus transformed electronically so that the singing would fill the envelopes of actual thunderclaps, and the playing of the strings those of actual raindrops, falling first on earth, successively on different materials down through history, and finally remaining in the air. Going to the concert would have been like going to a storm. I never started it. At the University of Illinois, where I was invited to work with a computer facility, the composition *HPSCHD* took two years rather than one.

It was through Mildred Constantine of the Museum of Modern Art in New York City (known in Rockland County, where I was living, as Connie Bettleheim) that I first heard of Marshall McLuhan. She was enthusiastic, and after reading *The Agenbite of Outwit*, Location 1:1 (1963) and, more recently *Tyuonyi 1* (1985), so was I ("Money is obsolete...work is obsolete," etc.). In my thoughts about world improvement I put McLuhan together with Buckminster Fuller ("No need for politicians, they may be sent off to the moon."). And for the source material of my current Norton lectures at Harvard I link them. They were often together at conferences in the sixties, once with Margaret Mead in Greece (1964) for a Doxiades Symposium held on a yacht in the Aegean Sea.

I remain stimulated and convinced, full of belief in Fuller and McLuhan. If as world people we ever come to our senses, their separate works will help us initiate intelligent action.

This book alternates articles by McLuhan himself with articles about him by people who knew him. I had been saddened in the late sixties to hear of his illness — described in the article by John Culkin. Matie Molinaro's article, which describes the lingering illness and silence from the time of his stroke in 1977 until his death in 1980, brought tears to my eyes. What a great loss it was for all those who are living that he died. I had lunch with him once in Toronto, and he asked me a question about pattern recognition that I couldn't answer. My mind doesn't work this way. I don't always understand McLuhan, nor do I understand anything else that I actually need and can use. Of my own work, that interests me most which I have not yet made, and I think that was McLuhan's attitude toward his own ideas. In his writings I like the way he leaps from one paragraph to the next without transition. This also happens in the *Journal* of Henry David Thoreau. ("The best form of government is no government at all.") Each one leaves space in his work in which a reader, stimulated, can do his or her own thinking.

SPORTS (1989)

Mesostics on the name Erik Satie, a translation from the French of Satie's Sports et Divertissements.

Preface

thE
fiRst
pIece is for those
who already disliKe me

it'S
A chorale
wiTh
nothIng
to rEcommend it

Swinging

sEe o swing
my heaRt
It is
walKing toward you

it haS tiny feet
when it's in your Arms
iT won't get
dIzzy
if it bothErs you tell it go home

Hunting

listEn
you'll heaR
the rabbIt singing
his voice is remarKable

the nightingale and the owl aren't liStening
they Are too busy
a wild boar plans To marry another boar a lady boar
me I'm using my gun
as a way of gEtting walnuts within reach

229

Commedia dell'Arte

Enlist
in the aRmy
you'll never regret It
you get to Know your way around

civilianS
Are careful
noT to rub you the wrong way
you can have gIrls at the drop of a hat
what a lifE

Waking up the Bride

the bridE got to bed
veRy late
she Is still sleeping
hear her guests trying to waKe her up

they are playing on guitarS
they mAde
ouT of old hats
a dog Is dancing
with his fiancEe

Blind Man's Bluff

you'vE just
bRushed past
hIm not guessing who he is
he is pale and can't speaK
becauSe of his trembling lips

why do you lAugh

he is holding his hearT
In the hands
hE is the one who loves you

Fishing

thE sounds
of wateR
from a rIverbed
fish going to Kindergarten one two two more

what'S going on
it's A fisherman
Thank you
everyone goes away Including
thE fisherman
water sounds from riverbed

Yachting

impossiblE
weatheR
yacht Is dancing
liKe a little fool

wind iS blowing
like A seal
ocean cannoT be controlled
It might
brEak on a rock

a prEtty
passengeR
Is not amused
i don't liKe it at all

anything elSe
would be preferAble
i wanT to leave
thIs
vEry minute   taxi!

Sea Bathing

thE sea
is veRy
wIde

i thinK
it'S less deep but deep enough
don't sit on the bottom though
it's very dAmp here come some really good waves
They're full of water

that one   dId it hit you
it cErtainly did   i'm all wet

Carnival

confEtti's
in the aiR
lIke snow
melancholy masK

now that pierrot iS tipsy he is pretending to be wicked
those mAsked ladies came in so gracefully
people are pushing each oTher around
just to get a good look at them
whIch
onE is the pretty one

Golf

of coursE i'll win
he weaRs
brIght green scotch tweeds
his weighted down caddy is walKing behind

the cloudS stop moving
the holes Are quaking
The colonel tees up
hIs club
bursts into splintErs

The Octopus

thE octopus
is in heR cave
teasIng a crab
maKing it run
thiS
wAy
and That
fInally
shE swallows it

but it goEs down
the wRong way
she Is
sicK
turnS
pAle
and sTeps
not meanIng to
on hEr
own fEet
she takes a glass of salt wateR
hopIng it will settle her stomach
actually the drinK
doeS her
A
greaT deal of good
It
changEs her mental attitude

The Races

thE weighing in
the cRowd
gettIng information
maKing a bet
at the gate   the race beginS   they're off
some horses Always go
The wrong way
here comes the losers   theIr
nosEs are up   their ears are drooping

Kitty in the Corner

micE
one two thRee four   cat   just one
the mIce
provoKe the cat

She gets
reAdy
To pounce
she dId it
now shE's alone undisturbed in her corner

Picnic

cold vEal
no one heRe
Is without it
i liKe
your white dreSs

good heAvens   an airplane
noT at all
that's a storm comIng up
a bad onE

Sleighing

my goodnEss it's cold
pRotect your noses
mIladies
Keep them
in your furS

the sleigh is reAlly whizzing along
The landscape doesn't know what to do
wIth
itsElf

The Roller Coaster

if you havE
    a stRong stomach
  you wIll
not get sicK

  it will Seem
    like fAlling
from a greaT
    heIght
  you'll bE
    amazEd
     it Really
      gIves you a strange feeling
here we go looK out you're turning pale

i don't feel So good
  i'm miserAble
    That just shows
  you are In
    nEed of a little amusement

Perpetual Tango

The devil
  neveR
takes tIme
to thinK

he juSt
  tAngos
insTead
he Is
quitE cool

hE
his daughteRs
  wIfe and servants
  Know

they'll never Stop
  dAncing
    They never do
  It's
  vEry hot

Flirting

thEy talk
in a modeRn way
are you all rIght
do you liKe me

you have Such big eyes
leAve me alone
i would like To be on the moon
he sIghs
hE shakes his head

Fireworks

wE have to wait
until it's daRk
oh! there they are   colored lIghts
a rocKet

one that'S
All blue
everyone admires iT
an old man Is slowly going mad
thEse are the last ones we'll see

Tennis

you want to play yEs   i do
he has a good seRve
and look at hIs legs
don't you thinK they are
handSome
And his nose is handsome too
That serve
made the ball spIn
gamE! set! match!

AN AUTOBIOGRAPHICAL STATEMENT
(1989)

I once asked Arragon, the historian, how history was written. He said, "You have to invent it." When I wish as now to tell of critical incidents, persons, and events that have influenced my life and work, the true answer is all of the incidents were critical, all of the people influenced me, everything that happened and that is still happening influences me.

My father was an inventor. He was able to find solutions for problems of various kinds, in the fields of electrical engineering, medicine, submarine travel, seeing through fog, and travel in space without the use of fuel. He told me that if someone says "can't" that shows you what to do. He also told me that my mother was always right even when she was wrong.

My mother had a sense of society. She was the founder of the Lincoln Study Club, first in Detroit, then in Los Angeles. She became the Women's Club editor for the Los Angeles Times. She was never happy. When after Dad's death I said, "Why don't you visit the family in Los Angeles? You'll have a good time," she replied, "Now, John, you know perfectly well I've never enjoyed having a good time." When we would go for a Sunday drive, she'd always regret that we hadn't brought so-and-so with us. Sometimes she would leave the house and say she was never coming back. Dad was patient, and always calmed my alarm by saying, "Don't worry, she'll be back in a little while."

Neither of my parents went to college. When I did, I dropped out after two years. Thinking I was going to be a writer, I told Mother and Dad I should travel to Europe and have experiences rather than continue in school. I was shocked at college to see one hundred of my classmates in the library all reading copies of the same book. Instead of doing as they did, I went into the stacks and read the first book written by an author whose name began with Z. I received the highest grade in the class. That convinced me that the institution was not being run correctly. I left.

In Europe after being kicked in the seat of my pants by José Pijoan for my study of flamboyant Gothic architecture and introduced by him to a modern architect who set me to work drawing Greek capitals,

Doric, Ionic, and Corinthian, I became interested in modern music and modern painting. One day I overheard the architect saying to some girl friends, "In order to be an architect, one must devote one's life to architecture." I then went to him and said I was leaving because I was interested in other things than architecture. At this time I was reading *Leaves of Grass* of Walt Whitman. Enthusiastic about America I wrote to Mother and Dad saying, "I am coming home." Mother wrote back, "Don't be a fool. Stay in Europe as long as possible. Soak up as much beauty as you can. You'll probably never get there again." I left Paris and began both painting and writing music, first in Mallorca. The music I wrote was composed in some mathematical way I no longer recall. It didn't seem like music to me so that when I left Mallorca I left it behind to lighten the weight of my baggage. In Sevilla on a street corner I noticed the multiplicity of simultaneous visual and audible events all going together in one's experience and producing enjoyment. It was the beginning for me of theatre and circus.

Later when I returned to California, in the Pacific Palisades, I wrote songs with texts by Gertrude Stein and choruses from *The Persians* of Aeschylus. I had studied Greek in high school. These compositions were improvised at the piano. The Stein songs are, so to speak, transcriptions from a repetitive language to a repetitive music. I met Richard Buhlig who was the first pianist to play the *Opus 11* of Schoenberg. Though he was not a teacher of composition, he agreed to take charge of my writing of music. From him I went to Henry Cowell and at Cowell's suggestion (based on my twenty-five tone compositions, which, though not serial, were chromatic and required the expression in a single voice of all twenty-five tones before any one of them was repeated) to Adolph Weiss in preparation for studies with Arnold Schoenberg. When I asked Schoenberg to teach me, he said, "You probably can't afford my price." I said, "Don't mention it; I don't have any money." He said, "Will you devote your life to music?" This time I said "Yes." He said he would teach me free of charge. I gave up painting and concentrated on music. After two years it became clear to both of us that I had no feeling for harmony. For Schoenberg harmony was not just coloristic: it was structural. It was the means one used to distinguish one part of a composition from another. Therefore he said I'd never be able to write music. "Why not?" "You'll come to a wall and won't be able to get through." "Then I'll spend my life knocking my head against that wall."

I became an assistant to Oskar Fischinger, the film maker, to prepare myself to write the music for one of his films. He happened to say one day, "Everything in the world has its own spirit which can be released by setting it into vibration." I began hitting, rubbing everything, listening, and then writing percussion music, and playing it with friends. These compositions were made up of short motives expressed either as sound or as silence of the same length, motives that were arranged on the perimeter of a circle on which one could proceed forward or backward. I wrote without specifying the instruments, using our rehearsals to try out found or rented instruments. I didn't rent many because I had little money. I did library research work for my father or for lawyers. I was married to Xenia Andreyevna Kashevaroff who was studying bookbinding with Hazel Dreis. Since we all lived in a big house my percussion music was played in the evening by the bookbinders. I invited Schoenberg to one of our performances. "I am not free." "Can you come a week later?" "No, I am not free at any time."

I found dancers, modern dancers, however, who were interested in my music and could put it to use. I was given a job at the Cornish School in Seattle. It was there that I discovered what I called micromacrocosmic rhythmic structure. The large parts of a composition had the same proportion as the phrases of a single unit. Thus an entire piece had that number of measures that had a square root. This rhythmic structure could be expressed with any sounds, including noises, or it could be expressed not as sound and silence but as stillness and movement in dance. It was my response to Schoenberg's structural harmony. It was also at the Cornish School that I became aware of Zen Buddhism, which later, as part of oriental philosophy, took the place for me of psychoanalysis. I was disturbed both in my private life and in my public life as a composer. I could not accept the academic idea that the purpose of music was communication, because I noticed that when I conscientiously wrote something sad, people and critics were often apt to laugh. I determined to give up composition unless I could find a better reason for doing it than communication. I found this answer from Gita Sarabhai, an Indian singer and tabla player: The purpose of music is to sober and quiet the mind, thus making it susceptible to divine influences. I also found in the writings of Ananda K. Coomaraswamy that the responsibility of the artist is to imitate nature in her manner of operation. I became less disturbed and went back to work.

Before I left the Cornish School I made the prepared piano. I needed percussion instruments for music for a dance that had an African character by Syvilla Fort. But the theatre in which she was to dance had no wings and there was no pit. There was only a small grand piano built in to the front and left of the audience. At the time I either wrote twelve-tone music for piano or I wrote percussion music. There was no room for the instruments. I couldn't find an African twelve-tone row. I finally realized I had to change the piano. I did so by placing objects between the strings. The piano was transformed into a percussion orchestra having the loudness, say, of a harpsichord.

It was also at the Cornish School, in a radio station there, that I made compositions using acoustic sounds mixed with amplified small sounds and recordings of sine waves. I began a series, *Imaginary Landscapes*.

I spent two years trying to establish a Center for Experimental Music, in a college or university or with corporate sponsorship. Though I found interest in my work I found no one willing to support it financially.

I joined the faculty of Moholy-Nagy's School of design in Chicago. While there I was commissioned to write sound effects music for a CBS Columbia Workshop Play. I was told by the sound effects engineer that anything I could imagine was possible. What I wrote, however, was impractical and too expensive; the work had to be rewritten for percussion orchestra, copied, and rehearsed in the few remaining days and nights before its broadcast. That was *The City Wears a Slouch Hat* by Kenneth Patchen. The response was enthusiastic in the West and Middle West. Xenia and I came to New York, but the response in the East had been less than enthusiastic. We had met Max Ernst in Chicago. We were staying with him and Peggy Guggenheim. We were penniless. No job was given to me for my composing of radio sound effects, which I had proposed. I began writing again for modern dancers and doing library research work for my father who was then with Mother in New Jersey. About this time I met my first virtuosi: Robert Fizdale and Arthur Gold. I wrote two large works for two prepared pianos. The criticism by Virgil Thomson was very favorable, both for their performance and for my composition. But there were only fifty people in the audience. I lost a great deal of money that I didn't have. I was obliged to beg for it, by letter and personally. I continued each year, however, to organize and present one or two programs of chamber music and one or two programs of Merce Cunningham's choreography and dancing. And to make tours with him throughout the United States. And later with David Tudor, the pianist, to Europe. Tudor is now a composer and performer of electronic music. For many years he and I were the two musicians for Merce Cunningham. And then for many more we had the help of David Behrman, Gordon Mumma, or Takehisa Kosugi. I have in recent years, in order to carry out other projects (an opera in Frankfurt and the Norton Lectures at Harvard University), left the Cunningham Company. Its musicians now are Tudor, Kosugi, and Michael Pugliese, the percussionist.

Just recently I received a request for a text on the relation between Zen Buddhism and my work. Rather than rewriting it now, I am inserting it here in this story. I call it *From Where'm'Now*. It repeats some of what is above and some of what is below.

When I was young and still writing an unstructured music, albeit methodical and not improvised, one of my teachers, Adolph Weiss, used to complain that no sooner had I started a piece than I brought it to an end. I introduced silence. I was a ground, so to speak, in which emptiness could grow.

At college I had given up high school thoughts about devoting my life to religion. But after dropping out and traveling to Europe I became interested in modern music and painting, listening-looking and making, finally devoting myself to writing music, which, twenty years later, becoming graphic, returned me now and then for visits to painting (prints, drawings, watercolors, the costumes and decors for *Europeras 1 & 2*).

In the late thirties I heard a lecture by Nancy Wilson Ross on Dada and Zen. I mention this in my foreword to *Silence* then adding that I did not want my work blamed on Zen, though I felt that Zen changes in different times and places and what it has become here and now, I am not certain. Whatever it is gives me delight and most recently by means of Stephen Addiss' book *The Art of Zen*. I had the good fortune to attend Daisetz Suzuki's classes in the late forties. And I visited him twice in Japan. I have never practiced sitting cross-legged nor do I meditate. My work is what I do and always involves writing materials, chairs, and tables. Before I get to it, I do some exercises for my back and I water the plants, of which I have around 200.

In the late forties I found out by experiment (I went into the anechoic chamber at Harvard University) that silence is not acoustic. It is a change of mind, a turning around. I devoted my music to it. My work became an exploration of non-intention. To carry it out faithfully, I have developed a complicated composing means using *I Ching* chance operations, making my responsibility that of asking questions instead of making choices.

The Buddhist texts to which I often return are the *Huang-Po Doctrine of Universal Mind* (in Chu Ch'an's first translation, published by the London Buddhist Society in 1947), *Neti Neti* by L.C. Beckett of which (as I say in the introduction to my Norton Lectures at Harvard) my life could be described as an illustration, and the *Ten Oxherding Pictures* (in the version that ends with the return to the village bearing gifts of a smiling and somewhat heavy monk, one who had experienced Nothingness). Apart from Buddhism and earlier I had read the *Gospel of Sri Ramakrishna*. It was Ramakrishna who said all religions are the same, like a lake to which people are thirsty come from different directions, calling its water by different names. Furthermore this water has many different tastes. The taste of Zen for me comes from the admixture of humor, intransigence, and detachment. It makes me think of Marcel Duchamp, though for him we would have to add the erotic.

As part of the source material for my Norton lectures at Harvard I thought of Buddhist texts. I remembered hearing of an Indian philosopher who was very uncompromising. I asked Dick Higgins, "Who is the Malevich of Buddhist philosophy?" He laughed. Reading *Emptiness—a Study in Religious Meaning* by Frederick J. Streng, I found out. He is Nagarjuna.

But since I finished writing the lectures before I found out, I included, instead of Nagarjuna, Ludwig Wittgenstein, the corpus, subjected to chance operations. And there is another good book, *Wittgenstein and Buddhism*, by Chris Gudmunsen, which I shall be reading off and on into the future.

My reading now makes use of time-brackets, sometimes flexible, sometimes not. There are no scores, no fixed relation of parts. Sometimes the parts are fully written out, sometimes not. The title of my Norton lectures is a reference to a brought-up-to-date version of *Composition in Retrospect*:

MethodStructureDisciplineNotationIndeterminacy
InterpentrationImitationDevotionCircumstancesVariableStructure
NonunderstandingContingencyInconsistencyPerformance (I-VI).

When it is published, for commercial convenience, it will just be called *I-VI*.

I found in the largely German community at Black Mountain College a lack of experience of the music of Erik Satie. Therefore, teaching there one summer and having no pupils, I arranged a festival of Satie's music, half-hour after-dinner concerts with introductory remarks. And in the center of the festival I placed a lecture that opposed Satie and Beethoven and found that Satie, not Beethoven, was right. Buckminster Fuller was the Baron Méduse in a performance of Satie's *Le Piége de Méduse*. That summer Fuller put up his first dome, which immediately collapsed. He was delighted. "I only learn what to do when I have failures." His remark made me think of Dad. That is what Dad would have said.

It was at Black Mountain College that I made what is sometimes said to be the first happening. The audience was seated in four isometric triangular sections, the apexes of which touched a small square performance area that they faced and that led through the aisles between them to the large performance area that surrounded them. Disparate activities, dancing by Merce Cunningham, the exhibition of paintings and the playing of a Victrola by Robert Rauschenberg, the reading of his poetry by Charles Olsen or hers by M.C. Richards from the top of a ladder outside the audience, the piano playing of David Tudor, my own reading of a lecture that included silences from the top of another ladder outside the audience, all took place within chance-determined periods of time within the over-all time of my lecture. It was later that summer that I was delighted to find in America's first synagogue in Newport, Rhode Island that the congregation was seated in the same way, facing itself.

From Rhode Island I went on to Cambridge and in the anechoic chamber at Harvard University heard that silence was not the absence of sound but was the unintended operation of my nervous system and the circulation of my blood. It was this experience and the white paintings of Rauschenberg that led me to compose *4'33"*, which I had described in a lecture at Vassar College some years before when I was in the flush of my studies with Suzuki (*A Composer's Confessions*, 1948), my silent piece.

In the early fifties with David Tudor and Louis and Bebe Barron I made several works on magnetic tape, works by Christian Wolff, Morton Feldman, Earle Brown, and myself. Just as my notion of rhythmic structure followed Schoenberg's structural harmony, and my silent piece followed Robert Rauschenberg's white paintings, so my *Music of Changes*, composed by means of *I Ching* chance operations, followed Morton Feldman's graph music, music written with numbers for any pitches, the pitches notated only as high, middle, or low. Not immediately, but a few years later, I was to move from structure to process, from music as an object having parts, to music without beginning, middle, or end; music as weather. In our collaborations Merce Cunningham's choreographies are not supported by my musical accompaniments. Music and dance are independent but coexistent.

It was in the fifties that I left the city and went to the country. There I found Guy Nearing, who guided me in my study of mushrooms and other wild edible plants. With three other friends we founded the New York Mycological Society. Nearing helped us also with the lichen about which he had written and printed a book. When the weather was dry and the mushrooms weren't growing we spent our time with the lichen.

In the sixties the publication of both my music and my writings began. Whatever I do in the society is made available for use. An experience I had in Hawaii turned my attention to the work of Buckminster Fuller and the work of Marshall McLuhan. Above the tunnel that connects the southern part of Oahu with the northern there are crenelations at the top of the mountain range as on a medieval castle. When I asked about them, I was told they had been used for self-protection while shooting poisoned arrows on the enemy below. Now both sides share the same utilities. Little more than a hundred years ago the island was a battlefield divided by a mountain range. Fuller's world map shows that we live on a single island. Global village (McLuhan). Spaceship Earth (Fuller). Make an equation between human needs and world resources (Fuller). I began my *Diary: How to Improve the World: You Will Only Make Matters Worse.* Mother said, "How dare you!"

I don't know when it began. But at Edwin Denby's loft on 21st Street, not at the time but about the place, I wrote my first mesostic. It was a regular paragraph with the letters of his name capitalized. Since then I have written them as poems, the capitals going down the middle, to celebrate whatever, to support whatever, to fulfill requests, to initiate my thinking or my nonthinking (*Themes and Variations* is the first of a series of mesostic works: to find a way of writing that, though coming from ideas, is not about them but produces them). I have found a variety of ways of writing mesostics: Writings through a source. Rengas (a mix of a plurality of source mesostics), "globally," letting the words come from here and there through chance operations in a source text.

I was invited by Irwin Hollander to make lithographs. Actually it was an idea Alice Weston had (Duchamp had died). I had been asked to say something about him. Jasper Johns was also asked to do this. He said, "I don't want to say anything about Marcel." I made *Not Wanting to Say Anything about Marcel*: eight plexigrams and two lithographs. Whether this brought about the invitation or not, I do not know. I was invited by Kathan Brown to the Crown Point Press, then in Oakland, California, to make etchings. I accepted the invitation because years before I had not accepted one from Gita Sarabhai to walk with her in the Himalayas. I had something else to do. When I was free, she was not. The walk never took place. I have always regretted this. It was to have been on elephants. It would have been unforgettable. . . .

Every year since then I have worked once or twice at the Crown Point Press. Etchings. Once Kathan Brown said, "You wouldn't just sit down and draw." Now I do: drawings around stones, stones placed on a grid at chance determined points. These drawings have also made musical notation: *Renga*, *Score and Twenty-three Parts*, and *Ryoanji* (but drawing from left to right, halfway around a stone). Ray Kass, an artist who teaches watercolor at Virginia Polytechnic Institute and State University, became interested in my graphic work with chance operations. With this aid and that of students he enlisted, I have made fifty-two watercolors. And those have led me to aquatints, brushes, acids, and their combination with fire, smoke, and stones with etchings.

These experiences led me in one instance to compose music in the way I had found to make a series of prints called *On the Surface*. I discovered that a horizontal line that determined graphic changes, to correspond, had to become a vertical line in the notation of music (*Thirty Pieces for Five Orchestras*). Time instead of space.

Invited by Heinz-Klaus Metzger and Rainer Riehn, with the assistance of Andrew Culver, I made *Europeras 1 & 2* for the Frankfurt Opera. This carries the independence but coexistence of music and dance with which Cunningham and I were familiar, to all the elements of theatre, including the lighting, program booklets, decors, properties, costumes, and stage action.

Eleven or twelve years ago I began the *Freeman Etudes* for violin solo. As with the *Etudes Australes* for piano solo, I wanted to make the music as difficult as possible so that a performance would show that the impossible is not impossible and to write 32 of them. The notes written so far for the Etudes 17-32 show, however, that there are too many notes to play. I have for years thought they would have to be synthesized, which I did not want to do. Therefore the work remains unfinished. Early last summer ('88) Irvine Arditti played the first 15 in fifty-six minutes. I asked why he played so fast. He said, "That's what you say in the preface: Play as fast as possible." As a result I now know how to finish the *Freeman Etudes*, a work that I hope to accomplish this year or next. Where there are too many notes I will write the direction, "Play as many as possible."

Thinking of orchestra not just as musicians but as people, I have made different relations of people to people in different pieces. *Etcetera* begins with the orchestra as soloists, letting them volunteer their services from time to time to any one of three conductors. *Etcetera 2/4 Orchestras* begins with four conductors, letting orchestra members from time to time leave the group and play as soloists. In *Atlas Eclipticalis* and *Concert for Piano and Orchestra* the conductor is not a governing agent but a utility, providing the time. In *Quartets* no more than four musicians play at a time, which four constantly changing. Each musician is a soloist. To bring to orchestral society the devotion to music that characterizes chamber music. To build a society one by one. To bring chamber music to the size of orchestra. *Music For* _____: So far I have written eighteen parts, any of which can be played together or omitted. Flexible time-brackets. Variable structure. A music so to speak that's earthquake-proof. Another series without an underlying idea is the group that began with *Two*, continued with *One, Five, Seven, Twenty-three, 101, Four, Two²*, *One², Three, Fourteen*, and *Seven²*. For each of these works I look for something I haven't yet found. My favorite music is the music I haven't yet heard. I don't hear the music I write. I write in order to hear the music I haven't yet heard.

We are living in a period in which many people have changed their minds about what the use of music is or could be for them. Something that doesn't speak or talk like a human being, that doesn't know its definition in the dictionary or its theory in the schools, that expresses itself simply by the fact of its vibrations. People paying attention to vibratory activity, not in relation to a fixed ideal performance, but each time attentively to how it happens to be this time, not necessarily two times the same. A music that transports the listener to the moment where he is.

Just the other day I received a request from Enzo Peruccio, a music editor in Torino. This is how I replied:

I have been asked to write a preface for this book, which is written in a language that I do not use for reading. This preface is therefore not to the book but to the subject of the book, percussion.

Percussion is completely open. It is not even open-ended. It has no end. It is not like the strings, the winds, the brass (I am thinking of the other sections of the orchestra), though when they fly the coop of harmony it can teach them a thing or two. If you are not hearing music, percussion is exemplified by the very next sound you actually hear wherever you are, in or out of doors or city. Planet?

Take any part of this book and go to the end of it. You will find yourself thinking of the next step to be taken in that direction. Perhaps you will need new material, new technologies. You have them. You are in the world of X, chaos, the new science.

The strings, the winds, the brass know more about music than they do about sound. To study noise they must go to the school of percussion. There they will discover silence, a way to change one's mind; and aspects of time that have not yet been put into practice. European musical history began the study (the isorhythmic motet), but it was put aside by the theory of harmony. Harmony through a percussion-composer, Edgard Varèse, is being brought to a new open-ended life by James Tenney. I called him last December after hearing his new work in Miami and said "If this is harmony, I take back everything I've ever said; I'm all for it." The spirit of percussion opens everything, even what was, so to speak, completely closed.

I could go on (two percussion instruments of the same kind are no more alike than two people who happen to have the same name) but I do not want to waste the reader's time. Open this book and all the doors wherever you find them. There is no end to life. And this book proves that music is part of it.

EUROPERAS 3 & 4 (1990)

To make a theatre which is the synergetic result of the coming together of its separate elements (the lighting, the singing, the piano-, the record-playing, the brief intrusions of the composite tape of more than a hundred operas superimposed (*Truckera*), brief flashes of light, the movement of the singers from one spot to another in the performance space or to one of the chairs at the back of the stage): seventy-five lights, 2,999 cues; six singers each singing six arias (Gluck-Puccini) of his or her own choice; 140 1–16 measure excerpts from Liszt's *Opern Phantasien*, two pianists; fragments of 300 78's played on twelve electric victrolas by six composers; the performance of *Truckera*; the performance of the lighting; 70 minutes, *Europera 3*.

Two singers, in the performance space or in the distance; 32 lights, 300 cues; complete *Phantasien* played so as to be suggested rather than heard, only one pianist; finally, the piano actually played, actually touched, *rubato*; a single victrola, one composer winding it up, carefully playing it; the performance of *Truckera* in another part of the building; no lights on the stage, light on the walls, light on the ceiling, perhaps; 30 minutes, *Europera 4*.　　　　　　　　　　**John Cage**

Lighting is conventionally the most constrained element of the theatre, restricted to an illuminating function. But a modern computer-controlled lighting rig can be taken as a rich compositional resource. In *Europeras 3 & 4*, even with a moderate number of lights, we have generated more than 6,000 changes of light grouped into 3,299 cues. A computer program was designed around parameter ranges and lists, and made requests to an internal *I Ching* chance operations module in order to determine all light intensities, positions, focuses and colors. In *Europera 3*, changes are rapid and focuses are primarily on the stage. In *Europera 4*, changes transpire more slowly and focuses are only on walls and ceiling. Light, both as a graphic and time-based element, enters as itself into the theatrical play.

Europeras 3 & 4 are concert operas. Staging plays a minor role. However, the chance-determined positions and rotations of tables and pianos, and the movements of singers between arias to new chance-determined positions on the grid, introduce direction and distance as acoustical elements.　　　　　　　　　　**Andrew Culver**
(Cage's collaborator, *Europeras*)

MIRAKUS: *MIRAGE VERBAL* (1990)

For Marcel Duchamp

These texts are derived from *Marcel Duchamp, Notes* (1983) by Alexina S. Duchamp and Paul Matisse with their kind permission. The same *I Ching*-determined collection of notes was used as for *Mirage Verbal*. These texts, however, are not a "writing through." They use MESOLIST (a computer program made at my request by Jim Rosenberg after consultation with Andrew Culver which lists all the words that satisfy the Mink rule for a pure 100% mesostic) in conjunction with *I* (a program by Culver which simulates the *I Ching* coin oracle). They are called *Mirakus* in reference to the first note obtained — "mirage verbal" — and haikus (unlike *Mirage Verbal*, they are short texts).

dynaMo
des aImants
entRe
lA

les joiGnant

suspEndu
pour Voir
instrumEnts à
tamis nombReuses et
calculaBles

mAtières
Looping the

on frappe bien propreMent sur
la saIson
                 tacks
à l'état de vapeuR

siphon Aux demi siphons
du Gaz

Etat
aVoir la
lE
paR
une ventilation B

gAuche
seuLs

poids
        forMe
de densIté

                de
        gRé
du gAz

        reGards

        rEady
            Voir plan
        attEntion
                    il y a
            tRois

    instaBle
                le jongleur revient
le lire des yeux ou A
        enLever

        dynaMo

        suffIsant en
        pRincipe
    l'échAppement
        leGaz

        dE
            Vous
        dE
        4
                    dimension
    d'omBre
        A
        expLosion

    instruMent
vascularIsée
        foRce
        pAr
        Grammar
                my
        piEd

            Voulant
        sEctions
        infRa mince voulant

    chamBre
        A
        Laisse

uniforMe
au ralent I

émanente sphèRe
lA couleur

explosion du Gaz
lE

aVant
la rEvolution
cRache la guèpe 18

chaque
Bien
est une trAduction
d'orgueiL

par ex.
aperçoIt

ayant leuR
section

chAque cercle
reGards
tablEau
suiVant

sont En
impRession
moBile
chAude
conventionneL

3ᵉ
droIte

paR des éléments
nécessAire et
reGards

sEra

d'aVant
toutE la nuit
paR ses
oBjets

pAsser
entre Les

fuMée de tabac la poussée
des cheveaux   pIèces
à bRûle
quoi
conséquences de l'Anthropocentrisme
du Gaz
couchE

Vision
liquidE
gRavité

d'équiliBre
chercher une Autre
le jongLeur

petite Méchanceté
la partIe
à nu en foRme de
2ᵉ plAn

filtre
reGards
tous
possiblE
j'aVais
c'Est à
d'instRuments à éclipse totale
même choses que les oBjets
conciliAtion
fou rires de La saison

oeuvre d'art
poëMe
Instant
de 2 ceRcles
les filAments ou
siGnification
dE
du pochoir Voir
misE à nu dans le dynamo
d'amouR
va et vient
elle va
un poids tomBe
expérience primAire de 2
descente de béLier est une

LETTER TO ZURICH (1991)

On June 20, 1991, Cage wrote a special note to the orchestra members of the Opernhaus Zurich, Switzerland.

Here is a story I was told years ago by an aging anarchist. He lived in New Jersey and had acquired a new house with new beds in it. While on a visit to Michigan he adopted two black children whom he brought back to New Jersey to live with him. The children were so happy in the new house that they jumped up and down on the beds. The old anarchist told me what trouble it had been for him to make a rule: No jumping up and down on the beds!

We all know that many of you are not playing the notes that appear in your parts. Instead, you are playing operatic melodies you remember, and, some of you, particularly the woodwinds, in parallel thirds, and a few others, particularly the brass, now and then, in conventional harmonies.

The melodic freedoms you have taken I gave to the singers who, as you know, sing arias of their own choice. The same freedoms were not given to you. Your parts are made up of excerpts from actual instrumental parts in the literature. We learn from these that many composers in the past used remarkably few notes, except for their melodies, just one or two and, exceptionally, three. That is, perhaps, not exciting news, but it gives to my work a certain space and lightness, which your licenses turn into thickness and heaviness. I am particularly unhappy when a well-known melody is played by many of you at nearly the same time: it's as though one of you had caught cold and were infecting the others. In *Europera 2* there are two sections where general inactivity gives a refreshing emptiness. You fill this up so that there is no rest of any kind. During the second of these sections some of you on June 15 began engaging in faulty tone production, suggesting your disgust with the work as a whole.

My work has been misrepresented, largely, I am sorry to say, by you musicians.

My work is characterized by nonintention and to bring this about, *I Ching* chance operations are employed in its composition in a very detailed way. On the other hand what many of you are playing is characterized by your intentions. We are on opposite sides of the future both musically and socially.

The future is either with the governments, their wars and their laws; or it is with the world as global village, spaceship earth as one society including the rich and the poor, without nations, everyone having what he needs for living. The future is either with the continuing pollution of the environment, or with giving the earth air we can breathe, water we can drink, and soil in which food can be grown.

The music of the future is not one with which we are familiar. It does not mean anything in particular. It is just evidence of "the ineluctable modality of the audible" to quote James Joyce in his *Ulysses*. Just vibratory activity needing no support to give us pleasure.

You may respond by saying you were not thinking about such things. You were just having fun. Or, in changing my work as you have you may have thought that you were improving it, making it more entertaining. In any case you did what you did, you may say, because of your "human nature." But human nature is not as bad as we are often told. People can actually change their minds. If we do change our minds, life on earth for all of us may become a success rather than, as now, like *Europeras 1 & 2*, a failure.

MACROBIOTIC COOKING (1991)

Since the early 1960s, when a strict macrobiotic diet cured Cage's debilitating arthritis, the composer became a devotee of macrobiotics. Here he compiles his favorite recipes, culled from trial and error in his kitchen.

The macrobiotic diet has a great deal to do with yin and yang and finding a balance between them. I have not studied this carefully. All I do is try to observe whether something suits me or not. Michio Kushi told me I should eat more root vegetables and less leafy ones, though he recommended watercress and parsley. The basis of the diet is the combination of brown rice and beans. This makes a protein and the rice is very balanced. I've become very fond of it. Nuts and seeds are good, and vegetables may be eaten. They are good when their sugars are slightly caramelized (slightly burned); this is a matter of taste rather than diet. Some vegetables should be avoided: potatoes, tomatoes, eggplant and peppers particularly for those who have arthritis. Turnips, carrots, celeriac, the large white Japanese radishes (daikon); all these are good. Winter squashes are excellent. When possible eat not only the root but the leaves too of vegetables (including the carrot leaves). In this direction (away from beans or rice towards the right or sugar) avoid sugar. Eat as little fruit as you fail to resist. Or become very choosy; insist on the best wild strawberries, raspberries and melons. Honey is sugar; don't use it. Alcohol also is sugar. Liquids should be reduced during a day (including water, tea, etc.) to two quarts.

Recently in Germany I met a doctor, Renata Kelleter who recommended more water, bananas, and apricots. I follow her advice. In the other direction towards meat, you can eat a little chicken or fish, avoid shellfish, and eat eggs not often, though they are permitted. Avoid red meat and all diary products. The idea is to make a shift from the animal fats to the vegetable oils, and to reduce the liquids. Instead of brown rice you can have cous-cous, kasha, boulghour (cracked wheat), quinoa. As far as quantities go, you should eat mostly grain, then beans, then vegetables, and least chicken or fish. Fresh salads are not good because they are too liquid. However, I eat tabouli which is not cooked. One very good way to prepare dandelion is to chop it up and saute it in a little oil; then add tamari (health food soy sauce). I use Braggs Amino Acids instead of tamari (less salt).

TABOULI (wheat salad)

2 C fine cracked wheat
1 C ice cold water
C minced fresh parsley
1 C finely chopped scallions
3 T minced fresh mint
¾ C lemon juice
1 C olive oil (health food store variety), or, better, Canola
1 t salt
½ t black pepper (or more) (black pepper is OK)

Combine wheat and water and refrigerate for 1 hour or longer. Add remaining ingredients. Refrigerate. Garnish with whatever (radishes, pitted olives, avocado).

This can be made with mustard greens. In that case omit the parsley, mint, and scallions. Or keep the scallions. I now use very little more than lemon juice; I measure the juice first and then combine it with just slightly more oil.

BROWN RICE

Twice as much water as rice. If you wish, substitute a very little wild rice for some of the brown rice. Wash or soak overnight then drain. Add a small amount of hijiki (seaweed) and some Braggs. Very often I add a small amount of wild rice. Bring to good boil. Cover with cloth and heavy lid and cook for twenty minutes over medium flame; reduce flame to very low and cook thirty minutes more. Uncover. If it is not sticking, cook it some more. If it is sticking to the bottom of the pan, stir it a little and then cover again and let it rest with the fire off. When you look at it again after ten minutes or so it will have loosened itself from the bottom of the pan.

Another way to cook rice: Using the same proportion of rice, bring to a boil and then simply cover with lid without the cloth, reducing the fire to low. After forty-five minutes, remove from fire but leave lid on for at least twenty minutes.

FRIED RICE

Saute scallions in a little sesame oil. Add sliced celery, sesame seeds if desired, and mushrooms, with tamari or Braggs at the end. A fair amount of tamari. Perhaps a little lemon juice. Or use leeks instead of scallions. Or chopped dandelions or chopped carrot tops or a mixture.

Another way (without oil): Add to cooked rice some lemon or orange juice, pine nuts or chopped pecans or walnuts, and some chopped parsley, Italian or Chinese (coriander).

WALNUT CHICKEN

Marinate chicken breasts cut into 1-inch cubes in 3 T tamari, 1 T sherry, ½ t ground ginger or ½-inch piece of ginger overnight. Heat 3 T sesame oil (total = ¼ C) over high flame and stir fry 2 sliced scallions, garlic clove cut in two pieces and 1 C of coarsely chopped walnuts. After three or four minutes remove garlic and transfer scallions and walnuts to a bowl. Add remaining oil and chicken pieces and marinade. Stir fry about five minutes, until chicken is tender and coated with soy mixture. Combine with walnuts and onions. Serve with rice.

ROAST CHICKEN

Get a good chicken not spoiled by agribusiness. Place in Rohmertopf (clay baking dish with cover) with giblets. Put a smashed clove of garlic and a slice of fresh ginger between legs and wings and breasts. Squeeze the juice of two or three lemons over the bird. Then an equal amount of tamari. Cover, place in cold oven turned up to 425°. Leave for 1 hr. Then uncover for 15 minutes, heat on, to brown.

Now I cook at 350°, 30' to the pound.

Or use hot mustard and cumin seeds instead of ginger. Keep lemon, tamari or Braggs and garlic. Instead of squeezing the lemon, it may be quartered then chopped fine in a Cuisinart with the garlic and ginger (or garlic, cumin and mustard). Add tamari. The chicken and sauce can be placed on a bed of carrots (or sliced ¾-inch thick bitter melon—obtainable in Chinatown).

GRUEL BREAD
(These ideas come from the Tassajara Book)

Go through refrigerator, collecting food you no longer wish to eat: rice, beans, cooked vegetables or raw (parsley that's turned yellow, etc.). Include any liquids you may have saved (such as water from parboiling string beans). Put through Cuisinart and measure. Add more than an equal amount of whole wheat flour. Do not work with more than 5-7 cups of gruel at the same time. Mix and then knead (adding dry dill weed if wished) for about 45 minutes or an hour until it is consistent ("all of a piece"). Then put in oiled bread pans. I use corn oil. After putting it in, take it out and put it back in upside down. (This oils the entire loaf.) Take a wide knife and make a deep indentation down the middle of the loaf. Cover with damp cloth and leave in warm place overnight. In the morning bake at 375° for one hour and 15-20 minutes.

NUT BREAD

Follow the recipe above, but use very few leftovers (rice and string bean water are fine). Add roasted unsalted nuts (walnuts, filberts, Brazil nuts, almonds, cashews, etc.). The nuts should be cut, but not very finely.

These breads are good with peanut butter (make your own in a Cuisinart). Or smoked salmon (the Gruel Bread only). Or a slice of avocado. Or alone.

TIBETAN BARLEY BREAD

2 C barley flour
4 C whole wheat flour
½ C sesame seeds (roasted)
1-½ t salt
2 T sesame oil
2 T corn oil
3-½ C boiling water
(spring water)

Mix flours together with salt. Add oil rubbing flour between hands until oily. Add boiling water, using spoon to mix until dough begins to form, then mixing with hands; knead until smooth (long time). Place in oiled pan. Cut top lengthwise. Proof (cover with damp cloth and put in warm place 2-6 hours or overnight). Bake at 450° for 20 minutes on middle shelf, then 400° for 40 minutes on top shelf.

GRANOLA

6 C rolled oats
1 C wheat germ
½ C sesame seeds
1 C wheat flakes
1 C barley, rye, or soy flakes
¾ C sunflower seeds
Pinch of salt (this is not necessary)

Mix together and add:

3/16 C of oil (sesame and olive and corn)
13/16 C water
Fill the cup of liquids to the brim with vanilla extract

Mix with hands. Bake at 325° ½ hour, stirring at 15 minutes and at end. Leave in hot oven. Wait 3-4 hours or even 6. Repeat ½-hour baking process again leaving in hot oven.

MISO SOUP

About three heaping tablespoons of miso paste. There are as many kinds of these as there are wines or cheeses. A few turnips, carrots, and scallions. Any other vegetables. A bunch of cress. In a little sesame oil, saute the cut-up scallion, then the carrots and turnips, not long. Then add 4 C of good water. When that comes to a boil, reduce the fire to low after removing a cup of water to put the miso paste in. Cover and don't simmer for longer than say 10 minutes. Meanwhile, you've soaked some WAKAME (seaweed). At the penultimate moment add the tenderest vegetables (seaweek and cress); others you've already put in. And after turning out the flame add the cup of miso paste dissolved. Serve. In hot weather, chill for about 20 minutes in the freezer.

ZUCCHINI SPICED

Add salt, turmeric sparingly, and finely chopped onion to heated oil. Stir for a minute, add zucchini cut in pieces. Stir (covered) for 5 minutes. Garnish with chopped nuts.

ZUCCHINI WITH SESAME BUTTER AND DILL

Cut each courgette lengthwise twice. Sear in hot oil, cooking as quickly and as little as possible. Then place in casserole with a small amount of oil and a sauce made of tamari, fresh dill (or dried) and sesame butter or tahini. Place in a moderate oven for, say, 45 minutes.

BEANS

Soak beans overnight after having washed them. In the morning change the water and add Kombu (seaweed). Also, if you wish, rosemary or cumin. Watch them so that they don't cook too long, just until tender. Then pour off most of the liquid, saving it, and replace it with tamari (or Braggs). But taste first: you may prefer it without tamari or with very little. Taste to see if it's too salty. If it is, add more bean liquid. Then, if you have the juice from a roasted chicken, put several teaspoons of this with the beans. If not, add some lemon juice. And the next time you have roast chicken, add some of the juice to the beans. Black turtle beans or small white beans can be cooked without soaking overnight. But large kidney beans or pinto beans, etc., are best soaked. (So are the others.)

Another way to cook beans which has become my favorite is with bay leaves, thyme, garlic salt and pepper. You can cook it with some kombu from the beginning. I now use the "shocking method." See Aveline Kushi's book.

And now I've changed again. A Guatemalan idea: Bury an entire plant of garlic in the beans without bothering to take the paper off. Cook for at least 3 hours.

CHICK PEAS (Garbanzos)

Soak several hours. Then boil in new water. Until tender. They can then be used in many ways.

1. Salad. Make a dressing of lemon or lime with olive oil (a little more oil than lemon), sea salt and black pepper, fresh dill-parsley, and a generous amount of fine French mustard (e.g., Pommery).
2. Or use with cous cous having cooked them with fresh ginger and a little saffron.
3. Or make hummous. Place, say, two cups of chick peas with ½ cup of their liquid in Cuisinart. Add a teaspoon salt, lots of black pepper, a little oil and lemon juice to taste. Add garlic and tahini. Now I no longer add salt, but instead a prepared gazpacho.

* MUSHROOMS

Cut in reasonable pieces and saute in canola oil (not too much oil). Cover a little and then uncover to reduce liquid. Before it is all gone, add a little Braggs. Taste to decide whether lemon is needed or pepper. (Use as a side dish or combine with rice to make Mushroom Rice.)

* Warning: Don't use any wild mushrooms that you don't know, or that some authority has not checked.

NORI

The thin seaweed. Can be used with tamari and then wrapped around rice or it can be toasted over a flame and then crushed and used as a garnish on rice.

COUS COUS

Get a good fowl. Put in couscousiere with finely chopped onion, slices of ginger and saffron and several cubes of chicken bouillon. After simmering for an hour and a half, cover with perforated part of couscousiere filled with cous cous that has been mixed with a cup or so of water. After half an hour of steaming this (uncovered) remove to a large bowl. Hand mix until no lumps are present. Add a little more water and mix. Then steam for another half hour. Etc. (Do this three times.) Add vegetables to stew at appropriate times, first carrots and turnips, finally zucchinis. Don't overcook these. Serve with chick peas.

GREEN VEGETABLES
(Broccoli, Mustard Greens, Kale, Collard Greens)

1. Get a good Chinese bamboo steamer. And a wok (or Metal Chinese steamer without wok). Arrange vegetables in the steamer. Steam briefly so that they're still crunchy.
2. Saute over high heat in heavy pan with a very little sesame oil. Without liquid. When slightly burnt, add Braggs.
3. Or parboil quickly, saving the liquid to use in soups or cooking of rice, etc. This is the way I prefer.

SQUASH (Acorn, etc.)

Bake without cutting open at 425° for 1 hour and 15-30 minutes. (Do the same with any root vegetables. Some, like rutabaga, need more time, if very large possibly 2½ to 3 hours.)

STRING BEANS

Parboil 7 minutes. Or if they are the fine small French ones or the very long Chinese ones, just 4 minutes. Make a dip of dampened wasabi (Japanese horseradish), enough water to form a ball, with tamari. Or hot mustard and tamari.

VEGETABLE PATE

Cook 2 cups of soaked split peas or lentils in 8 cups of water 15 minutes. Add 1 cup of boulghour and stir for 15 minutes (to avoid burning). Add sauteed sliced onion (plenty) and Dijon mustard (to taste) plus salt and pepper.

MATSUTAKE

In a shallow baking pan make a bed of coarse salt. Lay lengthwise slices of matsutake on it. Let the slices be ³⁄₁₆ to ¼ inch wide. Roast in a hot oven briefly; don't let them dry out. Serve with quartered juicy limes.

HYPOMYCES LACTIFLUORUM

Clean and prepare in thick slices (⅜ to ½ inch). Brush with sesame oil. Broil. Then brush again with tamari alone or tamari with dampened wasabi or tamari with dampened hot mustard. Serve.

PUFFBALL LASAGNA

Treat ½- to ¾-inch slices of puffball as though they were pasta. Make a mixture of flavorful mushrooms sauteed in sesame oil and then "salted" with tamari (*Polyporus fondosus, Craterellus cornucopiodes, Marasmius oreades, Lepiotas procera, rachodes, or americana*) and another of tofu mixed with miso to take the place of cheese. Alternate layers of these with the slices of puffball in a deep baking dish. Place in moderately hot oven until well amalgamated, about 45 minutes or an hour.

ROOT VEGETABLES

Carrots, Turnips, Jerusalem Artichokes, etc. Place in a Rohmertopf (clay baking dish) in a hot oven for an hour or more with a little, very little, sesame oil. They may be covered with leeks and topped with a mixture such as one of those suggested for roast chicken.

SOUP DES JOURS

Choose a large round pot (e.g., Le Creuset). Start with water from soaking seaweed (Mekabu is especially good) or from cooking 100% buckwheat soba. Add any vegetables (root and/or leafy ones and/or mushrooms: burdock, carrots, etc., first; at the last minute radish, turnip tops or even fresh carrot tops put through the Cuisinart) and/or beans, cooked rice, etc., but nothing cooked in oil. Keep on the stove, not necessarily on a fire except when warming up or adding new root vegetables. Change the flavor each day by the addition of leftovers or an entirely new ingredient such as freshly chopped (in a Cuisinart) parsley or mustard greens. Before each serving add Bragg's Liquid Aminos or some other vegetable protein or tamari to taste, and freshly ground pepper. When it gets too dry add more liquid and vice versa. It is especially good served with freshly cooked or leftover soba or rice.

PESTO SAUCE WITHOUT CHEESE

Make as usual with fresh basil, pine nuts and garlic. Then add miso paste instead of cheese. Delicious in the summer with cold soba. Or in the winter with hot.

OLIVE SPREAD

Pit about a pound of black olives or use about half a pound (plus) of olive paste. If green olives, add anchovies, not too many. Steam a cake of tempeh for about half an hour. Saute one large chopped onion in a little olive oil. Combine everything in the Cuisinart. Let cool.

A FANCIER PATE

Saute until dry ¾ of a pound of mushrooms, preferably wild and tasty, e.g., the black trumpet. Chop four large onions and finely 6 large cloves of garlic.

After cooking the onions in sesame oil (not much) and stirring in the garlic and cooking it, add the cooked mushrooms and then 2 cups of leftover beans and a little more than that of leftover rice or other grain. Put two-thirds of the mixture in a Cuisinart and puree. Mix all by hand (not Cuisinart) with chopped basil (plenty), pine nuts, salt and pepper, pinch of cayenne, and chopped parsley. Decorate with 3 pieces of bay leaf. Put in a Rohmertopf, cover and cook for 1½ hours at 400°.

EXQUISITE SALAD DRESSING

Proportions indeterminate: tahini, tamari, and lemon juice (optional).

BREAKFAST COOKED CEREAL

Find Indian Meal Cereal (Walnut Acres). For each serving (1 cup of water to ⅓ cup of cereal) add ½ piece of Lemon Broil Tempeh (made by White Wave, Boulder, Colorado).

TOFU TAMALE

Made by Colonel Sanchez, Santa Monica, California. Steam. Eat with beans & rice & chili sauce (Desert Rose or Miguel's Stow Away).

ICE CREAM

You need *Il Gelataio* (super) available through Lello (201-939-2555). Quite expensive. Use 3 large bananas processed in Cuisinart. Add Roma (Kaffree) drip blend (as desired). Fill container (about ½ inch below churner) with Carob Soy Milk.

MUSIC WITHOUT HORIZON
SOUNDSCAPE THAT NEVER STOPS
(1991)

This text is Cage's time-line representation of an interview with Anne Gibson of the Canadian Broadcasting Corporation. It originally appeared as a preface to the catalog of the 1991 Festival Weiner Klassik.

0'00"

*What I wondered was whether or not you would comment on
how you perceive the mind of*   05"
Bach   *whether you perceive it*
as   *uh . . . . .*   10"
. . . .   *a mind that was*
capable of pure mathematics or a mind that   15"
was tempered by emotions
do you see I think that it's   *through*   20"
the music we get an idea of the mind   *and*
I wondered what yours was.   25"

30"

35"

I   it seems   40"
to me when I thi when I think of Bach I I'm not
so sure that I think of a mm   a   45"
mind   as much as uh
uh   50"
as I think of a
a   55"
a person
whose life   was uh dedicated to music.   1'00"
It it's quite
uh   05"
I don't
I don't even know how   h   10"
how long his life was.

But I uh   I do know that he   *1'15"*
had   many   children,   that   many   of   them   became
                    uh   c   com-   *20"*
posers, that he was   uh constantly
          uh writing music, because each uh   *25"*
          each Sunday   must have
uhm   *30"*
been   the   occasion   for   another   first   (laughs)   performance.   And   *35"*
besides that   one hears of his visits
                                        to uh other mu-   *40"*
sicians.   In   And at
that time   it wa it was not   *45"*
easy to travel   but I'v I'v
I've often thought of his   uh   *50"*
leaving   wherever he was
                              and going   uh   *55"*
north   to   to visit Buxtehude.
                                                              2'00"

                                        H   h   he
          he. . . . . .uh   must   *05"*
                                        w   with all
those children,   and with his admir-   *10"*
ation for other musicians   and for his
own   constant activity,   *15"*
                                        he must not have
taken any time to divide   himself into   *20"*
                                                    on
the one hand a mind   and on the other   *25"*
hand uh   uh emotions hmm?
He must have been all   *30"*
          h   altogether   uh
one person constantly active.   *35"*
                                        I think what
          uh. . . . . . .   *40"*
                              what it's hard t ah what I find hard
to have explained is what it is   *45"*
                              in the conception of the music

                               which seems 2'50"

so mathematically intricate

     (interrupting) I I think mathematics is the 55"
wrong word.

               uhm 3'00"

            It h his his 05"
ah Bach's music is characterized
    I believe 10"
                    by
        uh. . . . 15"
      starting with a rather simple
          uh 20"
bu uh n simple's the wrong word uhw
uh starting with a short mu- 25"
sical   uh
         motive. 30"

And then   uh 35"
   through repetition and variation
    to   of that motive 40"
           to
bring 45"
a. . . .   piece of music into existence. 50"

           And 55"
  And uh   uh Schoenberg teaching us this
         said uhm 4'00"

when asked what variation was 05"
   he said variation is also   repetition 15"
       with some things
changed 15"
and some things not.
        20"

                             The uh   4'25"
          other thing that characterizes uhm
                        Bach's music   30"
           is that if you
                          if you take a   35"
given piece   and you
look at it   from the begin-   40"
ning to the end
             you see that there's something happen-   45"
ing at   at every
        smallest   uh   50"
                   division point
                so that the   55"
   so that the rhythm
                 is   if if th 5'00"
if for instance there's a gap in one line
                 or a long note   05"
      or a silence,
     the other lines all fill it up.   10"
            So that the rhythm is
is constant   and   15"
mechanical.
I mean to say as dependable as a machine hmm?   20"
          It's un it's not unpre-
dictable. Once it starts going,   it contin-   25"
ues going in exactly that same way until it's
(laughs)   finished.   30"
             Now . . . .*if* (interrupting)
  So you see if   if you're going   35"
to make a   a machine like that
         which isn't going to stop running the   40"
way it runs   and if
it's   uh   employing a motive   45"
      which it is using
      to make itself   50"
      which   is either repeated
or varied and if the variation is a repetition,   55"
       some things changed and some things not,
          uh   there you have 6'00"
it.

Now   (interrupting)   And furthermore e i th it has   6'05"
to be done before Sunday.

        (laughs)   10"

                  OK You have a

deadline. (laughs) *What is it*   that   15"
makes this machine

      capable   of astonishing some   20"
listeners   *spiritually?*

                            25"

                  e th There're   30"
so many possible answers to that question
           that I don't know whether we   35"
should even begin.   The
music is so often played in places where th they   40"
are e b giving attention to spiritual matters.

                          45"

             So that   uh .
. . .   it i it does it for that reason.   50"
  It's   it's the   it's the expected
         sound   in the spiritual en-   55"
vironment.   Hmm?

                        7'00"

       y Or you could say t two plus two equals
four.   (laughs)   05"
                  When it's
          not   *in a spiritual envi-*   10"
ronment?   Does it do it then?
            It has done.   15"
  OK.   Then then it has
       that's because of the action of memory.   20"
                    Oh,
    elaborate a bit on that.   25"
      You remember having been
in church hearing it.   And now   30"
you find yourself in the forest.

And someone happens to pass by with a radio   7'35"
playing *The Art of the Fugue.* Hmm? (laughs)

                                                   40"

            (laughs) *You're saying it's not inherent*   45"
in the music. No. It's a It's a qu   uh
                Do you Don't you know the   50"
story of the   man from Africa, black
    man who was   taken   55"
to a concert in London

                                    and   8'00"
    afterwards   uh the
music had gone from before Bach,   05"
            included Bach, and went on to uh some
modern music.   10"
            And they asked him afterwards what he
thought of the   of the music and he said   15"
why did they play the same piece over and over
again?   (laughs)   20"
                            (laughs) OK.
            Then this   *the next*   25"
question that comes to my mind is
                    given what you've said   30"
                            Differe differ-
ent cultures have different memories. *Tha*   35"
    Bach's music has been elevated above and beyond other
Baroque music   *by*   40"
us?
Is there an explanation for that within the music?   45"

                                                 50"

            I   55"

                                                 9'00"

I don't think anything has been   05"
        uh. . . . . .
    p say   as   as your remark   10"
                        suggests I don't think

that anything has been permanently   done   9'15"
                              to anything outside
of us   to   20"
put it   at   a   higher
     or   lower   point.   25"
                                    uh
              If if it has been done and if we think   30"
it has been done   then
we're simply not making use   35"
     of that   of that thing.
                              Because our   40"
              our way of using things
     is   within us.
                                                    50"
                         We   h
e must   make   55"
our own   uh . . . . . .
     experience.   10'00"
     And th   one thing w
uh will   uh will g   uh   05"
we will give our attention   to
one   thing   at   one   time and to another thing at   10"
another time.   And I will
at least I   uh will not   15"
automatically elevate
                              something   20"
or   or   a   whole   body   of
of work.   I remember   I m   25"
                         uh   loving
          Bach.   30"
                         And a
at the time that I did   10'35"
              I
knew a   a very great musician   40"
uh Richard Buhlig
who made an arrangement   45"
of   *The   Art   of   the   Fugue*   of   Bach
     for two pianos.   50"
          And I   had

the very great pleasure of hearing many perfor- 10'55"
mances of that *Art of the Fugue* in Southern Cali-
fornia when Buhlig was alive   11'00"

                              uh. . . .   I had   05"
the feeling   something like what
you've   expressed at that time   10"
                                      that uhm. . . .
        I needed no other   15"
        uh music   really   than that
                                      to hear.   I was   20"
so deeply involved in it.
                              And I remember being   25"
surprised   uh
        one day   when   30"
Buhlig said that uhm
                                      that he hoped   35"
he lived long enough   to play
Mozart.   40"
                                      And I said
what do you mean?   45"
                Because   m   my mind at
that point   being absorbed with   50"
Bach   when it moved
over t   to those six   letters   55"
                with a Z in it
                              uh. . . .   felt   12'00"
itself to be in a field of frivolity   hmm?
                                      I said   12'05"
what do you mean? And   he went
on I forget what he said I was so astonished   10"
                              but   e he
s   he went on to say that uh. . . .   15"
                Bach was all good and well   (laughs)
                                      but the great   20"
musician was Mozart.
                                                                    25"

Do you recall

what it was about And that he wanted to end   *12'30"*
his days   playing Mozart.   But that
he thought it would be too difficult.   *35"*

                                                                40"

   Do you recall what it was about Bach that absorbed
you at the time?   a All those things that I've just   *45"*
been talking about.   And
                              later fortunately I had the   *50"*
                                              I had
two experiences: one of listening to Mozart   *55"*
                                              and
another time   uhm. . . .   oh *13'00"*
kind of   a   study of Mozart
                                    that led me to   *05"*
a view of music that was different
                              uh than the view   *10"*
that   that the music of Bach gave.

                                                                15"
   uh. . . .   The difference is the difference
between everything fitting together   *20"*
as it does in Bach hmm?
and coming out to   to reassure us   *25"*
about   the. . . .   existence of
order. Hmm?   *30"*
                              uh. . . .   It
                        m Mozart does another thing.   *35"*
         He   he. . . . . .uh
   provides us with a m   *40"*
         with a music which is characterized by multi-
plicity.   Not character-   *45"*
ized by unity.   But
multiplicity.   And .   *50"*
. . .   uh. . . . .   you have
the feeling that if there were something   *55"*
         if he had been able to give us

some other thing   *14'00"*

than he did   in *Don*

Giovanni   that he would   *05"*

have willingly given it.

That th   *10"*

that he left the doors open

to   to X   *15"*

to the

unknown and the excitement   *20"*

and the. . . .uh. . . .

affirmation of life,   *25"*

rather than the affirm-

ation of order   hmm?   *30"*

is   what I love   *35"*

in Mozart.

Then this   *40"*

will seem an odd question, perhaps but maybe it's not

but   I am   *45"*

curious to know if there is any kinship between you as a

composer   *and the composer Bach.*   *50"*

   55"

   15'00"

   05"

My relation to

to uh. . . .   *10"*

Bach is through my   teachers.

   15"

And   I've already

mentioned them.   One was Richard Buhlig   *20"*

and the other was uh

Schoenberg.   *25"*

   30"

And that's a kind of kinship.

   35"

uhm. . . .   *15'40"*

Schoenberg

        45"

used to speak of the uhm. . . .   *50"*
      structural importance of
harmony.   *55"*
And I think he saw music
      as a   *16'00"*
     primarily

        05"

a concern for uh
pitch relationships.   *10"*

        15"

       My
    my uh. . . . .   *20"*

        25"

experience involved uhm. . . .

        30"

   at one point
  a remark from the filmmaker Oscar Fischin-   *35"*
ger   and he said everything   in. . . .uhm   *40"*
. . . .   creation has a spirit and the
the spirit of a. . . .m   *45"*
      a   e
that spirit can be released   *50"*
by it's being set into vibration.

        55"

uh That remark so inspired me that I went
around   hitting everything and   *17'00"*
touching everything and rubbing everything to
hear what   sound   *05"*
    could be produced.
     And so I entered into the world   *10"*
of noise   that

uhm. . . .   Varese had opened   *17'15"*
                and that

e much uh. . . .   what   *20"*
we now call world music has
has been in.   *25"*

                uh What I took   *30"*
then from   from uhm
             35"

I'm speaking of kinship now n
        what I took then from my   *40"*
    from the teaching that   that
Schoenberg gave me was not   *45"*
    harmony itself
but   the function that harmony   *50"*
    was playing which was   he said
structural   and I looked for   *55"*
        a structure that would
be hospitable to noises.   *18'00"*

        Because I knew that har-   *05"*
mony wouldn't be.
             10"
        And I found just
empty time.   *15"*
        It seems like kinship
is simply the open house   *for* The   *20"*
structure. The. . . .   the
perhaps then we come to the uhm   *25"*

        and that structure now in my   *30"*
work has uhm. . . .
given way to process,   *35"*
        just as a table would give
way to the   to the weather. Hmm?   *40"*

        So that uh .   *45"*

. . . . .

50"

I I don't know what the kinship is

55"

except

through uhm . . . . .   19'00"

05"

10"

Well   I'v   15"
I'm afraid w

we have to uhm . . . . side with   20"
Mozart   and his
uh   and   25"
at least Mozart as I see him uh
. . . . someone   concerned   with   multiplicity   30"
at that point   uh .
. . .   we we're glad to have Bach   35"
too.

(laughs)   Can you   40"
explain there is a renaissance amongst perfor-
mers Mmhmm *And most audience*   45"
from   *all kinds of walks of life*
for the music of Bach.   50"
We see it clearly.   *Now more than ever.*
Have you an explanation for   55"
that?

20'00"

Why they
want to go back to   *that*   05"
voice of the 18th century.

10"

15"

20"

I
I think it has to do with   25"

the uh   paying attention to
            or   order   20'30"
                                        and unity.

                                                                       35"
                                                  And so we
miss our t s so   40"
                  there's a general   (Interrupting) But I don't
    I don't think it's uhm . . . . .   45"
                                        I think it's a little bit look-
ing out the back window   50"
                      rather than moving ahead as Marshall
McLuhan would   would uh .   55"
                                        say we
                      whether we want   21'00"
to or not, we are   we are going
forward   hmm?   05"
                                        And that for-
wardness is definitely electronic.   10"

        And uhm . . . .   the   15"
Bach   uh   the
the sound of Bach and everything doesn't have   20"
to have to do with electronics. It has to do with machinery.   25"
                                    A machine that works quite
well.   30"
                                                  But
it   evide   But it doesn't have those mys-   35"
terious   uhm . . . . . .
    uh presences of   unpredictability   40"

                                    in it that it that are   45"
a almost the hallmark of uhm . . .
        of electronics.   50"
                              We have as McLuhan said
extended the central nervous system.   55"
                      And we're in a world where anything can

happen.   And that's not the   *22'00"*
world Bach was in.

                             So   *05"*
that   if   there   is   this   general   having-recourse-
to-Bach,   it is a retreat   *10"*
                                                  from
                   uh   a situation that the   *15"*
people are actually in   and that
sooner or later   they will   *20"*
have to enjoy.   (laughs)

                                                           25"

ABOUT THE EDITOR

Richard Kostelanetz (1940-) has written and edited many books of and about contemporary literature and art. His previous Limelight books are *Conversing with Cage* and *On Innovative Music(ian)s*. As a composer he has received annual Standards Awards from ASCAP; as a media artist he has received many grants and residencies for his work in radio, video, holography and film. His visual art has been exhibited around the world. He lives in New York City.